# PUBLIC POLICIES AND PRIVATE ACTIONS

This book is the product of a five year research project 'Consumer Energy Conservation Policies: A Multinational Study', initiated and coordinated by George Gaskell and Bernward Joerges. In addition the project's executive committee comprised:-


Peter Ester
Social Cultural Planning Office, Rijswijk, Netherlands

Tage Klingberg
National Swedish Institute for Building Research, Gaevle, Sweden

Cees Midden
Netherlands Energy Research Foundation, Petten, Netherlands

Eric Monnier
Centre Scientifique et Technique du Batiment, Paris, France

Marvin Olsen
Michigan State University, East Lansing, USA

Seymour Warkov
University of Connecticut, Storrs, USA

Kostas Zografos
University of Connecticut, Storrs, USA

We acknowledge with gratitude the support of the Directorate General for Environment, Consumer Protection and Nuclear Safety of the Commission of the European Communities for supporting the international coordination and comparative aspects of the research, and the publication of this book.

Camera-ready copy by Amoroso-Centeno

# Contents

# Preface

This book is in four parts. Perhaps the most important of these is Part II in which six empirical case studies of local energy conservation programmes in Britain, France, the Federal Republic of Germany, the Netherlands, Sweden and the United States of America are presented. While these programmes are in different countries and each one is unique, they share a common focus, that of local level implementation of public policies to change households' energy conservation actions. These case studies were guided by a common conceptual framework which we describe in Part I. The distinctive feature of this framework is an attempt to combine policy and behavioural analysis in the evaluation of the impacts of energy conservation programmes. In addition consumers' responses to programmes are conceived as a result of both programme characteristics - the 'top down' perspective - and consumers' contextual situation - the 'bottom up' perspective.

Part III takes an internationally comparative viewpoint. The case studies are discussed in terms of the two analytic approaches, the 'top down' and 'bottom up', highlighting key features of both the dynamics of conservation programmes and the process of energy conservation.

Finally in Part IV we draw together the conclusions and implications for policy and future research and expand on some ideas about the challenges and vexations of applied social research.

In the autumn of 1979 three of us - George Gaskell, Bernward Joerges and Marvin Olsen - met at the International Institute for Environment and Society in Berlin and began thinking of an international cooperative research project, later to be called 'Consumer Energy Conservation Policies: a Multinational Study', or more succinctly CECP. At the time, the second so-called 'energy crisis' had hit the oil-importing nations, and a series of circumstances had created a responsive climate in policy circles for studies going beyond conventional engineering and macro-economic approaches to energy planning. In particular, a number of major studies on 'alternative energy futures' had appeared which captured the imagination of both scientists and citizens, the most influential being Amory Lovins' 'Soft Energy Paths'.

Also, an articulate environmental movement had emerged, confronting in Barbara Ward's terms 'the hard and unforgiving' technologies of the oil and nuclear
industries, with a vision of transition to a 'conserver society'. At the same time, world-wide economic stagnation threatened 'fuel poverty' to a growing number of consumers, and a remarkable amount of behavioural research focusing on ways to improve the efficiency of private energy end-use was under way, especially in Canada and the United States.

In 1980, then, the conceptual groundwork for an international study on the ways and means to promote energy conservation in private households was carried out. It was our aim, from the start, to relate changes in private consumption to the 'triangle' of policy issues constituted by the links and conflicts between energy policy, consumer policy and environmental policy, and we were fortunate to receive, in 1981, a study grant from the Directorate General for Environment, Consumer Protection and Nuclear Safety of the Commission of the European Communities to set up a seven-country project. The initial participants from the Federal Republic of Germany, Great Britain and the United States were joined, in the order of their 'arrival', by teams from the Netherlands, Sweden, France, and Greece. An Australian team became associated with the project in 1982 without however drawing on funds provided by the CEC.

In the course of the project, two series of national studies and international comparisons were carried out. In a first phase, concluded in early 1983, comprehensive evaluations of consumer energy conservation policies and programmes were conducted in the participating countries and compared internationally. In the second phase, empirical studies of selected local energy conservation programmes directed at private households were conducted in six of the participating countries, and the present book draws on these case studies.

While national research was funded by some fifteen different academic and governmental institutions in the countries concerned, the Commission of the European Communities continued to support both the international coordination and comparative work. We should like to underline here our appreciation of the Commission's support and crucial role in making possible extensive cooperative research across countries by 'mobilizing' through seed-corn grants of, about 100,000 ECUs, national research funds of close to ten times that amount.

It is not possible to list here all the institutions who have supported this research, but we thank both the 'home institutions' of participating researchers and the many funding agencies involved and acknowledge their support with gratitude.

We have made a conscious attempt to present the findings and discussions assembled in the book in a way which makes them both accessible to readers outside academia, and palatable to fellow social scientists interested in more analytical approaches to social problems.

George Gaskell
Bernward Joerges

# The contributors

Peter Ester

Social and Cultural Planning Office, Rijswijk, Netherlands

Theo Van Eijk

Institute for Environmental Studies: Free University of Amsterdam, Amsterdam, Netherlands

Valencia Fonseca

Department of Sociology, Michigan State University, East Lansing, United States of America

George Gaskell

Department of Social Psychology, London School of Economics and Political Science, London, England.

Lutz Hildebrandt

Institute for Business Administration, Technical University, Berlin.

Bernward Joerges

International Institute for Environment and Society, Wissenschaftszentrum Berlin fuer Sozialforschung, Berlin.

Tage Klingberg

The National Swedish Institute for Building Reseach, Gaevle, Sweden.

Joop van der Linden

Institute for Environmental Studies, Free University of Amsterdam, Amsterdam, Netherlands

Cees Midden

Netherlands Energy Research Foundation, Petten, Netherlands

Eric Monnier

Centre Scientifique et Technique du Batiment, Paris, France

Harald Mueller

Peace Research Institute, Frankfurt, Federal Republic of Germany

Marvin Olsen

Department of Sociology, Michigan State University, East Lansing, United States of America

# PART I
# INTRODUCTION

# 1 Evaluating household energy conservation: concepts, approaches and hypotheses

GEORGE GASKELL and BERNWARD JOERGES

## Introduction

This book is about politics and consumers, on the relationship between political programmes and private concerns. C. Wright Mills (1959), in his 'Sociological Imagination', distinguishes between public issues and private troubles, and insists that social science is about relating both, without reducing one, the domain of politics, to the other, the domain of everyday life.

More particularly, the book is about research on energy politics and energy consumers. Energy is central in both domains, the political and the private. During the great disruptions of energy markets in the 1970s with the global shifts in political control and distribution of fossil fuel resources, energy issues played a major role in almost every policy area. In addition, energy policies impinged and often set major constraints on other policies, notably economic, environmental and security. In parallel to this crowding of policy arenas with energy issues, the everyday world of consumers was crowded with troubles related to energy. Almost every aspect of contemporary life styles is dependent on secure, safe and affordable energy supplies. Erratically rising energy prices have consequently had a pervasive impact and unsettling effect on consumers' daily affairs. Maintaining a commitment to increasing levels of energy generation, the typical response of the industrialized world to the 'energy crisis', has been a major source of deterioration of peoples environments. Some have responded through the political process, others with violence, and energy plants have become, in certain countries, the epitome of all that is undesirable in modern society.

More particularly still, the book is about local energy politics and less advantaged energy consumers. A series of preliminary investigations in the countries which provide the political and economic setting for the case studies presented here produced ample evidence that past energy policies have failed in two respects. They have, by and large, not been successfully translated into action programmes at the local level, and have increased the troubles of many less advantaged consumers. (DeBoer et al. 1983; Crossley 1983; Gaskell and Pike 1983; Hildebrandt and Joerges 1983; Klingberg et al. 1983; Leyral and Monnier 1983; Mueller 1984; Olsen 1983; Zografos et al. 1983).

Specifically, the book is about energy conservation, both as a distinct type of energy policy and as a distinct way of coping with consumer problems.


## On the meanings of energy crises

The disruptions in national and international energy-producing, energy-distributing and energy-using systems in 1973/74 and 1978/79 which have been termed the first and the second 'energy crises', were by and large defined, by central policy systems, as supply crises. Crises, that is, in the supply of cheap and readily available fuels, above all oil, for continued economic growth. Perceived as supply crises, emphasis in response varied somewhat from country to country and over time, to be sure. On the whole, the dominant strategy was to deal with them as 'price and consumption crises', that is as crises in the system of economic control over energy sources. Thus the typical responses were policies aimed at 'getting away from imported oil', translated into consumer policies as 'saving money by cutting back or switching to other fuels'. These policies were remarkably successful, until they lost momentum once certain immediately cost-effective adaptations in industrial as well as private energy uses and budgets were made and, especially once oil prices began to level-off or decline as a result of the global economic recession and over-supplies of various energy sources.

Another, less powerful definition was to look at energy crises as

4

'growth crises', that is as a profound maladjustment of Western economies with respect to the long-range availability of non-renewable energy resources. This coincided with the broader 'Club of Rome' perspective of limits to growth in the 1970s. Apart from being all but obsolete in official politics today, this view led to a range of policies to step up research and development in energy efficient technologies, 'new' technologies based on renewable sources, and programmes designed to promote 'low energy' modes of production and consumption. These policies have been only moderately successful and lost momentum once the 'limits to growth' mood had given way to a new-style mood of 'reindustrialization' to cope with unemployment and the recession (see e.g. Baumgartner and Burns 1984).

The fact that the 1970s energy crises were by and large constructed and responded to as supply crises meant that energy politics have, on the whole, been diverted away from conservation issues. And the crisis mood has since largely given way to a quite different set of definitions concerning industrial growth, and renewed confidence that markets can, and in fact did, deal remarkably well in adjusting to supply-side disturbances.

However, the energy crises of the 1970s were also defined in other ways. There are at least two social constructions, articulated primarily at the fringes of politics and at the social margins of industrial society. One relates energy to human survival issues, the other to issues of social equity. In both definitions, the predominant political response to the energy crises was challenged for failing to cope with the pressing issues of survival and equity.

For a long time, ecologists have argued that energy supply and demand are part of a wider debate on the conditions of survival for industrialized nations going far beyond the limited issue of preserving finite fossil fuel resources. Their main concern was not, and is not, the plundering of the earth's oil deposits but rather the threat to society and the environment posed by maintaining present levels of energy use in the industrial countries, by the imposition of these 'high energy' social forms on the rest of the world, and by expanding supplies through nuclear and other large-scale technologies. Ecologists have not been overly worried by OPEC-style pricing strategies which they saw as approaching ecologically sound marginal pricing. They have been more worried by the inability of industrial societies to reduce polluting and damaging levels of energy use, by responses to price increases which substitute one source of pollution with other, often riskier ones, such as nuclear and coal, and by the implications of continued high energy paths for almost every other major issue on the agenda of national and international politics, from peace to agriculture, from employment and technology to health and population.

Political responses to the energy crisis as defined by the ecology movement have become more tenuous in the early 1980s for a variety of reasons. Although in the late 1970s arguments were advanced for a 'soft path' of energy conservation in the strict sense of reducing consumption and the curtailment of nuclear development, this course was not adopted by any nation. Today even the early proponents have lost enthusiasm. The introduction of alternative technologies, once perceived as a vehicle of transition to less risky energy futures while safeguarding current consumption patterns, has met with a host of unforeseen social and economic obstacles (see Baumgartner and Burns 1984). These factors in themselves go a long way in explaining why environmental politics remain weak: they did not gain access to the king's road, which in this case is energy policy. Two other factors have to do with policy-making as a symbolic process. On the one hand, employment and economic revival have become paramount in the political rhetoric of national policies in the countries considered here. On the other hand there is a growing tendency for governments and other actors using the rhetoric of 'supply-side economics' to 'take over' certain environmental issues, such as acid rain, the preservation of the visual environment and the countryside. By assuming more or less nominally the rightful responsibility for such issues, at least some governments have transformed ecological core issues into ancillary aspects of policies that cannot, in the view of ecologists, be reconciled with policies for 'a sustainable future'.

It is almost commonplace to say that the energy crisis has hit the poor more than the rich. This is evidenced on a global scale, on a regional scale within countries, with respect to divisions between strong and weak industries and between well to do and disadvantaged consumer groups. In relation to disparities between consumers, there are three equity issues which have shaped the perception of the energy crisis by consumers at large and by the organizations representing them.

One has to do with the position of energy consumers vis-a-vis the energy industries and national energy policy. Should consumers have to accept supply patterns and policy options which are far more costly for them than they need be? Does the fact that energy utilities continue to invest in supply capacity in the face of much higher costs for producing an additional amount of energy than for saving the same amount of wasted energy reflect an unfair distribution of market power between producers and consumers of energy? Do windfall profits due to the deregulation of fuel prices reflect this? It is remarkable that consumer organizations in the countries considered here, and at the level of the European Community, have, with some notable exceptions, not taken a strong view in this respect, and the theme of basic inequities concerning the power to 'voice' interests and 'exit' markets has been articulated more vocally in environmentalist debates.

Another issue concerns social disparities resulting from energy price rises. The budget proportion devoted to energy services has always been higher for lower income groups, and has increased disproportionately as a result of rises in the relative prices for fuels. In Britain, Bradshaw and Harris (1983) talk about fuel poverty, an issue now recognized in other countries (Buxton and McGee 1986; Claxton et al. 1986; Warkov and Ferree 1986). Related to this is the question whether poorer consumers pay more for the same quantities of energy, which must generally be assumed to be the case. While these problems have indeed led to fuel poverty or at least to energy bills amounting to a second rent in some countries and areas, it has only recently been strongly articulated by consumer movements.

A third issue pertains not to social inequities related to energy consumption per se but to the distributional effects of energy conservation policies. Do the programmes initiated to promote energy efficiency discriminate between social groups? To what extent were the allocated public funds used to subsidize economic activities that would have been undertaken anyway? It seems to us that the acceptability of energy policies, particularly those intended to increase energy efficiency, hinges in a complex way on such questions. On the one hand, the readiness to support political departures that inevitably upset the balance of costs and benefits in many spheres of an economy may depend on the public's perception of 'who takes the burden'. It has been argued for example that the readiness of lower-income people to support environmental policies is linked to their perception of just income distribution in society at large (Schnaiberg 1975). To the extent that energy policy, as any other policy, is in part social policy, a failure to take distributional effects into account may be one of the reasons for the relative failure to maintain the momentum of conservation policies. At the other end of the political spectrum, the misallocation of state subsidies evidenced by widespread 'free-rider' effects in the implementation of loans and grants schemes for energy conservation has been used as an argument against state intervention in the energy economy, particularly with respect to investments in conservation. According to this school of thought, energy conservation policies of the past cannot be shown to have produced marked effects over those induced by changes in energy prices, and to the extent that the functioning of energy markets is judged satisfactory, allocation of public funds for conservation may not be a rational policy. This is of course an interpretation which accords well with the definition of the energy crisis prevalent in the producing industries. Again, such perceptions tend to weaken public support for conservation policies.

In sum, a dominant definition of the energy crisis as a supply crisis has led to policy responses in terms of supply, contributing to continued pressure on the environment. A less powerful definition of the energy crisis as an environmental crisis has led to partial policy responses in terms of energy conservation and technologies based on renewable energy sources, with little success, so far.

A failure, within energy policy, to define the energy crisis as a social crisis has contributed to the weakness of conservation policies and has itself produced inequities. This failure may be explained by the fact that such a definition implies policy responses that not only transcend energy policy but bring into focus a series of contradictions and conflicts over basic social values, over the distribution of costs and benefits of conservation policies, and over the division of authority to control energy policy.

While research into conservation policies and consumers' conservation actions cannot 'prove' any of these definitions 'right' or 'wrong', it also cannot uncritically accept the definitions underlying the policy process studied. Rather in this book we assume that there is a history of social definitions of energy and related crises which is embedded in the overall course of social, economic and cultural changes in industrialized societies. If, as might be expected, environmental and equity issues become more pervasive in the future, it is likely that future conflict over energy issues will be couched in these terms to a greater extent than in the past: unresolved policy issues tend to re-emerge if they relate to core issues in other policy arenas.

Of course, the crisis mentality of the late 1970s and early 1980s is now over and governments confront other pressing economic problems. Yet there are clouds on the horizon which presage renewed difficulties in relation to energy. In many countries the 'fall-out' from the disaster at Chernobyl is carrying implications for the whole future of nuclear generated electricity. While oil consumption has declined and prices slumped there is a body of opinion that price rises in the 1990s are likely. Thus, while energy conservation is, in the short term, well down the list of political priorities, if the past is ignored both governments and consumers may be forced to relive the painful history of the 1970s.

## Modelling the process of consumer energy conservation

Our approach to energy conservation is policy-oriented, interdisciplinary and cross-national. Before describing more specific features of the analytical scheme underlying the study, we will make a few comments concerning these three general characteristics of our research.

Research of the kind presented here is not strictly theory oriented, either in the sense of generating theory, or in the sense of testing theory. Rather, it uses theories of various kinds in interpreting social processes in terms of various criteria of 'success' or 'failure' with respect to policy goals. On the other hand, it is not programmatic in the sense of validating or prescribing policies. What then is it? Some would call it 'evaluation research' or 'policy implementation research', however, we are reluctant to use these labels with their strongly prescriptive connotations.

On the one hand, the studies assembled go beyond either of these two research orientations by seeking to combine analytically what we will call 'top-down' and 'bottom-up' perspectives. Policy makers in energy, consumer and environmental affairs should find this approach helpful in the sense that it empirically identifies a number of key factors related to the success or failure of local conservation programmes. However, this emphasis on the overall social dynamics of energy conservation processes does not easily translate into a simple set of recipes on 'how to do it' or prescriptions about 'what to do for whom'.

On the other hand, we make no claim to go beyond the evaluation research tradition which stays rather close to pragmatic issues as they are defined within the political and social settings studied. In other words, the more strictly descriptive-analytical study of the conflictual process of social and technological change in the modern welfare state is outside the scope of this undertaking. All implementation and evaluation research faces the dilemma either to assume a liberal-democratic stance implying the existence of legitimate policy goals which then are implemented more or less efficiently or a 'radical' stance implying that policy implementation is a product of conflicting interests, a game of power and compliance in which evaluation research itself tends to become identified with the aims of dominant actors (see for a discussion of these issues Barrett and Hill 1984). We do not claim to have resolved this dilemma. But we suggest that operating within the general perspective of evaluative research neither requires all participants to assume a common stance, nor precludes the view that the validity of the two positions may vary from case to case.

The 'energy crisis' has sparked off a tremendous amount of research in both the engineering and the economic disciplines, and much of it has been devoted to the issue of a 'more rational use of energy'. It is likely that policy-makers who know what they want and ask for specific technical and economic solutions to implement energy conservation strategies will have little trouble in finding answers. The same, in a sense, is true for householders: there is plenty of expert advice concerning the technical and economic details of solving most problems arising from a need to improve energy efficiency in the home. This is not so if one looks at non-technical and non-economic barriers to energy conservation, both at the levels of policy actors and at the level of consumers' actions. Indeed, we assume that major state programmes aimed at promoting 'rational' energy use have fallen short of their proclaimed objectives because they conspicuously failed to take into account institutional and behavioural factors (Gaskell 1983).

Institutional and behavioural, or structural and personal, contexts of energy use are in their turn domains of quite separate disciplinary approaches. Attempts to integrate the two approaches -- the socio-cultural and the psychological -- are quite rare in the area of consumer research. To put it differently: engineering and economic/econometric approaches have become quite interrelated and been comfortably linked with straightforward, quantifiable forms of policy analysis. However much needs to be done in the area of linking the qualitative analysis of policy and programme implementation to more integrated studies of the complex personal and socio-cultural factors shaping the end-uses of energy. Here we see our particular contribution.

A similar point can be made about cross-national research, both in the weak sense of a close-knit community of researchers exchanging data and converging on equivalent modes of analysis or in the strong sense of equivalent and comparative designs. Such co-operative/comparative research is well established in the engineering and economic fields. However, the study of the complex interplays between individual action, institutional context and political inter-vention does not lend itself to strictly comparative research across countries. Let it be said at the outset that we would consider the con-tention that this is feasible as either trivializing or pretentious. Still, a cross-national perspective is valuable, both from a conceptual and a practical point of view. Whilst saying this, it should be understood that the term cross-national, in this book, does not suggest a com-parison of nations or of national policies or of 'the consumer' in dif-ferent countries. It denotes the study of specific consumer groups, with comparable socio-economic positions in their societies, in specific and highly diverse local communities, exposed to specific conservation programmes covering a limited range of types of policy intervention in six highly industrialized Western countries confronted with the 'energy crisis'.

The studies contained in this book were preceded by an attempt at conceptualizing the process of consumer energy conservation and by a series of base-line studies on a very broad range of existing con-servation policies and programmes in the countries involved. Al-though consumer energy research had become a booming field at the time, no readily applicable 'model' for research linking policy analysis to an analysis of complex consumption behaviours had been developed in the literature.

The following five considerations seemed important to us in developing our own scheme.

* With regard to policy issues, it had to be broad enough to address, not only energy savings issues in a narrow sense, but related issues of environmental policy, consumer and social policy. Even a superficial inspection of energy conservation programmes shows that many of them include a broader range of objectives which must be taken into account in programme analysis. At the output end of programme implementation, furthermore, impacts of

11

relevance to other policy processes had to be addressed. Finally, since no one research team combined all the requisite foci, and indeed it is unlikely that such a group exists, participants had to be able to bring into the analysis their own particular policy orientations and institutional interests.

* The framework had to be comprehensive enough to take into account a wide spectrum, not only of national policy contexts, but especially of programme types and contextual factors shaping responses to programmes. Both viewed 'from the top', the perspective of programme makers, and 'from the bottom' the perspective of programme takers, any organized effort to change established routines of energy consumption involves a multitude of actors, action programmes and settings, and a hierarchy of social and temporal processes of differing scale. At least in principle, the model had to be able to analyse micro level as well as macro level processes and structures and to link actions taken by individuals, such as taking measures to improve their homes, with collective action, such as becoming aware of the energy crisis, and actions taken by all kinds of agencies, such as governments legislating building codes or utilities changing tariff structures.

* Our framework had to be general enough to accommodate hypotheses derived from a variety of disciplinary orientations, such as political theory, consumer behaviour theory, prescriptive theory of rational organization, sociological and social psychological theory of intentional social change. Approaches to be integrated were largely based on the backgrounds and theoretical predilections of participating researchers, and the main task initially was to find a terminology which could link them without unduly flattening concepts taken out of their 'natural' theoretical environments. This proved to be a major concern throughout the course of the study not only for the well known difficulties of, say, consumer researchers talking to policy analysts, but for more intangible reasons of achieving a dialogue between researchers from differing intellectual cultures.

* The model had to be specific enough to yield data that could be compared across programmes, across consumer groups and across national settings. The requirements of broadness, comprehensiveness and generality tend to produce abstract categories, like 'actor', 'organizational structure', 'consumer attitudes', which can be interpreted quite freely. The idea, on the other hand, of 'operational definitions', as derived from experimental research, is

quite useless in the context of research of an exploratory and evaluative character. We needed to indicate a range of acceptable indicators for specific concepts, rather than strict measurement rules.

* Finally, the framework had to be as neutral as possible with regard to certain a-priori assumptions about the process of consumer energy conservation. Again this proved to be a concern throughout the study because even the order of introducing certain terms, or representing a process graphically, predicates an analysis in a certain way which may not be shared by everybody. For example, representing conservation processes as an orderly sequence of steps from programme formulation through implementation to programme impacts should not preclude looking at conservation as a process that may not be an outcome of policy intervention of all. Similarly, constructing conservation actions as influenced by attitudes to energy conservation may blind the analysis of processes where conservation actions must be interpreted as reactions to institutional change and attitude change a result of this.

These requirements were not easily reconciled. As a consequence, conceptualization turned out to be a negotiated process of fitting different research interests and methodological approaches, and of redefining issues and hypotheses in the two consecutive stages of the overall study. Moreover, participating research teams have seen fit to emphasize, and elaborate, particular lines of analysis as set out in the overall 'model' guiding the research. In fact, we consider this an asset rather than a handicap to interdisciplinary, cross-national research.

In the following sections we will give an account of this process and the preliminary research leading up to the case studies presented in this book. First, the model of energy conservation processes we have used throughout will be summarized, followed by a summary of preliminary findings in eight countries. In the remainder of the chapter, the analytical perspective taken in the case studies and comparative evaluations in this book is discussed and a rationale for the case studies given.

*A conceptual framework*

Attempts to model processes of policy interventions for social change in the domain of private energy end-use are not new. Such models as have been presented in the literature (see Ellis and Gaskell 1978; McDougall and Ritchie 1979; Olsen and Goodnight 1977; Perlman and Warren 1977; Seligman et al. 1978; Shippee 1980; Stern and Gardner 1980; Stern et al. 1981; Warkov 1978; Winett and Neale 1979; and a number of contributions in Ester et al. 1984) are, however, typically limited in their range and appropriateness in terms of the requirements set out above.

In order to overcome such limitations, we have developed a model of the process of consumer energy conservation which has been described in great detail elsewhere (Olsen and Joerges 1981; Joerges and Olsen 1983). This model, which has itself developed and changed over time, has served as an 'intellectual management tool' throughout the phases of baseline studies, empirical studies of local conservation schemes, and within-country as well as cross-national comparisons. It has the following ten 'building blocks'.

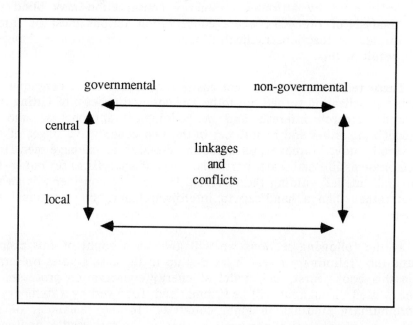

Figure 1.1 Main policy actors

* It is based on the notion of main policy actors, shaping the entire range of conservation policies and programmes directed at consumers or the structure of a programme directed at specific consumer groups in a locale. Policy actors may be governmental or non-governmental, or, as in the case of most energy utilities,

mixed. Governmental actors may be closely linked to energy and economic policy actors, or to other policy systems, such as urban and building policy, consumer or environmental protection policy. Similarly, non-governmental actors may be organizations representing consumer interests, environmental concerns, or other concerns such as social services for specific consumer groups. Policy actors may be central or local, and the focus here is on both vertical and horizontal linkages or conflicts between actors. Energy conservation programmes, as they are actually implemented, are thus seen as outcomes of complex 'actor games', embedded in broader policy interests concerning energy supply, environmental protection, and consumer welfare.

Policy actors' 'programmes', in the sense of declared goals, interests, strategies and justifications, are not taken as blueprints of programmes actually implemented, whose 'success' or 'failure' must then be evaluated against criteria derived from political rhetoric. Whether declared policies are matched by action programmes at the level of implementing agencies, and in the end at the level of household members' conservation actions, is seen as an empirical question. This is much the same as the issue of the relationship between consumers' expressed concerns or beliefs regarding energy conservation and their actual behaviours. In other words, policies may as much reflect what is not being done at the level of programmes as they may provide the rationale for programme design and implementation.

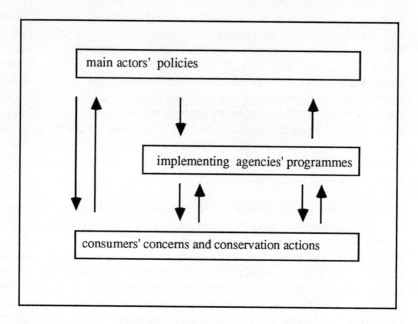

Figure 1.2 The interactive process

\* We conceptualize the process of consumer energy conservation as an interactive process of consumer involvement, policy formation, and programme implementation. This view partially reflects a belief in the value of involving the 'recipients' of policies in programme formulation and design. Partially it rests on evidence accumulated in many realms of public policy suggesting that the active participation of a programme's clientele, and the provisions a programme makes for such participation, can indeed improve conservation planning and facilitate programme implementation.

This conceptualization strongly reflects the preponderance of 'top-down' conservation planning and conservation programmes 'for' consumers, and indeed our wish to contribute to the art of programme design and implementation in the policy field of energy and environmental conservation. However the model also lends itself, in principle, to the analysis of self-organized, grass-roots initiatives and cases of 'counter-implementation from below'.

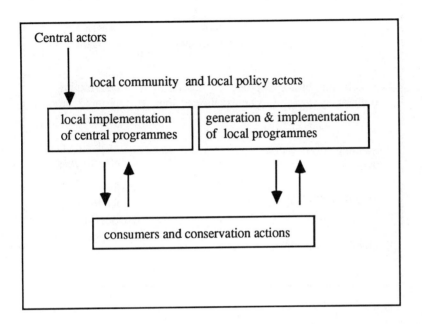

Figure 1.3 Focus on the local level

* The model emphasizes the local community as the most important setting for conservation programmes. Initial policy responses to the 'energy crisis' typically originated at central (national or state) levels. These were too general in their aims, restricted in their instruments and too rigid in their concrete objectives to be applicable to a wide range of conditions in local communities or to penetrate all but the most easily reached consumer groups.

Emphasis on the local level means both focusing on the issue of implementing central programmes at the local level and on the strengths and weaknesses of programmes generated locally, either by local authorities, local utilities or non-governmental organizations.

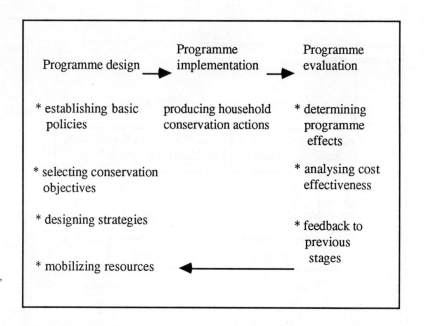

Figure 1.4 Stages of promoting energy conservation

\* At the level of implementing agencies and programmes, the model encompasses the entire process of promoting consumer energy conservation. Thus programme analysis begins with policy goals endorsed by implementing agencies and is carried through subsequent stages of specifying objectives, designing intervention strategies and mobilizing resources, implementing programme instruments, and producing desired changes, and evaluating effects.

We conceive here of programmes as a specific type of organization, set up to implement certain services for households in a planned and controlled fashion. The model defines minimum requirements for any such organization to be successful. Actual programmes may deviate from the 'logic' implied by this component and this would then be interpreted as a weakness, for instance if programmes lack some mechanisms to determine effects, or to account for the cost-effectiveness of particular measures.

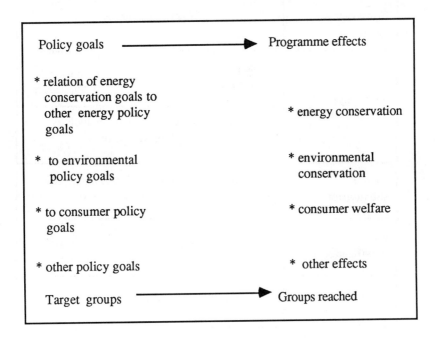

Figure 1.5 Multiple programme goals and effects

* At the stages of establishing policy goals as well as programme
outcomes, the model allows for an analysis of multiple policy
goals and effects. The reason for this is, again, to allow for a full
description of programmes which are often instrumental in the
achievement of a number of (sometimes conflicting) policies, and
to orient analysis towards certain normative assumptions underlying our research. That is to determine the degree to which energy
conservation goals are linked to environmental and consumer
policy goals and objectives.

Policy goals need not be explicit, but the absence of certain policy
goals, such as the avoidance of distributional effects or the environmental compatibility of measures advocated by a
programme, is as noteworthy, as the analysis of the explicit policy
goals by which a programme is justified. Similarly, choice of target groups, treated here as a basic policy decision, may not be explicit, and the absence of conscious targeting is as relevant a finding as decisions to benefit particular target groups.

| Conservation approaches | Energy use Areas | | |
|---|---|---|---|
| efficiency improvement | space heating | hot water | household appliances |
| | changing to more efficient technology (including insulation) | | |
| source substitution | changing from non-renewable to renewable sources and appropriate technologies | | |
| use modification | changing behavioural routines | | |
| life-style alterations | changing needs and preferences | | |

Figure 1.6. Programme objectives: energy conservation actions

* The model defines specific programme objectives in terms of those conservation actions a programme seeks to produce. In order to do that, a typology of conservation actions is derived from combinations of what we call 'conservation approaches' and 'energy use areas'. This allows us to compare in detail very different programmes, irrespective of their objectives in terms of, for example 'energy to be saved', or 'insulation level to be achieved'.

Household energy consumption is multiply determined. It is influenced by choice, or availability, of technology (including technical attributes of the house), the way these technologies are used in the provision of energy services such as waterheating, space-heating, or the use of electric appliances, and the life style of consumers, i.e. their preferences regarding activities which require these services. Changes in energy consumption can be a function of changes in all of these. Two main paths of achieving reductions in energy consumption can be distinguished: a 'technical' path, requiring decisions to (a) invest in improved technology - efficiency improvements resulting in reduced energy inputs (insulating the house, modernizing heating systems etc.) - or (b) in source substitution resulting in conservation of non-renewable energy sources; and a 'behavioural' path, requiring decisions to (c) re-organize the way household technology is used or operated - use modifications in the sense of more 'rational' or economical routines - or (d) alteration of life styles in the sense of choosing activities requiring less energy services. The first and the third of these approaches specify conservation objectives usually associated with policies for 'a rational use of energy', justified primarily on economic grounds. The second and the forth specify objectives often associated with 'soft' energy policy options, calling for resource conservation and more far-reaching social change as advocated, for example, by ecologically oriented programmes.

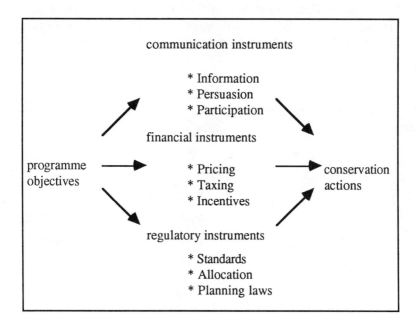

Figure 1.7 Programme instruments

* The model foresees, at the stage of implementing policy and programme instruments, an examination of a comprehensive range of instruments that can be used to promote energy conservation. It is commonplace in the literature to restrict analyses to instruments of a financial or informational nature, and to ask which of these

two categories is more effective. In using a more comprehensive scheme we have been guided by two considerations. On the one hand, the effectiveness of programme interventions seems not to be a matter of choosing either this or that instrument, but rather a matter of how to combine them in order to enable consumers at large, and especially less advantaged groups, to take conservation actions. On the other hand it seems that the attainment of efficient, fair and environmentally acceptable forms of providing energy services for consumers requires a differentiated repertoire of programme instruments.

It is unlikely that any single programme will use all of these instruments, and some will be outside the scope of most, particularly in local programmes. In the latter case, this component of the model is employed to characterize the 'policy environment' of specific programmes: no programme operates in a vacuum, and its interventions must be seen in the broader context of related policy interventions reaching (or not reaching) a programme's clientele through channels not operated by the programme itself.

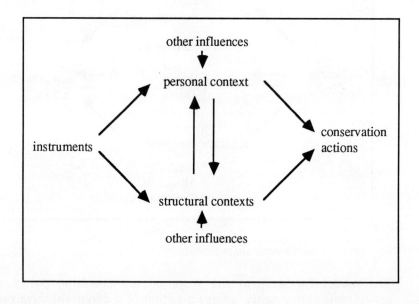

Figure 1.8 Conservation contexts

* In order to understand the process of consumer energy conservation, the mechanisms by which programmes succeed or fail in inducing conservation actions must be analysed. The model conceives of conservation actions as the combined product of changes in conservation contexts, both personal and structural. The term 'personal context' denotes the entire range of household members' dispositions to take conservation actions - past experience, specific skills and knowledge, general awareness of energy issues, attitudes concerning conservation, and broad value orientations. The term 'structural contexts' denotes the technical, economic, legal and socio-cultural environment constraining or facilitating conservation actions at the level of households.

Changes in these contexts can only partially be attributed to programme interventions. Changes brought about in either structural or personal contexts interact in complex ways to produce conservation actions. In addition, within both the personal context and the structural contexts, complex hierarchies of factors exist. Finally it must be noted that the conceptual distinction between 'personal' and 'structural' and their independent measurement poses difficult methodological problems.

For reasons of space, these issues cannot be spelt out here. While the basic notion of interacting contexts has guided our research throughout, their broad definition and the indicators used to measure them have changed from study to study, and even, as a result of variation in programme scope and level, target groups characteristics etc., from programme to programme.

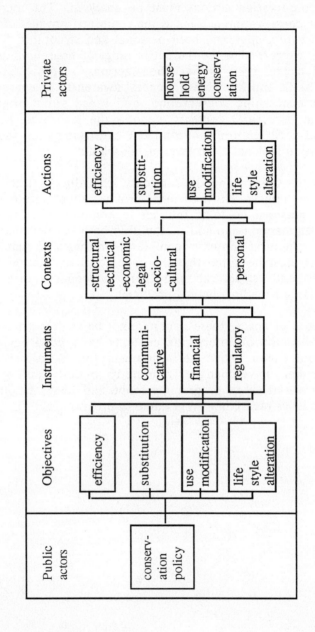

Figure 1.9 Programme strategies

* The model defines programme strategies as particular ways to link programme objectives, programme instruments, conservation contexts and conservation actions. The diagram gives a complete grid of possible links, and a particular programme's strategy can be defined by the particular combination of links it manages to put into operation.

* Finally, the model foresees, or lends itself to, two types of analysis. We term these 'top-down' and 'bottom-up' respectively, and we believe that both are essential for a full understanding of the conservation process. The application of rather complex, and at the same time quite loose, models of the type introduced above yields great amounts of data of different character and quality. At the same time, it does not specify a finite set of hypotheses concerning functional relationships between its major elements. Its purpose is to guide data collection and structurization, and to put many partial relationships into an overall perspective. This can best be achieved by looking at the entire process from both the point of view of programme-makers and programme-takers.

Thus the 'top-down' perspective entails a detailed analysis of the history and structure of programme design and implementation, and relates relevant findings to characteristics of programme clientele, levels of programme take-up, and effects in terms of conservation actions induced as well as other intended or unintended effects.

The 'bottom-up' perspective, in contrast, entails a detailed analysis of the way conservation actions are shaped by consumers' personal, economic, legal, socio-cultural and technical situation, and of the way, the overall community context shapes programme development.

## Initial assumptions and preliminary findings

The empirical case studies presented in this book did not start ab initio. They were preceded by a series of evaluations, in the countries here represented and, in addition, in Greece (see Zografos et al. 1983), and in Australia (see Crossley 1983), documenting existing energy conservation policies and programmes both at central and local levels, and by governmental and non-governmental agencies. Both policies and programmes were then assessed, in a largely 'top-down' perspective, on the basis of information and data made available by programme agencies.

Apart from the very practical objective of providing critical overviews on the 'state of the art' in programme development, these studies focused on a series of issues and assumptions which we felt needed clarification before embarking on necessarily highly selective empirical analyses. These initial assumptions, stated in terms of the overall conceptual framework, (see Olsen and Joerges 1981), were:

* Private households in all countries included have, in response to the 'energy crisis', reduced their consumption of non-renewable energy by only a small fraction of what is theoretically and practically possible. Therefore, adopting purposeful energy conservation policies could improve this situation markedly.

* All energy conservation involves a combination of technical and social factors which comprise an integrated socio-technical system, so that there can be neither a purely 'technical fix' or a 'social fix' for energy conservation. Therefore, any conservation policy must systematically include both types of action.

* The process of enacting policies for consumer energy conservation must involve consumers in decision-making roles at every stage or at least represent the citizens' perspective, if the process is to be successful. Therefore, conservation programmes should seek to maximize meaningful consumer involvement.

* As a process of intentional social change, consumer energy conservation programmes must create changes in the structural contexts - technical, economic, legal, and socio-cultural - that shape patterns of energy consumption. Therefore, conservation programmes must be designed to change whatever features of the various structural contexts are relevant.

* As a process of intentional social change, consumer energy conservation programmes must alter the personal context of energy
use by mobilizing individuals through increasing energy awareness, motivation to act, knowledge of conservation actions,
capability to take those actions, and confirmation of outcomes.
Therefore, conservation programmes must be designed to promote
this mobilization process as fully as possible.

* A wide variety of communicative, financial, and regulatory instruments can be used to implement changes in the structural and
personal contexts of energy use. Therefore, a successful conservation programme will strategically combine different instruments
that are relevant to the contexts being changed.

* Energy conservation programmes are most likely to be effective
when they are designed and implemented at the local level, utilising existing community organizations and networks of interpersonal relationships, and adapting higher-level programmes to local
conditions. Therefore, the local community should be the operational setting for all consumer energy conservation programmes.

* Energy conservation programmes are most likely to be effective
when they provide a complete package of all necessary services to
consumers. Therefore, conservation programmes should be organized and conducted in the manner that is most accessible to
consumers and tailored to their requirements.

* Energy conservation programmes are most likely to be effective
when they are specifically oriented toward particular target
populations or groups. Therefore, a comprehensive community
conservation programme should contain many different kinds of
activities aimed at various specified targets.

* Intentional social change programmes require an element of
evaluation to determine if they are being successfully implemented, are achieving their intended objectives, and are having
any other unintended or indirect effects. Therefore, consumer
energy conservation programmes should be continually and
thoroughly evaluated.

The results of these preliminary studies have been documented
elsewhere (De Boer et al. 1983; Crossley 1983; Gaskell and Pike 1983;
Hildebrandt and Joerges 1983; Klingberg et al. 1983; Leyral and
Monnier 1983; Olsen 1983; Zografos et al. 1983). From a comparative

analysis delineating and identifying types of programmes developed by 1982 in the countries covered, a certain number of trends, strengths and weaknesses of public policies in the realm of household energy conservation emerge. Here is a brief summary (for more detailed comparative analyses see Joerges and Mueller 1984; Mueller 1984).

Generally it was found that the development of conservation programmes had, by the time these studies were concluded, lost momentum as a result of, presumably, the world oil markets having turned into 'buyers markets' and a wide spread waning of a 'crisis mood', in public awareness. In particular a series of successful local 'model schemes' described in these studies cannot hide the fact that energy conservation has not yet become a routine policy function at the municipal level. Also, the 'synergetic' effects to be derived from vigorous energy conservation policies, particularly with regard to environmental, consumer and other social policy goals, very rarely appear to be systematically taken into account in formulating and conducting programmes.

The kind of programme most typically developed in all the countries covered (with the exception of Greece which still lacked a coherent set of programmes targeted at private households) was conducted under the auspices of some central agency with a broad range of policy goals where energy conservation is only a subordinate goal. The focus was clearly on home heating and on communication instruments of the general campaign type, supplemented by a scheme of financial incentives; the dominant approach was the 'technical fix' aimed at improving the thermal efficiency of houses and equipment, implicitly targeted at the well-educated, middle-class homeowner. The areas of household appliances and private cars were addressed to a much lesser degree, and regulatory instruments, particularly local planning and community organization, not given priority; comprehensive changes in life-style were not advocated, and tenants/low income consumers were seldom reached by these programmes.

Several factors limit the success of this type of programme, the most important being the unequal distribution of financial incentives to energy conservation and the institutional barriers to undertake conservation actions implicit in landlord/tenant relationships.

With respect to the locus of authority to initiate and implement programmes, it appears that there is no one 'ideal agent' but that each type of agency possesses specific advantages and limitations.

Central (national) government agencies dealing with energy conservation are indispensable in setting overall conditions by formulating broad objectives, creating a stable regulatory environment (building codes, appliances standards), offering flexible schemes of financial incentives, and monitoring the performance of lower level implementing agencies. Local authorities have a unique advantage in transforming central provisions into programmes adapted to specific situations and local requirements, and in using established communication channels to target programme recipients. The energy industries and utilities have a formidable potential of technical competence and efficient supply which could be linked to consumer choices concerning the rational use of energy; however, by and large utilities have not taken a lead in household energy conservation. Consumer organizations, environmental associations and a range of voluntary social groups were shown to be able, and indeed almost uniquely so, to address specific consumer groups and their particular problems, e.g. low income or otherwise disadvantaged groups, and a growing number of citizens with 'alternative' orientations and life-styles.

Another finding concerns those local programmes with reportedly outstanding success in terms of mobilization of consumers and energy savings achieved. They seem to share certain pertinent attributes such as an active and prudent channelling of central-level programmes, a high commitment of key persons or a core group of citizens, an imaginative and extensive use of local communication channels, a combination of various instruments and services into 'packages', and the active involvement of local business and utilities.

Our preliminary studies led to a number of critical conclusions with respect to certain major flaws in the overall political response to the 'energy challenge' as it presents itself at the level of private end-use. One is, that programmes are by and large based on the notion of 'sovereign consumers', that is private households are pictured as rational economic actors who could do something about their domestic energy problems if they only wanted and were given appropriate information and some financial incentive; programmes are not geared to the issue of removing institutional barriers to energy conservation.

Secondly, programmes tend to be distant from consumers. That is, they are not well adapted to widely varying local conditions and they are not offered in the context of consumers immediate living environment; programme penetration has therefore remained weak. At the same time, conservation programmes often remain isolated from other relevant policies and programmes, in particular energy supply policies at both central and municipal level; consumers have been induced to invest heavily in energy conservation while similar efforts at the level of energy generation and distribution have lagged behind.

Finally, conservation policies and programmes have had distinct distributional effects. That is the notable public subsidies channelled into the residential sector were disproportionately taken up by relatively well-to-do homeowners, who as a result have been able to reduce their energy bills; less advantaged consumers, particularly those in rented or older properties, have not benefited. As in other spheres of consumption, there is evidence of a series of social disparities: the poorer a household, the more inefficient its energy use, the higher the price for useful end-energy, and the more environmentally polluting its energy consumption.

**The focus of the case studies: decentralization and the disadvantaged**

It is against the background of these findings that the case studies of local energy conservation schemes which make up the bulk of this book were conducted, choosing as their common focus the twin issue of programme decentralization and of tailoring programmes to the requirements of disadvantaged consumer groups.

It seems important to point out, that - with the exception of the United States and Sweden - more comprehensive community level programmes are still a recent and novel departure from the typical official and centrally administered information campaigns and loans and grants-schemes directed at 'consumers at large'. The decision to concentrate on local programmes in itself precluded the selection, in each country, of programmes of equal intrinsic interest yet similar organizational structure, policy focus, and targets. Instead, we set out to identify one (or several) cases of particular interest in terms of either their 'model' character as a localized conservation scheme or their particular focus on disadvantaged groups (or both) in the six countries covered here.

As a result, the six cases (or series of cases) chosen represent widely different solutions to, as it were, a similar challenge: how to bring energy conservation services closer to consumers, how to integrate them as fully as possible with the particular community context, and how to adapt them to the requirements of consumer groups not reached generally by 'conventional' programmes.

While this research strategy imposes limitations for the application of a unified design, the choice, as we saw it, was between studying 'comparable' communities/programmes/target groups, but missing the more exciting national experiences, or studying intrinsically interesting cases and attempting to identify their particular strengths and weaknesses in their proper context.

The option for a case-study approach implies differences in design which must be kept in mind in an attempt at comparative interpretation, while not precluding, on the other hand, a certain degree of commonality at the level of data collection and analysis based on a common set of general research questions.

Guided by the conceptual framework, programme analysis was based on a series of hypotheses concerning the role of various programme attributes for programme success. Thus in the studies the 'top-down' approach investigated such issues as the relationships between positive and negative programme outcomes and

- the *flexibility* of programmes in terms of allocation of funds, targeting specific groups, selection of instruments and linkages with other agencies

- the nature of *linkages* with other agencies both within the locality and outside it

- more elusive factors such as the degree of *commitment* of key persons and programme staff to energy conservation and other objectives

- the degree of *targeting* of programme services, particularly with respect to disadvantaged consumer groups

- the programme's *comprehensiveness* in terms of goals, instruments and channels

- the *credibility* of the agency conducting the programme

- and finally the issue of *conflict management* during the stages of programme instigation and implementation.

In terms of the 'bottom-up' analysis the choice of mediating or contextual variables for empirical study was to a great extent dictated by the choice of programme(s). In other words, the design of each case study had to reflect the idiosyncrasies of the specific programmes and their target groups, rather than implement a preconceived or ideal model of the conservation process. However, at minimum the studies were designed to investigate at least three broad categories of contextual variables hypothesized to play a role in shaping consumers reactions to a programme

- their attitudes, values and behaviours, the *personal* context
- their socio-demographic position, economic and family situation, the *household* context
- and the social characteristics of the community in which the programme operates, the *community* context.

With respect to overall design differences, the six studies in the following chapters can be grouped as shown in Figure 1.10.

| <u>Level</u> | <u>Variants</u> | <u>Cases</u> |
|---|---|---|
| Community | | |
| | one community/one programme | NL, USA |
| | one community/several programmes | FRG |
| | several communities/similar programmes | GB |
| | several communities/different programmes | F; S |
| Programme | | |
| | one programme | NL; USA |
| | several similar programmes | GB |
| | several different programmes | FRG; S; F |
| | locally generated programme | FRG; F; NL; USA |
| | local programme with strong central linkage | FRG; F; GB |
| | local implementation of central programme | FRG; S; F |
| Households | | |
| | client sample & comparison non-client sample | all cases |
| | no sub-sample of disadvantaged clients | F; S; USA |
| | sub-sample of disadvantaged clients/tenants | FRG |
| | disadvantaged clients/tenants only | GB; NL |

Figure 1.10 The focus of the case studies

Policy implementation and evaluation research must, by its very nature, be pragmatic in both design and reporting, that is it must stay close to national and local peculiarities of the subject under evaluation and to the expectations and requirements of public policy agencies. This, and the fact that the number of parameters potentially important for programme success is very large and cannot possibly be 'controlled' within the type of study presented here, implies that generalization and conclusions must be drawn prudently. The interpretations of national findings in a cross-national perspective presented in Part III of this book should therefore not be mistaken for a rigorous cross-national analysis of empirical data produced by a quasi-experimental research design. We will rather look at the body of national findings as a pool both of social scientific expertise in policy oriented research and as evidence of the hierarchy of factors determining success or failure of conservation programmes for consumers.

## References

Barrett, S. and Hill, M. 1984. Policy, bargaining and structure in implementation theory: towards an integrated perspective. *Policy and Politics*, 12, 3, 219-240.

Baumgartner, T. and Burns, T.R. 1984. *Transitions to alternative energy systems: entrepreneurs, new technologies and social change.* Westview Press, Boulder/London

Bradshaw, J. and Harris, T. 1983. *Energy and social policy.* Routledge and Kegan Paul, London.

Buxton, M. and McGee, C. 1986. Energy, employment and welfare: Process and policy in Australian domestic energy programmes. In E. Monnier, G. Gaskell, P. Ester, B. Joerges, B. LaPillonne, C. Midden, and L. Puiseux, *Consumer Behaviour and Energy Policy: An International Perspective.* Praeger, New York.

Claxton, J.D., Gorn, G.J. and Wienberg, C.B. 1986. Energy policy to serve low income households. In E. Monnier, G. Gaskell, P. Ester, B. Joerges, B. LaPillonne, C. Midden, and L. Puiseux, *Consumer Behaviour and Energy Policy: An International Perspective.* Praeger, New York.

Crossley, D.J., 1983. *Consumer energy conservation policies and programmes in Australia.* CECP Technical Report Vol. XI, IIUG. Wissenschaftszentrum, Berlin.

De Boer, J., Ester, P., Mindell, C. and Schopman, M., 1983. *Consumer energy conservation policies and programmes in the Netherlands/energiebesparingsprogramma's ten Behoeve van Consumenten in Nederland. (Bilingual)* CECP Technical Report Vol.

VIII, IIUG. Wissenschaftszentrum, Berlin.

Ellis, P. and Gaskell, G. 1978. *A review of social research on the individual energy consumer.* LSE, London.

Ester, P., Gaskell, G., Joerges, B., Midden, C., Van Raaij, W.F. and De Vries, T., 1984. *Consumer Behaviour and Energy Policy.* North Holland, Amsterdam.

Gaskell, G. 1983. Consumer energy research: progress and prospects. *Journal of Economic Psychology,* 3, 185-191.

Gaskell, G. and Pike, R. 1983. *Consumer energy conservation policies and programmes in Britain.* CECP Technical Report Vol. VI. IIUG. Wissenschaftszentrum, Berlin.

Hildebrandt, L. and Joerges, B. 1983. *Consumer energy conservation policies and programmes in the Federal Republic of Germany/energiesparprogramme fur private Haushalte in der Bundesrepublik Deutschland (Bilingual)* CECP Technical Report IV, IIUG, Wissenschaftszentrum, Berlin.

Hildebrandt, L. and Joerges, B. 1984. Energieberatung fur private Haushalte auf der ortlichen Ebene: ein Vergleich von vier Programmen, In *einer suddeutschen Gemeinde.* IIUG. Wissenschaftszentrum, Berlin.

Hutton, S., Gaskell, G., Pike, R., Bradshaw, J., and Corden, A., 1985. *Energy efficiency in low income households. An evaluation of local insulation projects,* Department of Energy. HMSO, London.

Joerges, B., 1983. *Consumer energy research: An international bibliography.* CECP Technical Report, XII, IIUG. Wissenschaftszentrum, Berlin.

Joerges, B. and Mueller, H. 1983. *Energy conservation programmes for consumers: A comparative overview of findings.* CECP Technical Report I, IIUG. Wissenschaftszentrum, Berlin.

Joerges, B. and Olsen, M.E. 1983. *The process of consumer energy conservation: A conceptual framework for programme analysis.* CECP Technical Report I, IIUG, Wissenschaftszentrum, Berlin.

Joerges, B. and Mueller, H. 1984. Energy conservation programmes for consumers: a comparative analysis of policy conflicts and programme response in eight western countries. In P. Ester, G. Gaskell, B. Joerges, C. Midden, W.F. Van Raaij and T. DeVries, eds. *Consumer Behavior and Energy Policy.* North Holland, Amsterdam.

Klingberg, T. et al. 1983. *Consumer energy conservation policies and programmes in Sweden.* CECP Technical Report IX, IIUG, Wissenschaftszentrum, Berlin.

Klingberg, T. 1984. *Local implementation of two Swedish energy conservation programmes in the household sector.* National Swedish Institute for Building Research, Gaevle.

Klingberg, T. and Wickman, K. 1984. *Energy trends and policy impacts: An analysis of energy statistics from seven countries within the CECP project.* CECP Technical Report III, IIUG. Wissenschaftszentrum, Berlin.

Leyral, R. and Monnier, E. 1983. *Politiques de maitrise de l'energie domestic en France.* CECP Technical Report V, IIUG, Wissenschaftszentrum, Berlin.

Leyral, R., 1984. *Impacts sociaux de programme locaux pour la maitrise de l'energie. Les cas de Veynes, La Rochelle, Conflans-ste-Honorine, I, Analyse des programmes et des leurs contexts.* CSTB/AFME, Paris.

McDougall, G.J.R. and Ritchie, J.R.B. 1979. Consumer energy conservation. A framework for policy research. In Olsen, J.(ed.) *Advances in Consumer Research,* 7, Association for Consumer Research, San Francisco, CA.

Mills, C.W. 1959. *The Sociological Imagination* Oxford University Press: Oxford.

Monnier, E. 1984. *Impacts sociaux de programmes locaux pour la maitrise de l'energie. Les cas de Veynes, La Rochelle, Conflans-Ste-Honorine, II, Evaluation des Effets Induits.* CSTB/AFME, Paris.

Mueller, H. 1984. *Consumer energy conservation policies and programmes. A comparative analysis of programme design and implementation in eight western countries.* CECP Technical Report II, IIUG, Wissenschaftszentrum, Berlin.

Olsen, M. 1983. *Consumer energy conservation policies and programmes in the United States and the Pacific North West region.* CECP Technical Report X, IIUG, Wissenschaftszentrum, Berlin.

Olsen, M.E. and Fonseca, V. 1984. *Linkages between community energy conservation programmes and household energy use.* Social Research Center. WA:Washington State Univ. Pullman.

Olsen, M. and Goodnight, J.A. 1977. *Social aspects of energy conservation.* Northwest Energy Policy Project.

Olsen, M. and Joerges, B. 1981. *The process of consumer energy conservation: an international perspective.* IIUG, Wissenschaftszentrum, Berlin.

Perlman, R.R.L. and Warren, R.L. 1977 *Families in the energy crisis: impacts and implications for theory and policy.* Ballinger, Cambridge, Mass.

Schnaiberg, A. 1975. Social syntheses of the societal - environmental dialectic: the role of distributional impacts. *Social Science Quarterly,* 56, 1, 5-20.

Seligman, C., Darley, J.M. and Becker, L.J. 1978. Behavioral approaches to residential energy conservation. *Energy and Buildings* 1, 3, 324-337.

Shippee, G. 1980. Energy conservation and conservation psychology: A review and conceptual analysis. *Environmental Management* 4, 4, 297-314.

Stern, P.C., Black, J.S. and Elworth, J.T. 1981. *Home energy conservation: programs and strategies for the 1980's.* Consumer Union Foundation, New York.

Stern, P.C. and Gardner,, G.T. 1980. A review and critique of energy research in psychology. *Social Science Energy Review,* 3, Yale University Press, New Haven N.J.

Warkov, S. 1978. *Energy policy in the United States: Social and behavioural dimensions.* Praeger, New York.

Warkov, S. and Ferree, J.D. 1986 Residential energy assistance in Connecticut: social inequity and institutional response. In E. Monnier, G. Gaskell, P. Ester, B. Joerges, B. LaPillonne, C. Midden, and L. Puiseux, *Consumer Behaviour and Energy Policy: An International Perspective.* Praeger, New York.

Wickman, R. 1984. *International residential energy statistics: A compilation of data from eight Western countries.* CECP Technical Report III, IIUG, Wissenschaftszentrum, Berlin.

Winett, R.A. and Neale, M.S. 1979. Psychological framework for energy conservation in buildings: strategies, outcomes, and directions. *Energy and Buildings,* 2, 101-116.

Zografos, K., Warkov, S., Joerges, B. and Megaloconomos, G. 1983. *Consumer energy conservation policies and programmes in Greece. (Greek version by K. Zografos; bilingual).* CECP Technical Report VII, IIUG, Wissenschaftszentrum, Berlin.

# PART II
# THE NATIONAL CASE STUDIES

# 2 Local insulation projects for disadvantaged consumers in Britain

GEORGE GASKELL

## Policy background

*Energy efficiency policies in Britain*

In Britain about 28 percent of energy consumption in Britain occurs in the residential sector (Select Committee on Energy 1982). When economic viability and possible take up of energy efficiency investments are taken into account it is estimated that savings of 25 percent could be made by the year 2000 (ACEC 1983). Since 1973 government policy has promoted energy efficiency in this sector by the use of a variety of economic, informational and regulatory strategies.

Up to 1981 these are described in detail in Gaskell and Pike (1983a). For more recent developments see the Third Report of the Select Committee on Energy (1986). Here a summary of the major elements is presented.

*Market forces:* The fundamental objective of the present government's energy efficiency policy is to price fuel at 'realistic', long-run marginal cost levels. The emphasis on pricing policy is a result of a broader free market economic strategy. In the context of energy it is argued that pricing policies both encourage consumers to use energy more efficiently and make energy saving investments more cost-effective and attractive. Thus appropriately set prices are the signals to consumers to make optimum decisions on energy efficiency. In pursuit of this policy electricity prices rose 5 percent above the increase in the industry's costs, and gas prices rose 10 percent above the rate of inflation during the period 1980-82.

*Incentives:* Households are encouraged to insulate their lofts and hot water tanks with the help of home insulation grants administered by local authorities on behalf of the Department of the Environment. Householders in dwellings with less than 25mm of loft insulation qualify for a 66 percent grant up to a maximum of £69 to increase the insulation to 100mm. For pensioners a 90 percent grant, up to a maximum of £95, is available. Local authorities can improve insulation standards in their own housing stock using the home improvement programme. The Department of Health and Social Security make a contribution to conservation policy by paying single payments to enable claimants of supplementary benefit to purchase materials for lagging hot water tanks and draught proofing their dwellings.

*Information campaigns:* Campaigns of exhortation and practical advice in the national and local media using the themes of 'Save it', 'Make the most of Energy' and more recently 'Get more for your Monergy' and, for example, the Energy Saver Shows and Energy Efficiency Year, attempt to increase awareness and change attitudes and behaviour by informing consumers about energy efficiency and the benefits to be derived from it.

*Regulation* has been used most extensively in setting standards for conservation in new buildings. Mandatory standards for insulation of roofs and walls have recently been improved from 0.6 and 1.0 to 0.35 and 0.60 respectively (maximum 'u' values, w/m 2 deg. C).

These three strategies have had an impact. By 1983, 83 percent of homes whose lofts could be insulated had been, 28 percent had some double glazing, and 90 percent of hot water tanks had been lagged (National Domestic Equipment Survey). However, the potential for energy saving in the domestic sector is still very large. Only 25 percent of local authority homes have loft insulation to the present standards and less than 14 percent of dwellings where it is possible have cavity infill. The Building Research Establishment estimate that only 45 percent of the potential energy savings in the residential sector have been achieved.

*Disadvantaged consumers and the growth of the voluntary sector schemes*

These policies have been pursued at the cost of increasing social disparities. As a result of the priority given to pricing policy, fuel poverty, the inability to afford adequate warmth in the home, is now more prevalent (Bradshaw and Harris 1983). The incentives given for insulation investments have been taken up by the better-off householders but less so by tenants and other disadvantaged groups. For example, while 90 percent of upper and middle class households now have insulated loft spaces, the figure for the working class is only 74 percent. In the English House Conditions Survey 1981, it was found that only 36 percent of private tenants and only 62 percent of single pensioners had loft insulation compared with 73 percent overall (Bradshaw and Hutton 1984).

The reason for these differences is that in practice these energy conservation programmes have been most relevant and attractive to owner occupiers, who have the incentive to improve their properties, the funds available and the ability to cope with grant procedures. As result these policies have had inequitable distributive consequences. Typically the poor and the elderly, who have the greatest need to use energy efficiently for reasons of both economy and comfort, spend a much larger proportion of their budget on fuel, and are more likely to live in old or low standard homes with inefficient and costly heating systems. Price rises hit their budgets hardest but because of their circumstances they are least able to respond to price signals and exhortation. Even the homes insulation scheme which provides capital grants requires them to find the balance between the grant allowed and the total cost of insulation. Furthermore many of the poorest consumers live in the rented sector bringing into focus the vexed and unresolved issue of whether landlords or tenants are responsible for energy efficiency house improvements. Findings from the English House Conditions Survey highlight the outcomes of these various problems. Of the single pensioners without loft insulation, 21 percent had not insulated because they were not responsible for the property, 8 percent because they felt it was not worth it, 15 percent because they could not afford it and 27 percent because they had never thought about it. The finding that as many as 41 percent did not know about loft insulation grants highlights the limited impact of present energy conservation programmes on this group.

A contributory factor to these disparities in the scope and effectiveness of current programmes is the historic division of responsibility between government departments for energy conservation and related social policy. The Department of Environment deals with insulation grants as part of its housing improvement policy, the Department of Health and Social Security gives selective grants to poorer families for hot water tank insulation and draught proofing, an aspect of social policy, and the Department of Energy is concerned with general energy conservation policy. Although energy conservation within government is now co-ordinated by the Energy Efficiency Office, the key spending on domestic insulation takes place in other departments for whom energy efficiency is a secondary priority. With limited resources and an objective of achieving cost-effective energy savings the Energy Efficiency Office has concentrated its efforts on the industrial sector while relying on price policies and information campaigns for residential consumers. Low-income consumers, although almost 20 percent of households, are accorded low priority in terms of government spending perhaps because it is assumed that the potential for energy savings from this group is small.

However, recognizing that disadvantaged consumers were not benefiting from present national energy efficiency programmes, the government supported the development of community based voluntary sector projects operating under the aegis of Neighbourhood Energy Action (NEA). NEA is a National Council of Voluntary Organizations (NCVO) service that was set up to encourage community based action to help low income families cope with rising energy costs. It advises community groups and other local bodies about setting up and running projects using government grants to provide energy advice and low or no-cost home insulation for poorer families. In providing this service local projects meet a second objective, creating jobs and training opportunities in areas of high unemployment. NEA is co-ordinated from the NEA Information Centre in Newcastle, where the pioneering Keeping Newcastle Warm project was a precursor to the NEA initiative.

*Local energy initiatives*

The first voluntary sector project 'Insulate a Pensioner' was established by the environmental group 'Friends of the Earth' in Durham, with financial assistance from Age Concern. Initially using volunteers and then employing regular workers under a national job creation programme, this provided a highly subsidized insulation service to pensioners and disabled people living in Durham. FOE Durham produced a pack describing how other groups could set up, run and maintain a local insulation project, and in 1977 set up an Energy Advice Service to provide information to other voluntary organizations and local advice agencies.

The Durham initiative and a similar project in Birmingham, showing that the same principles could be applied successfully in an inner city context, provided a stimulus for further schemes. In showing that local organizations could cater for consumer groups who had fallen through the net of national programmes, these projects generated considerable interest nationally. Subsequently the Department of Energy encouraged local authorities to use the job creation programme to establish insulation projects for their public sector housing and a number of voluntary organizations set up similar schemes for disadvantaged householders in the private rented and owner occupied sectors.

Following the run down of the Durham initiative, the city of Newcastle became the focal point for the development of local energy projects, when the City Council supported the establishment of an Energy Advice Unit and an insulation project. The number of projects increased rapidly in 1981 when the National Council for Voluntary Organizations (NCVO) set up Neighbourhood Energy Action (NEA) to provide support, advice, information and training for existing projects and to stimulate the creation of new schemes. The Department of Energy provided financial support for NEA by contributing to its running costs and by offering seedcorn grants to help with the planning and promotion costs (£500 maximum) of intended projects, and a grant (£5000 maximum) to cover the initial expenditure required to establish a project, for example transport, equipment and materials.

When established the funding for the voluntary sector projects comes from a variety of different sources. The staffing, labour and administration costs are usually met by various government schemes designed to create jobs and regenerate deprived urban areas. The cost of materials for loft and tank insulation is paid by the home insulation grants scheme (HIGS) from the Department of the Environment administered by the local authorities. For those on supplementary benefit with savings of less that £500, a single payment from the Department of Health and Social Security for materials for simple draught proofing and hot water tank insulation is available. Where the grants for materials are insufficient, the client is often required to pay the balance. Other sources of funds to run schemes come from local authorities, charities, businesses and commerce. The projects use a variety of techniques to target clients including direct canvassing, leaflets, local media, visits to clubs, referrals from local agencies and social networks.

## The research strategy

By 1982, although these voluntary sector initiatives had received considerable recognition and support from both local and central government and from other interested bodies there was little independent evidence concerning the efficiency of their operation or indeed about the effectiveness of the service they provided. Thus the present research was conducted with the objective of making a detailed evaluation of both the projects themselves and the impact they have had on their clients. The potential contribution of these projects to national policy for the efficient use of energy is not the only reason for studying them. Local energy projects may also be important in contributing to four other policy goals.

*Job creation:* They have potential in providing socially useful work which would not be done otherwise. At the local level they give work to the unskilled and unemployed, nationally they help to develop the domestic sector insulation industry (Association for the Conservation of Energy 1983).

*Relief of fuel poverty:* It is now widely recognized that attempts to relieve fuel poverty by social security payments and/or adjustments to prices, are both wasteful and ineffective unless poor consumers' homes are well insulated and have efficient heating systems. Improving the insulation level of the houses of low income families is an important contribution to relieving the problems of debt, discomfort and distress caused by high energy prices.

*Improving the housing stock:* The target population for local conservation projects - the poor and elderly - tend to live in the most dilapidated housing. The projects therefore may contribute to the improvement of this housing stock.

*A model for community energy projects:* While the NEA schemes are focused on disadvantaged consumers it is possible that a development and extension of NEA would offer an effective mechanism for the delivery of more comprehensive energy conservation services at the local level. Of particular interest, is the extent to which these decentralized schemes are more successful in targeting and attracting

44

clients than the typical government/local authority programme.

The design of the evaluation involved three stages: a postal survey of all projects known to NEA: an in-depth study of 5 selected projects: and a survey of clients and a comparison sample of non-clients of these five projects. The postal questionnaire achieved a response rate of 85 percent and in this details were elicited of the aims and origins of the project, contacts with NEA, deployment and funding of manpower, financial support, links with other agencies and services offered to clients. Five projects were then chosen for detailed case studies. They were selected on a variety of criteria including their clientele, location, sponsor and the range of services provided. The projects selected of which the first two have been described were:

Midland - a long established Friends of the Earth project.

Northern - the largest project in the country in terms of workforce and jobs accomplished.

Lothian - a project in a rural area in Scotland with a very high level of unemployment set up as part of a scheme to stimulate community owned business ventures.

Tees - a project covering a wide area in Cleveland and part of a Community Enterprise Scheme to provide jobs for the unemployed.

Borough - a new project in London, sponsored by the local council to create employment opportunities.

The sampling frame for the consumer survey was the record of work completed by the five projects. The sample was selected to achieve equal numbers of households who had had loft insulation and draught proofing installed. Clients were interviewed in their homes and details elicited of socio-demographic characteristics, fuel use and heating arrangements, level of insulation, the work done by the project and its effects. A response rate of 82 percent was achieved giving a sample of 310. The comparison sample was restricted to pensioner clients only and obtained by a random route method. 92 percent of the pensioner clients were successfully matched. (N = 167)

# The institutional arrangements for the local energy projects

A variety of agencies, national and local, statutory and non-statutory, may be involved in local projects either directly or indirectly, formally or informally and in terms of financial support and/or other resources. In Figure 2.1 overleaf, a general model of the agencies involved and their particular roles is presented.

There is no agency on which all projects are formally dependent in terms of definition of goals, finance or accountability. A quasi-legitimating agency is the Energy Efficiency Office of the Department of Energy which reports on their progress in Parliament, provides part financial support for central NEA and grants to help for local projects in their initial stages.

The Energy Efficiency Office is represented on the NEA funding bodies liaison group which was set up to oversee the development of the NEA programme. Other members of this committee include the Manpower Services Commission, which provides staff costs for most projects through the Community Programme and the National Council for Voluntary Organizations, the charity which from the outset has sponsored the central NEA in its support of local schemes. It should be noted that this describes the situation at the time the research was conducted. The Manpower Services Commission has withdrawn from the liaison group since it no longer funds the central NEA but the Department of the Environment is now involved in so far as it funds a special NEA post for promoting local authority support for projects.

Although the projects could not function without grants to clients for insulation materials from the Department of Environment and e Department of Health and Social Security, these two Departments, whose support is essential but indirect, are not represented on the Liaison Group. At the local level projects have direct contact with the Energy Efficiency Office and the Manpower Services Commission and are encouraged to use the support services of NEA. NEA's role is entirely advisory and it has no authority over the projects. Informal contacts may also be established with local offices of the Department of Health and Social Security, the offices of the gas and electricity utilities, local authorities who administer the home insulation grants scheme and other voluntary bodies.

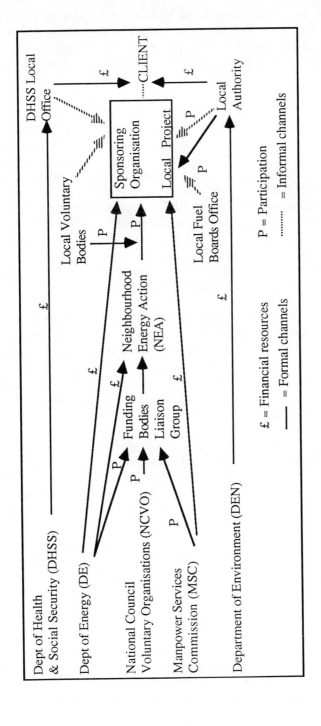

Figure 2.1 The agencies involved in local energy project programmes

The extent to which these local bodies participate in and the type of contact they have with projects varies. In the minimal case the local authorities and DHSS offices pay grants to the clients for insulation materials fitted by the project but have no dealings with the project itself. In other situations, a local agreement is reached, normally initiated by the project, whereby the grants are paid directly to it and the two statutory bodies along with the utilities may help with project promotion and client referrals. In some instances local authorities take a much more active role in setting up a project, providing part or complete funding for the enterprise and giving a variety of other forms of of assistance, for example premises, management advice and staff training. The extent of local voluntary groups' participation is also variable. In some cases they take an active role in project management while in others they have no formal involvement and may or may not take part in project promotion and client referrals. Such a variety of arrangements is perhaps typical of the flexibility and opportunism of the voluntary sector but they carry with them certain costs to the programme as a whole.

There is imbalance and potential tension both within local projects and between the various participating agencies with respect to the primary objectives of the programme. The provision of energy conservation services for low income households is the main objective of the programme and job creation a product of this. However, the balance of funding of local projects by the Department of Energy(DEN) and the Manpower Services Commission (MSC) is the reverse of this - the majority being provided by the job creating MSC and much less by the DEN. If improving the thermal comfort of disadvantaged consumers is the overall objective then both of those bodies are less directly involved than the DHSS which has only informal links with the local projects, although providing some basic funding through single payments. The role of the Department of the Environment in providing home insulation grants is peripheral to all these objectives except that improving the housing stock through increased insulation does have an effect on comfort. Thus as an instrument, NEA is not ideally designed to promote the aims of any one government department; it tends to operate in the gaps between departments, some projects emphasizing one objective and some another. The effect of this is evidenced in the priority which many projects now in the development stage give to job creation above energy related work. Job creation was reported by 37 percent as their major objective while 56 percent mentioned energy related services. This contrasts with the established projects where the respective percentages were 21 and 78. There is a danger in this shift in main focus for the longer term success of the scheme. An overriding commitment to job creation is a potential weakness because if running an insulation project becomes too difficult, organizers may change their activities to a variety of other pursuits acceptable to sponsoring organizations.

## The impacts of the programme

The description of programme impacts is divided into two sections concerning (a) the growth of the programme as a whole and the achievements of the active projects, as assessed by responses in the postal survey of projects and (b) the aggregate performance of the five projects selected for detailed investigation, drawing on both the in depth study of the projects and the survey of the client and comparison groups.

*The evolution and achievements of the programme*

In a short period NEA and the projects it has helped to establish have made considerable achievements. When NEA was set up in 1981 there were less than 10 local projects. By September 1982 there were 28 active insulation projects, five energy advice units giving a service to clients of advice and information about energy use and welfare benefits and 57 schemes in the planning stages. In total all these employed 234 people. In 1984, after this study was completed there were 90 active projects projects employed some 3000 people.

In the year ending 30th September 1982 the 28 active insulation projects, which varied both in size (from 3 to 19 employees) and length of operation, had carried out insulation work in a total of 7979 homes. This figure includes draught proofing in 6,281 homes and the insulation of 2,396 lofts. 91 percent of the clients received a home insulation grant reducing the average cost of loft insulation from £83 to £20. The single payment for draught proofing reduced the average cost of this service from £22 to £8, although many clients received this service free of charge. In addition to insulation services a number of schemes reported that they gave energy advice and services to clients. In general, however, the provision of advice did not appear to be high priority and only a few schemes could be described as offering a comprehensive service.

The survey of projects underlined the importance of an advisory agency in the development of local projects. All 57 schemes in the planning stage had made contact with NEA and of these 46 had not been offering services of any kind prior to this contact. The schemes reported receiving a wide variety of assistance from NEA, including provision of information, general advice and assistance, help with grant applications, provision of training opportunities, advice regarding government policy, publicity materials and liaison with other schemes. Of the relevant cases 95 percent said that NEA had been useful in helping them set up and 86 percent of established projects said NEA had been useful in helping them to develop and expand. For many projects, NEA is a catalyst for their interest in energy conservation, their link with central government in respect of funding applications, and a central resources for information and advice on project planning and organization.

*The overall achievements of the five selected projects*

To assess the achievements of the projects the following criteria were chosen: penetration into the community assessed by general awareness of its existence, knowledge of its services and reasons for participation; services in terms of the insulation and other work carried out for clients and the impacts of these in terms of comfort, satisfaction, energy savings and cost and benefits.

*Awareness and knowledge of the projects:* By definition all the clients are aware of the projects existence. To assess the general penetration of the project in the locality the comparison sample were asked whether they had heard of it. Although the projects are small in scale, with limited resources, and some had been active for only a year, 37 percent of the comparison group had heard of their local project. Approximately half became aware as a result of direct canvassing, promotional activities and the local media, and 40 percent through social networks, that is from friends, relatives and neighbours. However, 57 percent of those who knew about a project had no idea of the services which were being offered. It is generally acknowledged that pensioners are a difficult group to target and to achieve familiarity with available services. These findings suggest on the one hand that the projects have already had a considerable impact within their communities, but that local channels of communication, including social networks while creating awareness appear to be limited in terms of the specific information they disseminate.

*Reasons for participating:* Clients decisions to participate were based on expectations of improved comfort, mentioned by 95 percent and lower energy costs, mentioned by 49 percent. Significantly over half the sample had never thought of installing insulation prior to their contact with the project showing the lack of success of existing publicity in raising awareness among low income consumers. For those who had considered doing such work the main reason for not doing it was financial.

*Insulation and other work carried out by the five projects:* Turning to the clients, the five projects installed loft insulation into 52 percent of the households with an accessible uninsulated loft; fitted a hot water tank jacket in 44 percent of households with an uninsulated hot water tank; and fitted draught proofing in 93 percent of client households (in almost half the homes the project added to, and improved, existing draught proofing.)

As a result of this work, the percentage of clients with loft insulation went above the 1982 national average (81 and 74 percent respectively), but were still below the national average for hot water tank insulation (77 and 84 percent respectively). When contrasted with the comparison sample, clients having been much more poorly insulated prior to intervention, had overtaken the levels within the comparison by a considerable percentage (see Table 2.1). In addition, not only were a greater percentage of client households equipped with draught proofing, but the extent of draught proofing was also greater than the comparison group.

Table 2.1
Levels of insulation pre and post NEA in client, matched client and comparison samples

|  | Matched clients | | Matched comparison group | All clients | |
|---|---|---|---|---|---|
|  | % N=167 | | % N=167 | % N=310 | |
|  | Pre | Post | | Pre | Post |
| Loft insulation | 29 | 93 | 71 | 59 | 81 |
| Hot water tank insulation | 59 | 87 | 75 | 59 | 77 |
| Draught proofing | 47 | 86 | 52 | 47 | 97 |

In addition to technical improvements, some projects described their work as including advice and information on both energy use and related social welfare issues. In the survey, however, 91 percent of the clients claimed to have received no advice from the scheme, a finding that will be discussed later.

*Impacts of the projects' work on clients*

*Comfort:* The work was found to have made a noticeable impact on the clients subjective comfort levels. 89 percent of them described their homes as warmer and 92 percent as less draughty. Comparisons between clients with different insulation improvements showed that draught proofing had the greatest effect on reported comfort levels.

*Satisfaction and project credibility:* In terms of quality of service, standard of work and value for money, the projects' activities were described as satisfactory. Although one in four jobs gave some problems later on, for example draught stripping coming loose, difficulties opening and closing doors. As an indication of the projects credibility with clients it was found that 47 percent had recommended other people to contact the local scheme for insulation services.

*Energy Savings:* With the respondents' permission, gas and electricity consumption figures were obtained from the fuel boards. Data for both gas and electricity for the first two complete quarters after the project's work was compared with the consumption data for the corresponding period in the previous year. A base-line for consumption was established using the same four quarters for the comparison households. Changes in gas and electricity consumption were aggregated and expressed in gigajoules and clients and the comparison group compared to give an estimate of the effects of the insulation work on energy use. Owing to the frequency in the company records of estimated data, the sample size for this analysis was reduced to approximately 180 households.

The analysis showed that the insulation measures installed enabled clients to reduce energy consumption relative to the comparison group by between 2 and 5 percent. Analysis showed that loft insulation produced savings of 2 percent and draught proofing 5.0 percent. These reductions are not as great as might be expected if all the benefits of insulation had been taken up in reduced consumption. The Watt Committee estimates that loft insulation and draught proofing would lead to reductions of 8 and 12  percent respectively.

However, as has been noted above, the clients are taking at least some of the benefits of insulation in increased comfort rather than reduced consumption. At the same time, the relatively small reductions are to be expected since pensioners tend not to use whole house heating for reasons of economy. With zoned heating focused particularly on living rooms the benefits of loft insulation in terms of energy savings can be expected to be small.

*Cost and pay back periods:* The average cost of materials for loft insulation was £78; 34 percent of clients received a 66 percent grant amounting to £58, and 63 percent received the 90 percent grant amounting to £69. The average contribution made by the clients was £15. For draught proofing the average cost of materials was £19, but for those receiving a DHSS single payment, the cost was £25 in comparison to £13 for non-recipients; 45 percent of clients received a single payment. The DHSS single payment clearly leads to more extensive works - 5 windows and 4 doors on average in comparison to 2 windows and 3 doors for non-recipients. While 75 percent of clients were able to find the money for their contribution to work without difficulty, the remaining 25 percent had experienced difficulty.

With an average weekly fuel expenditure for client households of £8.60, the saving due to loft insulation is estimated at 26p, and to draught proofing at 46p per week; an estimated annual saving of £13.52 and £23.92 respectively. Assuming a rate of inflation of 5 percent in the price of fuel, the pay back period for insulation and draught proofing in this instance are shown in Table 2.2.

Table 2.2
Pay back period for loft insulation and draught proofing

|  | Payback Period |
|---|---|
| loft insulation | |
| client's contribution | 2.1 years |
| total cost of loft insulation excluding labour | 11.6 years |
| draught proofing | |
| client's contribution | 9 months |
| total cost of draught proofing excluding labour | 1.1 years |

Hutton et al (1985) conducted a simple cost benefit analysis of NEA projects based on a telephone survey in 1984 in which various performance indicators of the projects working at that time were determined. This cost benefit analysis estimated the total private savings in terms of reduced fuel expenditure and increased comfort against total public expenditure. This showed that within two years there was a net benefit to society on fuel savings and increased comfort after accounting for the cost of the manpower and materials used by NEA, assuming a discount rate of 5 percent. The pay-back period was increased by a year when more pessimistic assumptions were made about the benefits to be gained from draught proofing and loft insulation.

*Strengths and weaknesses of the service to clients*

Overall, the five projects are having a positive and clearly beneficial effect on their clients. The projects are successfully targeting disadvantaged consumers achieving satisfactory levels of awareness of the available service and giving eligible clients improvements to their home insulation which lead to greater comfort and lower fuel costs.

On two criteria the service was found to be limited. Approximately 20 percent of all clients still had uninsulated lofts and no hot water tank jacket after the project had visited them. There are a number of possible explanations for this, for example ineligibility for grants and client refusal, but there must be some cases where needed work was not done without good reason. Secondly only a small percentage of clients (less than 10 percent) said that they had received advice or information about energy use from the projects. Some projects staff argue that advice is irrelevant to those living at low levels of thermal comfort but while this may be true for some it is not necessarily true for all. 60 percent of the clients had central heating and some 15 percent were using it continuously during the winter. Those in rented property seldom receive instructions on system control and may well be using it inefficiently. Other research has shown that personal advice on more efficient energy use can lead to greater economy without less comfort (Gaskell and Pike 1983b). Given the difficulties faced by projects in contacting disadvantaged consumers it would seem to be a lost opportunity not to provide more comprehensive services.

## Project characteristics and performance

The objective of this section is to determine whether the way in which projects are organized and managed influences the extent to which they give satisfactory services to their clients. To investigate this issue, which may have implications for the development of the programme, the five projects are firstly evaluated on a number of criteria which together give an overall ranking of the projects in terms of effectiveness. Secondly the projects are contrasted on a number of organizational characteristics which are hypothesized to influence effectiveness. A comparison of these two analyses highlights those organizational variables which may explain differences in the performance of the projects.

### Project effectiveness

The following criteria of effectiveness were selected:

* awareness of the project in the wider community, assessed by the percentage of comparison group households who had heard of the project.

* knowledge of project services assessed by the percentage in the comparison sample knowing what services the project offers.

* the number of conservation actions achieved, that is, the number of clients per worker per year for each project.

* the quality of the work, assessed by the percentage of clients who report problems with draught proofing fitted by the project.

* the project's credibility with clients, assessed by the percentage of clients who have recommended the project to other people.

The rank ordering of projects on each of these five criteria is presented in Table 2.3 a score of 5 denotes most successful on the particular criterion.

The rank ordering for individual characteristics must be interpreted with some caution given the differing contexts in which the projects operate and the small sample sizes. However, it seems fair to conclude from the overall ranking that Midland and Northern provide the most effective service followed by Lothian, Tees and Borough.

## Table 2.3
### Assessments of five criteria of project effectiveness

|          | A | K | C | Q | Cr | R  |
|----------|---|---|---|---|----|----|
| Northern | 3 | 5 | 5 | 4 | 4  | 21 |
| Midlands | 4 | 3 | 4 | 5 | 5  | 21 |
| Lothian  | 5 | 4 | 2 | 1 | 3  | 15 |
| Tees     | 1 | 1 | 3 | 3 | 2  | 10 |
| Borough  | 2 | 1 | 1 | 2 | 1  | 7  |

Key:
- A     Awareness
- K     Knowledge
- C     Conservation
- Q     Quality
- Cr     Credibility
- R     Ranking overall

*Project organizational characteristics*

To what extent can such differences in effectiveness be attributed to the characteristics of the projects themselves. To investigate this the projects are assessed on five general organizational attributes.

*Maturity:* It is hypothesized that maturity, that is length of operation and the experience accruing from it, is of value to projects giving employees work and management skills and the project time to establish itself in the locality. The latter aspect was frequently mentioned by newly established projects who had to spend a great deal of their time promoting services and contacting clients.

*Financial flexibility:* Many projects rely on job creation funds for staff costs but these are relatively inflexible having certain conditions of use which may limit project effectiveness. Workers on job creation funds can be employed for a maximum of one year and the average wage for workers in any project is limited to £60. Funds from this scheme are also reassessed annually. On account of this attracting and keeping good quality staff particularly in senior positions is difficult, as is longer term planning. Projects with additional and more flexible resources are in a better position to employ experienced staff for management functions. Furthermore the major alternative source of funds is from the Urban Programme from which resources are allocated for a five year time span.

Most projects are in receipt of Department of Energy start-up grants which cover the expenses necessary for establishment. But these are limited and one-off. Projects with other funds which can be used to finance essential remedial work in homes prior to installing insulation or to top-up the grants for those clients who cannot afford their contribution may be more able to provide an effective service.

*Size:* In terms of organizational structure projects usually have a manager, a stock controller, a finance officer and a project leader to organize and administer a team of insulation workers. Economies of scale may accrue within larger projects since the same management/administrative complement is necessary whether the project is relatively large for example 20 employees, or small with perhaps 8 staff.

*Commitment:* The extent to which the project or its sponsoring agency is committed to energy related work may be related to effectiveness. In practice such commitment usually arises out of the interests and enthusiasm of a key person. Projects with a strong commitment to job creation but with a weak orientation towards energy services might be expected to be less effective than those which have home insulation and relief of fuel poverty as their primary goal.

*Linkages:* We define a linkage as a participating agency with whom the project co-operates to receive support of the following kinds:-

* financial: for example, resources from local authorities, business charities.

* administrative: for example, management services and advice on accountancy

* political: for example, positive or negative support from local political leaders, trade unions.

* operational : for example, promotion of project services and help with client referrals from fuel boards, statutory agencies and voluntary bodies.

Table 2.4

Project Characteristics

| | M | F staff costs | F other costs | S | C | L finan-cial | L adminis-trative | L polit-ical | L operat-ional | Overall Ranking |
|---|---|---|---|---|---|---|---|---|---|---|
| Northern | 4 | 5 | 5 | 5 | 5 | 5 | 5 | 5 | 5 | 44 |
| Midland | 5 | 4 | 3 | 2 | 5 | 3 | 2 | 3 | 4 | 31 |
| Falkirk | 3 | 2 | 3 | 4 | 1 | 2 | 4 | 1 | 3 | 23 |
| Tees | 3 | 2 | 3 | 4 | 3 | 2 | 2 | 3 | 2 | 24 |
| Borough | 1 | 2 | 3 | 1 | 3 | 4 | 2 | 3 | 2 | 21 |

Key:

M = Maturity

F = Flexibility of Funding

S = Size

C = Commitment

L = Linkages

It is predicted that the greater the number of linkages, indicative of a more developed network of participating agencies at the local level the more effective will the project be. As shown in Table 2.4 the five projects are ranked on these characteristics. Again, a rank of 5 denotes the project in the most favourable situation.

*The characteristics of the successful projects*

The overall rank ordering of the projects on the characteristics thought to be determinants of effectiveness is first Northern, second Midland, followed by Lothian, Tees and Borough. Contrasting Table 2.4 and Table 2.3, that is the project characteristics with effectiveness, we find that maturity, flexibility with respect to staff costs, commitment to energy work and operational linkages are the more important characteristics when judged against effectiveness. Two further characteristics should be included in this list. These are size, and flexibility with respect to other costs. The reason for this is that the Northern project, the largest of the five by far and the only one with additional resources to help clients, was achieving 50 percent more conservation actions than Midland.

In summary, the more successful projects judged on the criteria of awareness in the locality, knowledge of project services, quality and quantity of conservation actions and credibility with clients are larger and have been in operation longer, have more financial flexibility for the employment of staff and the provision of extra help to clients, are more committed to energy services and have more operational linkages with local participating agencies helping to promote the services of the project.

These carry implications for the optimal structure and staff resources, financing and external relations of projects. While maturity cannot be bought its importance in project effectiveness may need recognizing in type of advice that projects receive when starting up and in the setting of priorities for work in their early days of operation.

## Consumer contexts mediating projects impacts

Here we are concerned to find out what are the characteristics of the client and comparison samples that differentiate between those who are able or not able, and willing or not willing to participate in a local project. To do this the role of personal and structural context factors which might influence clients' awareness, knowledge and participation in project services are investigated. Following the conceptual model the community, technical, economic and legal contexts of the three following groups are contrasted.

* 'clients': the projects' clients

* 'non-participants': those in the comparison group who were aware of the project's existence but did not make use of the service

* 'non-awares': those in the comparison group who had not heard of the project

Taken together the analyses of these contexts of consumption may show both the extent to which the projects are successful in targeting their services to disadvantaged consumers and the nature of the obstacles that prevent some from participating.

*The personal context:* No analysis of the personal context, that is consumer's attitudes and values was included in the study, although in the conceptual framework for this multinational project it is seen as an important mediating factor in programme take up. In pilot research it was found that traditional methods for assessing attitudes were unsuccessful with the older respondents that formed the sample. Given an already long and taxing interview it was decided to exclude the personal context since other elicitation techniques proved to be too time consuming.

*The community context:* The finding that 40 percent of 'clients' heard about the local project through friends, relatives and neighbours, suggests that social networks may be an important factor in a project's success in attracting its target group. The questionnaire included a number of items measuring the extent to which households were socially integrated in their locality. These were, length of residence, the amount of communication between households and membership of local organizations. A combination of these was computed to form a measure of social integration for each household. In line with other research, this measure of social integration was related to the degree of urbanization of the area. Households in the rural scheme (Lothian) showing highest social integration scores while those in the largest urban area (Borough) had the lowest. Of these measures of social integration, the index of degree inter-household communication differed significantly between the five projects. In the rural and provincial areas households were more likely to have friends and family living close by and more social contacts than their urban counterparts. Since such social networks have been shown to be important in the diffusion of innovations, an ex post facto analysis was conducted relating the way in which clients contacted the scheme to their level of social integration, measured by the inter-household communication indicator. This analysis might show how projects working in different types of localities might tailor promotional strategies to maximize client referrals. Social psychological research would predict that in areas of high social integration, working through social networks would be most effective while local media/direct canvassing would be better in an area of low integration (Midden and Ritsema 1984).

In Table 2.5 the percentages of clients hearing of the project through the different channels are shown. The project localities have been ordered by level of social integration from low to high.

Table 2.5
How clients became aware of the project

low integration ------------> high integration

|  | B | M | N | T | L |
|---|---|---|---|---|---|
|  | % | % | % | % | % |
| Local media | 44 | 21 | 45 | 41 | 3 |
| Local agency | 12 | 24 | 9 | 2 | 2 |
| Direct canvas | 12 | 3 | 3 | 22 | 71 |
| Social networks | 21 | 52 | 43 | 34 | 24 |

Key:
B  Borough
M  Midland
N  Northern
T  Tees
L  Lothian

It can be seen that the two projects making greatest use of social networks, Midlands and Northern, are not operating in the most socially integrated localities. This is contrary to expectation but can be explained on the basis of an important characteristic determining project effectiveness. Both the Midland and Northern projects had been established for a comparatively long time, had developed some standing in the area, and were thus able to rely on the recommendations of satisfied clients and their acquaintances for new referrals. In addition, Lothian, operating in the most integrated area, relied on direct canvassing as a result of a misunderstanding about the legitimate promotional activities for projects funded under the Community Programme. These findings suggest that the use of social networks for client referrals evolves with the development of a scheme and that in time social networks become a major source of client referrals.

Comparisons between the three groups, 'clients', 'non-participants' and 'non-awares', underline the importance of social integration in determining project awareness. The 'non-aware' group was found to be significantly less socially integrated than either the 'clients' or the 'non-participants'. This suggests that projects are reaching more socially integrated homes and illustrates the importance, on the one hand, of stimulating social networks for client referrals, but equally the importance of other channels, for example, local media, direct canvassing and referrals from statutory and other agencies, in order to reach the more socially isolated households that are eligible for assistance.

In conclusion two factors appear to interact in determining whether awareness of a project diffuses through a community. First, the project's length of operation within that community - the longer a scheme has been operating, the more likely it is that eligible households will have heard of it. Secondly, the degree of social integration of households within the community - the more socially integrated the household, the more likely it is to hear about the project from others.

*The technical context:* Setting aside existing levels of insulation no differences between the three groups were found in terms of house type, the age of the house or heating arrangements. The technical context is most relevant in accounting for the reason why some of those who had heard of the scheme had not participated. A comparison of the 'clients' and 'non-participants' showed that the former lived in homes with considerably poorer insulation characteristics than the latter. The 'clients' were less likely to have any loft insulation or draught proofing and were more likely to complain of dampness and condensation in their homes. Thus the reason why some of those who were aware of the project did not participate is most likely to be that they were not eligible for grants for insulation materials. This is not to say that they had well insulated homes, since any existing loft insulation disqualifies households from the grants.

*The economic context:* As with the technical context the 'clients' were found to be in a less favourable position and to be more disadvantaged than the other groups. A larger percentage of 'clients' were in receipt of supplementary benefit, fewer had other sources of income and they were more likely to be living alone. The need for a low cost insulation service is evidenced by the finding that 60 per cent of the clients said that they could not have afforded to have the work done if their contribution had been £10 more.

*The legal context:* While many local authorities have encouraged the activities of insulation projects, tenants in the private accommodation face particular problems. They need to obtain permission from landlords to have work done but there is also the matter of who is responsible for the client's contribution to the insulation work? Since there is no legislation on this matter the situation is unclear. Comparing the three groups we find that private tenants were well represented in the 'client group' but there were many more in the 'non-aware' than in the 'non-participant groups'. This points to the conclusion that achieving awareness amongst private tenants is difficult but that take-up of service, following awareness is less of a problem.

*Mediating contexts: summary*

It must be remembered that the local projects studied are small in scale and could not be expected to have succeeded in reaching anything but a small percentage of potential clients. The analysis of the 'clients,' 'non-participants' and 'non-awares' indicates that the projects are reaching their target group - their clients are personally and economically disadvantaged and their homes are poorly insulated. To this extent here is a programme that has at least partially managed to reverse the apparent 'law of the free rider'. At the same time it the more socially integrated in the community that are aware of the projects existence. As the schemes expand new efforts will be required to target the more isolated pensioners.

# Conclusions, social scientific and policy implications

## Conclusions

The main finding of this evaluation of the insulation services offered by local projects is that clients gain a considerable benefit from the service. The projects reach households which can be considered to be in fuel poverty. Their homes are poorly insulated, cold and draughty and costly to heat. The service provided by the projects, mainly draught proofing windows and doors and to a lesser extent insulating lofts, results in greater comfort levels (a social benefit) and to reductions of around 5 percent in their use of fuel (an energy saving benefit).

While some of the benefits of insulation are taken up in increased comfort levels, the insulation is still cost effective when judged on the criterion of pay back period. In terms of the clients' own contribution, the pay back period for draught proofing is estimated at about nine months and for total cost excluding labour charges, thirteen months. For loft insulation the figures are 2.1 years and 11.6 years respectively. From the national perspective the cost of manpower and materials in the scheme is paid back in reduced fuel costs and increased comfort within two years.

The projects are found to be meeting a need that would not be alleviated by other means. They cater for those who 'have fallen through the net' of existing national insulation programmes and underline the need for low cost service provided at a local level in order to reach such consumers. As a result of the projects' work, clients have overtaken the insulation standards of similar people living in the neighbourhood. There was no evidence of a 'free rider' effect. It is only through the provision of non-cost labour and subsidized insulation that the clients are able to accept the service offered. In terms of quality of service, standard of work and value for money, the NEA projects are judged to be more than satisfactory by their clients.

The more successful local projects judged on five criteria of effectiveness are larger, have been operating longer, have more flexibility th respect to resources, are more committed to providing an energy service for low income consumers and have more contacts with local agencies who help to promote their services. To increase effectiveness projects must give more effort to targeting less socially integrated households and aim to provide a full insulation service including energy advice rather than just draught proofing or loft insulation.

A task for the supporting government departments is to find resources and the appropriate mechanisms for the funding of materials for remedial building work which is often essential before insulation services can be carried out in clients homes. There is little point in insulating rotten windows and leaking roofs. Which government department should take the lead in these matters is a key issue in determining the longer term success of the programme. We have already discussed the lack of correspondence between the objectives of the sponsoring agencies. One step towards resolving this problem would be a restructuring of the NEA Funding Bodies Liaison Committee into a more general steering committee with representatives from the four rather than the present two government departments.

However, since this may not be feasible, responsibility for the programme could be devolved to NEA or some development of it. To be effective a regional network of initiating/advisory agencies is required with resources to provide the necessary services to developing projects. An important task for this initiating/advisory body would be that of establishing formal mechanisms for the type of operational linkages which we have found to be vital in project effectiveness. For example, the Fuel Boards could be encouraged to give energy advice, training to projects and provide relevant part-time management expertise. In addition, any customers in fuel debt should be informed of the local projects services.

*Social Scientific Implications*

*The innovation process:* In a broader analytic context the local energy conservation projects studied in this research are attempting to create social change: to turn public policy into innovative actions among disadvantaged householders. The rationale for these projects is that equivalent policy instruments organized centrally have had little impact on this group of consumers.

It is interesting to see how the present findings, which confirm the greater effectiveness of local as against central policy instruments, accord with social scientific analyses of the innovation process. Perhaps the most important general analysis is that of Rogers (1983) in which innovation is conceived as a five-stage process. Initially people become aware of an innovation often through the mass media, then they seek out information about it. In this persuasion stage more active communication channels such as interpersonal networks are thought to be influential. Next a decision is made whether to adopt the innovation. The decision to adopt is followed by stages of implementation and confirmation. The decision to adopt is based on characteristics both of the potential adopter and the innovation itself. Adoption is more likely if the innovation has advantages over the present situation, is compatible with the persons values, is not too complex to implement, can be tried out and has observable benefits. Early adopters have been found to be of higher social class, to have favourable attitudes to change and have more exposure to the mass media and more social contacts. While many of these ideas have parallels in the adoption of domestic energy conservation in Britain, the present research was not a direct test of the model since this would have necessitated a broad sample of the population in the vicinity of the projects from which differential awareness, knowledge and participation could have been related to consumers' personal characteristics and contextual conditions. Such an investigation was beyond the scope of this research.

There are two particular issues highlighted by this study that depart from Rogers' general model. The first arises out of the target population, one which Rogers would describe as late adopters. Rogers describes late adopters as those with traditional value orientations who are dubious of innovations and change agents. Adoption lags far behind their awareness. Suspicious of new ideas and a precarious economic position forces them to be cautious about innovations. A somewhat different picture of late adopters emerges in this research. On the one hand the obstacles to adoption are awareness, knowledge and economic considerations. But it is not found that adoption, in circumstances where the economic incentives are favourable, lags behind awareness and knowledge. On the contrary, once low income consumers know of an attractive opportunity they are prepared to take the initiative and request project services. In terms of energy related innovations slow take up may be due more to programme characteristics (poor targeting, information and inadequate incentives) than to the characteristics of consumers themselves.

Secondly, we find that social networks, as predicted by Rogers are important elements in the innovation process. In Rogers' model the mass media are seen as more effective in conveying knowledge about the existence of an innovation but they are not a useful channel for the type of detailed information required at the persuasion and decision stages. This is most effectively gained through the more active interpersonal channels of friends talking to one another about their experiences. These social channels are better able to convey the type of information that is required before a person decides on the appropriateness of an innovation for their personal circumstances. In contrast to Rogers we find social networks contributing to awareness but being less successful in disseminating even basic details of what is on offer. Of course this may be a result of the nature of the sample, old aged pensioners, but it suggests that some social networks may need prompting and educating before they make a contribution to the diffusion of innovations.

*Social policy implications*

Two general issues are highlighted by this research. First, in terms of social policy it illustrates the inequitable distributive consequences of energy conservation policies based on energy pricing and subsidies for insulation. The present sample of low income consumers spend 18 percent of their income on fuel, have poorly insulated homes and live at low levels of thermal comfort (16 degrees C). In contrast, the national average budget share for fuel for the same quarter is 14 percent for all pensioners and 9 percent for all households. The middle classes who have proportionally lower fuel costs and more available resources, are relatively unaffected by price rises and take advantage of home insulation grants. Those most in need of better insulated homes are penalized by high prices and are least able to take advantage of subsidies because of personal circumstances and the nature of the incentive schemes themselves. This contributes in part to the extraordinary imbalance between capital expenditure for energy efficiency in low income households, £18m in 1982-3 and revenue expenditure on heating bills, £1,147m in the same year. This finding led the Select Committee on Energy (1985) to recommend that steps be taken to implement a programme to fully insulate the houses of those on low incomes. In the absence of other policy initiatives the NEA scheme of local energy conservation projects, giving as it does a unique, beneficial and cost effective service to disadvantaged consumers, deserves support.

This research suggests that the minimum requirements for the voluntary sector energy programme to develop and make a substantial contribution to national energy efficiency policy are

* Retaining a strong commitment to energy efficiency work rather than treating it as a convenient vehicle for job creation.

* Providing comprehensive insulation and energy advice services to clients.

* Encouraging local authorities, social security departments and the fuel boards to take an active role in support of local schemes.

* Strengthening the management of projects, by both training courses and the availability of funds such that at least one post in each local scheme is funded independently of the current job creation scheme programme.

* Providing longer term and more adequate funding to the schemes so that they are viable in terms of operating costs independent of other sources.

* Expanding the role of the central co-ordinating body to include regional offices and more resources to promote train and monitor schemes.

Such measures would inevitably demand a greater commitment of financial resources from Government, but even with these measures it must be said it will take decades rather than years to improve the thermal insulation of the homes of the majority of disadvantaged consumers.

## Postscript: official reactions

In its 8th Report the House of Commons Select Committee on Energy (1985), an all party committee of members of parliament with the responsibility of monitoring and commenting on the policies of the Department of Energy, devotes a paragraph to the research from which the present chapter is drawn.

"We welcome the recent publication by the Department of Energy of the Research Study 'Energy Efficiency Low Income Households: An Evaluation of Local Insulation Projects' with its endorsement of the value of the work of Neighbourhood Energy Action (NEA). Some of the conclusions of the study do concern us: the allegation that NEA has only weak support in official circles, the description of turf wars between different Departments of State and the analysis of the hampering effect of the rules of the Homes

Insulation Scheme on the NEA's work. We think it is worth repeating some sentences from the Study's concluding paragraph: 'Despite progress with conservation in the domestic sector, there is still room for a major investment programme to cover uninsulated hot water tanks, lofts, walls and draught proofing. This remaining potential is concentrated in lower income households. Therefore the first priority must be to develop policies that reach out to these households.' We agree, and while we applaud the Department for publishing a study which does not shy away from criticism, we also hope that action will be taken to meet the research study's analysis of defects in Government policy." (para. 23 p.xvii)

The Government's official response is included in an appendix to a subsequent report from the Select Committee on Energy (3rd Report Session 85-6).

"Some consumers on low incomes are unable to contemplate energy efficiency measures unless they are free or virtually free. Others live in rented premises. The Energy Efficiency Office continues to support the work of the voluntary sector insulation project groups and Neighbourhood Energy Action - the co-ordinating charitable organization - as an effective channel through which Government help can be given to improve energy efficiency and standards of heating in low income households. These projects utilise resources drawn from four different Departments - labour and associated operating costs from the Department of Employment's Community Programme (administered by Manpower Services Commission), grants from the Department of the Environment for tank and loft insulation, single payments from the Department of Health and Social Security for draught-stripping and grants to help establish project groups from the Energy Efficiency Office. They thus illustrate how different Department's programmes can be combined to improve energy efficiency." (para 46 p.xviii)

Clearly the Energy Committee were less than satisfied with this reaction from the Secretary of State for Energy, for in the main body of the report they say:

"The Government's observations on fuel poverty do not provide any glimpse of policies that 'reach out' to lower-income households as its own Research Study recommends. The Committee endorsed this study and the Government's response itself implies that the recommended policies are necessary ... we emphasize again the Secretary of State's own words on fuel poverty - 'much more needs to be done'." (para 7 p.vi)

## References

Advisory Council on Energy Conservation, 5th Report, 1984, *Energy Paper 52*, HMSO, London.

Association for the Conservation of Energy 1983, *Jobs and Energy Conservation*, ACE, London.

Bradshaw, J. and Harris, T. 1983, *Energy and Social Policy*, Routledge and Kegan Paul, London.

Bradshaw, J.R. and Hutton, S. 1984, *Expenditure on Fuels 1982*, National Gas Consumers' Council and Electricity Consumers' Council, London.

Gaskell, G. and Pike, R. 1983a, *Consumer energy conservation policies and programmes in Britain*, CECP Technical Reports Vol VI. IIUG Wissenschaftszentrum, Berlin.

Gaskell, G. and Pike, R. 1983b, Residential energy use: an investigation of consumers and conservation strategies', *Journal of Consumer Policy* 6, pp 285-302.

Hutton, S., Gaskell, G., Pike, R., Bradshaw & Corden, A. *Energy Efficiency in Low Income Households*, HMSO, London.

Midden, C.J.H. and Ritsema, B.S.M. 1984, The meaning of normative processes for energy conservation. In P. Ester, G. Gaskell, B. Joerges, C. Midden, W.F. Van Raaij and T. DeVries, eds. *Consumer Behavior and Energy Policy*. North Holland, Amsterdam.

Roger, E.M. 1983, *The Diffusion of Innovations*, 3rd Edition, Free Press, New York.

Select Committee on Energy 1982, *Energy Conservation in Buildings*, House of Commons: HMSO, London.

Select Committee on Energy 1985, *8th Report. The Energy Efficiency Office*, House of Commons: HMSO, London.

Select Committee on Energy 1986, *3rd Report. The Government's response to the Committee's 8th Report (Session 1984-85) on the Energy Efficiency Office.* House of Commons: HMSO, London.

This research was conducted in collaboration with Jonathan Bradshaw, Sandra Hutton and Anne Corden (University of York) and with Richard Pike (LSE). The Economic and Social Research Council supported this research.

# 3 An evaluation of local programmes in France

ERIC MONNIER

**French energy conservation policy: new developments**

In recent years there have been some new developments in French energy conservation policy but the main characteristics of this policy can be summarized as follows.

* in 1981 a new concept emerged: that of 'Energy Management'. This innovation was the result of a plan to carry out a co-ordinated action programme to include all those involved in the energy field in different ways and to integrate factors from demand to supply. This plan found concrete form in the setting up of new French Energy Management Agency (AFME) in which a number of bodies were grouped together.

* as well as the usual range of financial measures and regulations, the emphasis has been on helping consumers in their decision-making (in various sectors: industrial, agricultural and residential), on thermal improvements to existing homes, and finally on a large scale research and development programme on technologies aimed at halving energy consumption in new homes.

* the decentralized and democratic energy planning called for by Parliament in 1981 has not taken place to the desired extent.

From the point of view of the energy producers, mention should be made of a recent trend: the reduction of the nuclear programme. By a historical irony this comes at a time when the ecology movement has lost a lot of support and the anti-nuclear movement is practically non-existent. However, a growing awareness of the likelihood of large surpluses in the production of electricity is certainly at the root of the reduction in the number of nuclear power stations built each year, but the big financial deficit of Electricite de France (EDF) undoubtedly also played a part in this change of direction. In general, government policy in the field of energy is concentrating less and less on the domestic sector, since studies have clearly shown that this sector has already contributed a great deal to energy conservation. Nowadays efforts are focused more on the industrial sector, and on public buildings.

In our area of concern, that of action affecting the consumer and housing, the local programmes called for in our early study (Monnier 1984; Leyral 1984) have been implemented very quickly (not that we would presume to believe it was our recommendations that brought about such speedy results!) The development of this form of action is all the more remarkable in that it constitutes an exception in the context of the French administrative system. Local programmes in the sense that we understand them, with precise objectives, appropriate resources in terms of manpower, materials and finance, and an assessment system, are still rare at present.

In September 1982, for the first time, AFME decided to launch experimental local programmes in three average towns with different types of housing, Conflans St. Honorine, Meaux and Blois. Since the results seemed very positive, eight new local programmes were designed in January 1984, this time more closely associated with the local authorities, both financially and organizationally. These new programmes are being developed and should be implemented in the coming months. Focusing, in our research, on local programmes has therefore proved very relevant in view of new energy policy developments in France.

**Selection of local programmes**

Our criteria for selecting programmes for study were the following: they should be organized at the local level, have individual consumers as their target, in particular 'disadvantaged' households, be participative in character and, finally, be considered exemplary in the wider national context. In view of the fact the organization of local programmes is too often the exception rather than the rule in France, it has proved impossible, despite all our efforts, to find schemes which combine these characteristics. For this reason, the three programmes chosen, although all organized at the local level, have quite different characteristics.

We must acknowledged that none of them is directed specifically towards disadvantaged social groups, since in France these groups are mostly tenants in the public sector, and hence decisions relating to energy are taken mainly by the estate management body and not by the consumers themselves.

Our three programmes were selected to test a hypothesis about the influence of greater or lesser participation by the State at central level on the design and implementation of programmes. Thus, one of the programmes was implemented by local bodies with little assistance from regional and national organizations, the second by the local authorities with the aid of national subsidies, and the third, although organized in a town, was implemented by a national agency. These three programmes were analysed in detail with respect to their organization and relationships between the actors.

**Analysis of the programmes**

*Concepts and methodology used in the 'top-down' approach:*

On the left hand side of the conceptual diagram (see Figure 3.1) the relationships between the different 'organized actors' are set out.

The key actors in the system are the initiator or supervisor of the programme. It is rare, however, for initiators not to make use of intermediaries, called here relays, for the information campaign or to provide a consumer advice service. Our approach concentrates on these relays, since we consider that the success of a programme depends on their financial and structural linkages with the initiator (arrow 2 on the left hand side of Figure 3.1) but also on the nature of their activities prior to the programme (type of action usually taken, whether or not they are established locally).

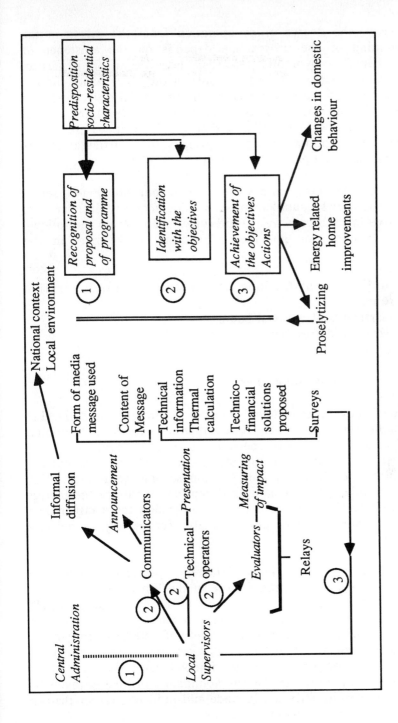

Figure 3.1 Elements of a programme: conceptual diagram

In our view, the degree of co-operation from the relays in the smooth running of the programme depends on the existence of secondary benefits (symbolic rewards, acquisition of expertise, economic and political advantages...), but, on the other hand, the individual interests of the relays may distort the initial objectives of a programme. In addition, the links between the local level and central administration (arrow 1) must be studied carefully if we are to understand why a programme has given priority to a particular objective, or implemented a particular measure.

For each of the programmes we carried out about ten semi-structured interviews, supplemented by documentary information. Our objective in each case was to interview people from the following groups (whether or not they played an active part in the programme):

* local public administrations : technical and administrative departments;
* local departments of national bodies;
* companies or tradespeople;
* leaders of local organizations.

*Programme A : 'Veynes, solar town'.*

In the case of 'Veynes, solar town', there is no programme delivering services to households as such, but rather a series of promotional events targeted at a variety of specialist groups. However, it seemed important to us to include in this study one of the few, if not the only, genuinely local energy conservation scheme in France. Why does 'Veynes, solar town' remain an exception? What are the factors which made it possible for these actions to develop there rather than elsewhere? It is impossible, unfortunately, for us to give definite answers to such questions.

Like many other villages in the Hautes-Alpes département, the population of Veynes has been falling in the last decade (3178 inhabitants in 1982, 3330 in 1975). The village community would probably have shown no more enthusiasm for stemming this tide than its neighbours, had it not been severely affected by reorganization at SNCF (French National Railway Company), the biggest local employer. To compensate for the loss of jobs locally, the local council decided to take advantage of the abundant sunshine enjoyed by the area to develop its activities in trade and industry, rather than in the traditional field of tourism.

On the initiative of a local councillor, the Association for the Study of Solar Energy (ADES) was set up in 1976, and became the supervisory body for this new policy, the four main objectives of this non-profit organization are as follows:

* to create jobs: to do this, the local council and the ADES have helped to set up a company to manufacture solar panels, by the loan of a building, and by developing a market for the solar panels produced.

* to develop domestic uses of solar energy: since 1976, a solar fair has been organized in the village, including an international solar film festival.

* to encourage professionals to design and use solar equipment: an architectural competition and training sessions have added to the expertise of local builders.

* finally, to show the feasibility of solar heating systems, by means of demonstration projects: municipal swimming baths, houses and greenhouses.

The funding of the programme was modest, some 325,000 francs, obtained from a variety of public agencies at local and national level but since all the staff were volunteers the budget was sufficient. The town's other cultural, tourist and even sporting associations help in these activities. Their assistance has been all the more easy to obtain since these associations are 'para-municipal' and the chairperson held important positions in the municipality.

The fame of this programme spread outside the region. It was even featured in the national media: the development of local 'self-help' programmes and the development of solar energy became two major themes following the election of the Socialist Party. It seems that the national interest in these initiatives completely changed the issues at local level, giving rise in particular to internal rivalry. Of late, the ideological credibility of the principal actors has faded considerably as a result of the decline of the ecologist movement in France since 1981, and of the solar energy movement since 1982.

With the death of the former Mayor in 1982, the key person suddenly found himself without his main source of legitimation (political legitimacy), and became opposed and gradually dispossessed by the new team at the Town Hall. This new team supported a new organization in competition to the first. At the same time, an internal dispute at the solar panels factory ended in the dismissal of eight of the staff, who set up a new company a few yards from the first. In short, as Leyral (1984) notes in his report, 'conflicts pile up because of lack of space'.

In analysing this situation, it appears that such conflicts could not have occurred if the programme had been able to create a real consensus in the village community. In spite of all their efforts, the organizers were never able to really mobilize the inhabitants of Veynes. This failure was caused, in our view, by the difficulty the inhabitants had in identifying themselves with the programme: the identity suggested by the slogan 'Veynes, solar town' conflicted with the pre-existing 'Veynes, railway town'. The latter slogan has associations with a national undertaking, with something serious and safe, whereas the associations with the 'solar town' are local, light-weight and speculative. In spite of these reservations, the programme 'Veynes, solar town', is a successful model because of the number and the originality of the schemes. It would also seem, according to the people interviewed, that the level of ownership of solar powered water heaters is distinctly higher in this department than in the rest of France.

*Programme B : 'La Rochelle Trade Fair Exhibition'*

Action by the District Council of the Charente Maritime Department and by the Local Council at La Rochelle in the field of energy has increased in recent years, especially in thermal improvements to public buildings (hospitals, schools, etc.). The key person in this programme is an elected member of the District Council. After several attempts, for example selective collection of recyclable waste, an association for the development of new energies, which had varying degrees of success he initiated a more traditional type of programme: a technical/administrative programme based on existing structures.

In fact, he got the District Civil Engineering Department (DDE) to act as the real supervisor of the programme. This was possible because since 1980 a very active 'energy unit' has existed in this local government department which keeps files on behalf of the local authority and follows up projects from the technical angle. Also involved in this initiative from the beginning were regional representatives from AFME (French Energy Control Agency) and Electricite de France (EDF). The main objective of this programme was to convince residents of single-family houses to carry out energy-related home improvements. The District Council, for its part, also hoped to help the building trades sector, but at the same time to protect the environment by developing appropriate technological solutions to energy saving. In order to reach the target audience, the annual trade exhibition and fair of La Rochelle was used and a stand was organized there offering a number of free services, including:

* a simplified energy audit (calculated by computer)
* technical advice on the solutions proposed
* help with the administrative paperwork (application for planning permission, for subsidies etc. )
* financial aid: favourable credit rates.

The supervisors of the programme succeeded in mobilizing an impressive number of people from different government departments and public services onto this stand including representatives from the District Civil Engineering Department (DDE), AFME, the National Home Improvement Agency (ANAH) and EDF The banks were also approached and agreed to offer favourable credit conditions. A private technical studies office was given the job of carrying out the energy audits. Indeed, four more computer consoles had to be added to the one provided initially to cope with the flow of customers, which increased as the days went on. The information campaign, which was well thought out, was also given to a specialist company. A letter signed by the district councillor with a questionnaire attached was circulated to 60,000 households in single-family house dwellings, inviting them to come to the stand at the trade fair, with the questionnaire duly completed giving the necessary information about their accommodation, their energy consumption etc. In addition to the traditional methods - newspapers, radio, posters - prizes were given each day at the stand for a draw using the participants' files. The prizes - insulating materials, heat pumps - were themselves donated by local companies. The cost of the programme, not including the ten or so staff seconded by their respective organizations, remained fairly moderate: 600,000 francs (or approximately 700 francs per audit).

From the strictly organizational point of view, this programme was undeniably a success, in so far as a large number of agencies or bodies succeeded in working together for the ten days of the trade fair. In addition, the system set up showed its capacity to react quickly to satisfy a demand which was four times greater than expected (850 energy audits were carried out). Finally, this programme was a success because the DDE used the experience to create a permanent telephone advice service 'SOS Energy', and organized the stand again in 1984 (though with reduced resources).

In contrast to the programme in Veynes, this one succeeded in avoiding a conflict between the partners. Two factors made relations between the actors much easier:

* on the one hand, because the initiator had once worked for the DDE, the supervisor of this programme, and still appears in the organization chart of this body;

* on the other hand, the four main representatives of the District Council, the DDE, AFME and EDF involved in the programme all belonged to the National Association of Civil Engineers[1].

However, it should be stressed that, unlike programme A, this programme did not seek (and perhaps even went so far as to avoid) consumer participation, and was restricted to one action of short duration.

*Programme C: 'The Conflans Challenge'*

In 1982, AFME wanted to experiment for the first time with the use of local programmes to implement its new policy of aids to consumer decision-making. It decided to organize three experimental operations (known as 'pilot schemes') in three medium-size towns in the Paris region. The town of Conflans-Ste-Honorine, which became the focus of our evaluation, was chosen by the organizers because of the high proportion of single-family houses there. The objective of this programme, similar to that of programme B but more ambitious, was to carry out energy audits in all public and private buildings (including the industrial and tertiary sector) and to follow this through by persuading all property owners in Conflans to make the necessary improvements. The design and implementation of these experimental programmes, given their importance for AFME, were the direct responsibility of the Agency and more particularly of one of its Directors. Large sums of money were made available so that many specialist professional or private bodies could be called upon.

The participation of the Conflans Town Council in programme was marginal: the only significant assistance was given by the Communications department which produces the local freesheet and organizes various public events. The attitude of the Town Council to the initiatives taken by the organizers was however a determining factor in the sense that nothing could be done on its 'territory' without its agreement.

AFME did encounter difficulties in making a success of the programme: firstly in convincing the banks to grant credit facilities, and secondly in getting local companies to come to an agreement on price guidelines for carrying out the improvements. These price lists were then sent to consumers at the same time as their expert report. Not wishing to leave anything to chance, AFME had a survey carried out before designing the programme to find out what were the most appropriate methods of informing and sensitizing single-family home owners. In the first few days of the programme it set up a permanent branch office on the spot, which above all made it possible to follow and to co-ordinate the different operations on the spot.

The private agency dealing with the information campaign adopted a strategy aimed:

* first, at identification with the programme, and thanks to its evocative title, 'The Conflans Challenge', at mobilizing the whole of the local community collectively.

* second, at preventing the public from becoming bored, since the programme was to last a year. For this reason, the campaign was designed in four phases: presentation of the operation, an awareness campaign for the energy audits, a phase of persuasion to get the improvements carried out and lastly, final information on the results obtained. Each of these phases was to be marked by fresh 'events' - public presentations, articles in the local freesheet, posters and exhibitions.

Almost all the available information channels were used: personal letters, presentations in schools, local meetings, and local association meetings. Because of this, and despite their initial anxieties, the organizers did not meet with much resistance when infra-red pictures were taken of roofs from an aeroplane and of house frontages from the street, or even when thermal engineers went from door to door through the streets of the town in groups of about ten.

The results of our analysis show, however, that the reception given to the experts varied a lot from one social group to another. The difficulties came, surprisingly, from the experts themselves who found it difficult to be placed in the position of asking for something from the households: an apparently humiliating situation for some of them. This interesting finding emerged from a process evaluation ordered by organizer.

Finally, the programme made it possible to provide very full audit reports (containing infra-red photographs of the house and a graded list of work to be carried out) to rather more than 3,000 households. The penetration rate was therefore exceptionally high: 54 percent of households living in single-family houses. It would probably be difficult to achieve a higher figure than this, since the organization of the programme was particularly efficient and its cost particularly high. AFME spent about 5 million francs (not including the audits of blocks of flats or in industry), of which 1 million francs went on the information campaign.

It should be mentioned in this connection that the organizers of this programme had considerable help from local tradespeople. It is to AFME's credit that they were able to make the Union of Traders and Craftsmen realize that they would be the main beneficiaries of the programme, but also that they organized several information meetings and training courses for them (free and well-adapted to their requirements). The tradespeople themselves took charge of the organization of two commercial exhibitions (presenting equipment and materials for energy conservation).

Co-operation with the Town Hall was more difficult, however. The Council was somewhat reluctant in view of the size of the programme, fearing that it would be rejected by the public. Fortunately, the agency running the information campaign, used to working with local authorities, was able to act as mediator in the most delicate moments. AFME wisely had left it to the Town Hall to choose the agency to carry out the information campaign. Since the impact on the residents was positive, however, the Council then resumed its involvement with the operation by deciding to prolong it at its own expense. The President of the French Republic came to Conflans - Ste - Honorine to see at first hand this local programme which is considered by government to be exemplary.

However detailed it is, the analysis of the three programmes does not of course support any hypotheses relating to the organization of programmes in general. Our results, although they are exploratory, can certainly make a useful contribution by defining more precisely both the main elements of the structure of actors, and the modes of operation within the structure, the actors game.

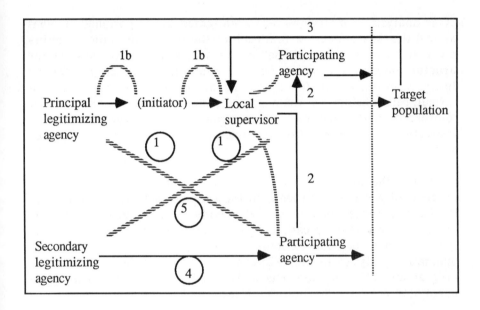

Figure 3.2 Actors and their linkages

At the centre of the structure are the initiator of the programme and the main relay: the local programme supervisor. The part of the supervisor may be played by a non-profit making body (programme A), or by a local authority (programme B), or by a private company (programme C). In all cases the supervisor, along with the initiator, carries out the executive functions (programme design and im-plementation and co-ordination of those involved). This function can only be carried out effectively if decisions can be taken at this level. This decision-making presupposes of course that evaluations have been carried out (arrow 3 in Figure 3.2). However, it is also essential that the decisions should have some financial and above all some political security, provided by a body whose legitimacy is recognized by the other actors, which we will call the 'principal legitimizing body'.

This legitimacy may come from a local electoral mandate (programmes A and B) or from central government (programme C). We should note that in all three cases, the initiator always belongs to the 'principal legitimizing body', but this still does not ensure legitimation (in case A, the death of the Mayor led to the breakdown of the structure).

Our analysis of interviews also highlighted the importance of what we call the 'key person': within each of the important bodies, one individual becomes the principal spokesman. The effectiveness of the structure depends on the key person's commitment to the programme and relationships with the other key actors. It seems necessary for formal relationships between one organization and another to be reinforced (and sometimes 'short-circuited') by informal relationships (family, friends, professional associations) between the key actors.

Finally, the analysis of the conflicts which inevitably mark the progress of a programme leads to the conclusion that, in the case of local programmes, some legitimizing bodies have a secondary role to play, but their attitude can be a determining factor. For this reason, the existence or non-existence of a 'system of mediation' or 'mediating body' (5 in Fig. 3.2) can be crucial for the success of the programme, allowing conflicts to be resolved or compromises to be negotiated between conflicting interests.

## Evaluation of impact on households

*The 'bottom-up' analysis of the diffusion of the programme*

This part of our analysis is in some sense like a market research study, in that it offers an understanding of the potential market for an idea: that of domestic energy conservation. Bolstered by the legitimacy of their intentions, initiators of programmes too often forget that the households which are the recipients of their message are not uniformly convinced about the importance of the issues; that they have more or less favourable cultural attitudes; or that they live in (objective) material conditions which vary a great deal. For these reasons, not all of them will espouse the objectives of the programme.

Approached in this way, a programme is seen as a device producing effects on consumers with the aim of changing their behaviour. The elements which make up this instrument are firstly the 'announcement' (the promotional campaign: posters, media messages, events....) used to present the 'offer'. In the cases studied here a free energy audit for the home and related financial aids. It should also be noted that to be complete the programme should always include an evaluation, but this is precisely the actual objective of our work. Amongst the main effects which this instrument can produce, we have concentrated on the following (see Roux 1980).

* the 'signature effect', by which the public can identify those operating the programme;

* the 'proximity effect', by which the instrument seeks to reduce the symbolic distance between the public and the proposal, making possible the identification which is essential if the public is to accept the proposal;

* the 'science effect', which ensures the legitimacy of the proposal, hence its authority and persuasive force;

* and finally, the 'uniqueness effect', in other words, because the programme is a special one (local and/or experimental), it offers the community the chance to distinguish itself from the wider social environment.

In our study we attempt to understand how this process operates by determining which consumers:

* recognize the offer
* identify with its objectives
* achieve these objectives (cf. the right hand side of Figure 3.1)

For each of these three phases of the process, separate hypotheses have been formulated which link the attitudes and behaviour of households vis-a-vis the programme to their socio-economic and residential contexts. This analysis of social impacts is based on a comparative analysis between the programmes at Conflans and La Rochelle, that is between four samples (for each programme a sample of 'participants' of the programme and of 'non-participants').

Participants were randomly selected from the records of the organizers. In Conflans, non-participants were randomly selected from the list of households which had not had an audit and in La Rochelle a census based quota sample was taken. The total sample was 1014 households. For these cross-comparisons a questionnaire was drawn up comprising four sections:

* general attitudes to energy conservation;

* detailed description of conservation actions taken in the home (improvements carried out and planned);

* attitudes to the programme;

* description of the dwelling and the household: financial resources, composition etc.

There was also a fifth section for households which had had an energy audit report. The data in the audit were included as far as they were available: volume of the house, its thermal coefficient 'G', its total energy consumption, and the various works recommended in the report sent to the household as part of the programme.

As regards data analysis, we chose a method of qualitative statistical analysis of the quantitative data gathered. Our interpretations were based on a process of analysing corresponding factors, which enabled multiple correlations to be drawn and thus reduced the risk of partial interpretations of phenomena. For a description of this statistical method see Lebart et al (1984).

Finally, to conclude these comments on methodology, it should be emphasized that multidimensional configurations - spaces - have been constructed on the basis of attitudes and reactions to the programme, taken as 'active variables', socio-economic indicators were then projected onto the space, becoming what we call the 'illustrative' variables.

In the next sections, this bottom-up approach is applied on programmes B and C. Unfortunately in the case of the first programme at Veynes, it was of no use to assess the impact on the consumers since households were not one of the specific aims of the organizers.

With the aim of measuring the effectiveness of the information campaigns of the two programmes B and C, we carried out an independent analysis of the attitudes of households in each case. In this section the analysis presented has been calculated on the sample of all the households that were informed about programme 'B' - 'La Rochelle Trade Fair'. Thus, in addition to the sample of participants, there were some 'non-participants' who remembered the programme implemented at the Trade Fair a year before (26 percent of the sample). The term participants refers to households having asked for an energy audit in La Rochelle (programme B) or having accepted the expert report offered in Conflans - St. Honorine (programme C).

Table 3.1
Participants and non-participants in La Rochelle

|  | non-participants n=298 % | participants n=200 % |
|---|---|---|
| executives | 21 | 10 |
| blue-collar workers | 13 | 41 |
| civil servants and public sector employees | 43 | 33 |
| self-employed and freelance | 5 | 8 |
| the higher paid (>9500FFr/month) | 53 | 19 |
| the lower paid (<9500FFr/month) | 47 | 81 |
| home owners | 82 | 45 |
| tenants | 3 | 39 |
| individual detached houses | 59 | 28 |
| terraced and semi-detached | 41 | 72 |
| homes with oil fired heating | 39 | 29 |
| homes with town gas-fired heating | 33 | 43 |

The division between 'participants' and 'non-participants' is the basis of the strongest differentiation within the sample. In Table 3.1 six cross tabulations contrasting the two groups are shown.

Table 3.2 Topology of attitudes to the programme: La Rochelle (N=259)

| Type — Dependent Variables | Attitudes / Opinions Regarding Energy | Socio-Residential Characteristics |
|---|---|---|
| type 1 (42%) Had an audit carried out. No criticism of the programme. Took part in an exhibition but never in a meeting to promote the diffusion of the unchanged programme. Did not advise others to take part in the program. | Energy consumption quoted was correct. Energy-saving behaviour. Unfamiliar with national programmes. Energy saving because of cost of heating. | Takes some part in Associations / interest groups. M retired. F at home. Has lived in the house for 26 years. M Farmer. F: Primary Education. Frequent help given amongst neighbours. |
| type 2 (32%) Had an audit carried out. In favour of the diffusion of the programme if improvements were made to it. Criticism of programme. Took part in a number of trade shows and exhibitions. Advised and recommended others to take part. | Has had several types of improvements carried out (heating and insulation). Difficulties in financing improvements. Energy consumption higher than average. Familiar with local government initiatives. Uses an open fire. | F: works. Participates a lot in associations / interest groups. Very frequent help given amongst neighbours. M: civil servant or local government employee. Belongs to a trades union political party or cultural associations. |
| type 3 (11%) Did not have an audit carried out. Took part in a number of trade shows and exhibitions. Advised others to take part. Several criticisms. In favour of the diffusion of the programme with several improvements. Did not find the presentation very effective. | Does not ask for advice from parents or neighbours. Very concerned by energy saving in towns. Very familiar with national energy conservation programmes. Good knowledge of consumption of domestic appliances. | Person interviewed: M Takes part in a number of associations (sporting, cultural) M: tradesman / shopkeeper. House built recently. Individual heating appliances. Area of the house: 120 to 170m$^2$ M: teacher. |
| type 2 (15%) No opinion about the programme, nor concerning wider diffusion. Did not take part in the trade fair - exhibition. Did not have an audit carried out. Did not advise others to take part. | No improvements of any type. No actor consulted. | Terraced house with no garden. Tenant. Energy: town gas for hot water. Person interviewed: f. Area of the accommodation: 120 to 150m$^2$. |

Key: Type: Consumer Type & Percentage of Sample N=259 M: Male F: Female
Note: These items arranged in categories, have been listed according to their degree of importance. Thus these are the factors which cause one subsample to differ most from the other three.

88

The second basis of differentiation on the other hand, reveals a more unexpected sample structure. According to this, the division is between households which were relatively passive about the programme and those who showed a more active attitude: the latter took part in the trade fair and in meetings on the subject of energy, but at the same time formed a critical attitude to the programme. Among these critical households were people who were already active in interest groups and associations (people who are politically involved in community life), tradesmen and craftsmen, and more generally the self-employed (who are typically against public initiatives and in favour of the private sector). On the other hand, households typical of the attitude of passive acceptance included retired people, office workers and women (especially women at home); in general, these were concerned, conventional people. These analyses support the model of programme diffusion outlined above. We find that recognition by the public of the programme offer and identification with the programme offer are two important consumer reactions. These can be represented schematically as shown in Figure 3.3.

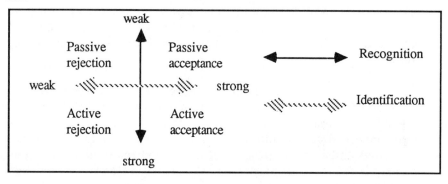

Figure 3.3 Schematic Representation of Attitudes

*Reactions to the programme at 'La Rochelle'*

The correspondence analysis of attitudes to this programme points to four separate consumer types. In Table 3.2 the characteristics of these types are shown with respect to their reactions to the programme, attitudes about energy use and socio-residential characteristics. The four types can be characterized as follows:

* the 'not interesteds' (type 2). These represent only a small proportion of our sample (approx. 15 percent of the households which remembered the programme) but, of the total population of the

89

La Rochelle area, they represent about 55 percent of residents in individual houses according to our calculations. These are households who feel that the programme does not concern them because they live in a terraced house, because they are tenants or because they are supplied with town gas (reputed to be the cheapest form of energy); but this group also includes people with little technical background: women and blue-collar workers.

* the 'critics' (type 4). Of the critics (about 42 percent of the non-participants who had been informed about the programme) a distinction should be made between those households who were predisposed to be critical of the programme because it was a State initiative, and supporters of special interest groups who were also critical of the programme, but in a spirit of one-upmanship.

* the 'opportunists' (type 1) About 56 percent of households who had the audit carried out did so, it seems, because the opportunity was offered, because prizes were given and/or because they had the time. These were mainly retired people, people from modest backgrounds, and households where the wife stays at home: in fact the traditional clientele of the trade fair. These people probably did not have genuine motivations for having the energy audit.

* finally, the 'specific clientele' (type 3). 43 percent of the households who had the audit carried out came to the trade fair specially for that purpose. The households represented here are those involved in community affairs: they participate in local associations and interest groups and have good relations with neighbours. Some of the supporters of special interest groups had therefore adopted a positive attitude to the programme.

*Reactions to the Conflans programme*

An analysis was conducted using the same method for the households interviewed at Conflans (programme C) whether or not they had an audit carried out. At first sight, it appears to show a picture very similar to that obtained in La Rochelle. The interpretation of the differentiating characteristics is almost identical: the first distinguishes between households according to their level of recognition of the offer, and the second according to the degree of identification with the objectives of the programme. However, we find that these two comparisons are less dramatic. The attitudes to the programme are therefore organized according to the same structure, but are less clear cut at Conflans than at La Rochelle.

Thus it would seem that a process of social selectivity is at work in Conflans more so than in La Rochelle. This had not been expected. The selectivity is all the more surprising since the programme succeeded in reaching about 54 percent of residents of individual houses; an undeniable success, given the traditional resistance in the suburban sector to any intrusion into private territory.

In Conflans the distinction between participants and non-participants are shown in Table 3.3.

Table 3.3
Participants and non-participants in Conflans

|  | participants | non-participants |
|---|---|---|
|  | n=373 | n=143 |
|  | % | % |
| middle and higher executives | 55 | 36 |
| blue collar workers (women) | 17 (14) | 41 (32) |
| the high paid (>11500FFr/month) | 39 | 23 |
| the low paid (<5500FFr/month) | 14 | 38 |
| holders of higher education diplomas and degrees | 21 | 9 |
| those with no higher qualification | 30 | 54 |

The consumer types within the sample of households in Conflans is similar to that in La Rochelle (see Table 3.4). The changes in distribution are more significant:

* the 'not interesteds' This covers about 65 percent of non-participant households in single family dwellings in the town of Conflans. Their socio-residential characteristics correspond exactly to those of the 'non-participant' households described in the previous paragraph.

* the 'opponents' (type 4). Here there are 12 percent of non-participating households but also 6 percent of participating households who had 'forgotten' about having had an expert report. This group, whose attitude was one of clear opposition to the programme, shows the existence of a 'political effect', to the extent that where a programme has a local dimension it inevitably enters a political arena. It will come as no surprise that these opponents were from the highest social group reacting against the Mayor, a socialist minister.

* the 'consenters' (type 1) comprising 63 percent of participants, and 34 percent households in single family dwellings belong to this group. They are interested in taking steps to save energy by changing their behaviour rather than by having improvements carried out. These are also the households living in areas where there was a positive impetus, a 'snowball' effect, the opposite of what happened in the area of the previous group.

* the 'converts' (type 3) approximately 18 percent of participants, it seems, identified completely with the objectives of the programme. This group more or less corresponds to the 'specific clientele' in the analysis of La Rochelle.

Table 3.4 Typology of attitudes to the programme: Conflans (N=498)

| Type | Dependent Variables | Attitudes / Opinions Regarding Energy | Socio-Residential Characteristics |
|---|---|---|---|
| type 1 (51%) | Accepted the audit. Favourable to diffusion of programme, without modification. No criticism of the programme. Several positive comments. Thinks the presentation of the programme was "very effective". Never took part in a meeting or trade show. | Very economical energy habits. Good knowledge of consumption of domestic appliances. Concerned by energy savings in their tow. Very familiar with the "weather heating campaign." Energy saving: an important matter. | Volume of house: $(200,350m^3)$ Energy bill: $(3000F,12000F)$ F: Technical education. Administration C.L.S. "To be loved, close family".Hollow Brick Wall. Modern, cheap furniture. M: middle grade executive |
| type 3 (14%) | Has advised and recommend other to take part in the programme. Has taken part in formation meetings. Asked for the audit to be carried out. Consulted several actors. Favours the diffusion of the programme if several changes are made to it. Numerous criticisms. Has taken part in trade shows. | Concerned by energy savings in the town. Familiar with nation programmes. Improvements carried out: double glazing, external insulation, draught excluders on doors and windows. A lot of improvements carried out. Energy saving: an important matter. | Owns dishwasher. M: higher education. Participates a lot in associations. Standard of living declining. F: secondary education + A levels. Help given amongst neighbours: very frequent. F: middle grade executive. M: civil servant or local government employee. |
| type 4 (8%) | No positive comments on programme. Found presentation of the programme "not very effective". Opposed to diffusion of programme. Has not advised others to participate. Expert report refused or "forgotten". Numerous criticisms of programme. | Energy saving: not important. Opposed to development of solar energy more than that of nuclear energy, and to make big energy consumers pay more. Very familiar with national energy conservation programmes. Thinks this does not contribute at national level to reducing own energy consumption. | M: high grade executive. Owns second home. Reception of researcher "distant". Belongs to the associations +4 cm of insulation in roof. "Like to be well thought of". M: technical education, administration. Standard of living: declining |
| type 2 (27%) | Indifferent opinion on the programme and its presentation. Quite favours diffusion of programme. Did not accept audit. Did not take part in trade shows or exhibitions. | Has not had and does not intend to have any improvements carried out. Not at all concerned by energy savings in the town. Completely unaware of EDF campaign. | F. & M.: primary education. Area of accommodation:$60M^2$.Does not participate in associations. M & F: blue collar workers. One living in the house. Single F.Age > 65 years. Income > 4000F. |

Key:  Type: Consumer Type & Percentage of Sample N=498    M: Male    F: Female
Note:  These items arranged in categories, have been listed according to their degree of importance. Thus these are the factors which cause one subsample to differ most from the other three.

*The achievement of objectives: improvements carried out*

The energy audit had an important impact on households in terms of energy conservation improvements carried out. The results of the straight classification summarized in Table 3.5 are sufficient to illustrate this impact.

* the proportion of households taking conservation actions almost doubled;
* the average number of actions per household increased from 1.7 to 2.6;
* the average cost of actions increased by approx. 80 percent.

In addition our analyses show that the audit had the effect of improving energy literacy (Gaskell and Pike 1983); this is a no less important result, though less spectacular than those listed previously. We find that people's criteria for decisions are also more rational in terms of economics and energy for example less double glazing, for which the payback time is rarely less than 30 years. The audit therefore encourages a clear qualitative improvement in home improvements for the purposes of energy conservation and in this context we find that the most detailed audit in Conflans had a greater qualitative impact.

However, this undeniably positive result has to be tempered by the following observations:

* households where the audit recommended a large number of improvements are not those which carried out most conservation actions;

* the households which carried out the greatest number of actions were those who said they had already envisaged doing a large proportion of the recommended improvements before the audit was carried out;

* finally and on the other hand, the absence of conservation actions was linked to opinions like: 'the energy savings promised are not credible' or 'these improvements are not essential'

Table 3.5
Energy conservation actions taken

| | Afme Sofres | La Rochelle | | Conflans | |
|---|---|---|---|---|---|
| | | no audit | audit | audit | no audit |
| **Conservation actions** | | | | | |
| Households which had taken conservation actions (% of sample) | 20%* | 20%* | 38% | 37% | 17% |
| Average number of types of actions per households where actions were taken | 1.7* | 1.7 | 2.6 | 2.7 | 2.0 |
| Average cost of actions per household where taken (francs) | 8812* | 9960 | 17,870 | 16,950 | 13,750 |
| Total cost of actions carried out by households (million francs) | | | 5.8 | 18.8 | 5.9 |
| **Conservation Intended** | | | | | |
| Households planning conservation actions (% of sample) | 12%* | 11%* | 18% | 24% | ** |
| Average number of types of future actions per household planned by households | 1.4* | 2.1 | 2.2 | 2.1 | |
| Estimated total cost of actions planned by households (million francs) | | | 2.7 | 12.2 | |

* Estimation on the basis of an annual survey AFME.SOFRES 'Energy savings: attitudes and behaviours of individuals' National sample (N=5000) **Sample size too small

The findings tend to show that the influence of the audit is certainly important, but is limited. Its aim is to convince, and its conclusions, however well founded, are more acceptable if the reader is already prepared to accept them. It is not easy to produce the essential 'effect of persuasion' in all the participants in the same way. The effect can, it seems, be reinforced by the use of a 'visibility effect', in other words by the use of visual aids brought into play with participants. Thus the households who took the most conservation actions were those most impressed by the infra-red pictures (visualisation of the problem), and the authority of the report was disputed rather less at La Rochelle than at Conflans, because participants could see the 'computers' actually operating on the stand at the trade fair.

*Disadvantaged households: negligible impact*

Among the characteristics of households, who had carried out or were planning to carry out a lot of actions, were some that have already appeared in our analysis of attitudes to the programme. They include the homes of the highly paid, of middle range executives and of people who are very active in local interest groups and associations. Gender differences are important: men living alone are very active when it comes to taking conservation actions, women living alone not at all. The connection between taking conservation actions and energy bills is made more often than in our previous analyses (which leads us to think that the expert report is succeeding in introducing a new rational element into the decision-making process). Finally, taking conservation actions is linked to the size of the house and its age; it is also, more unexpectedly, connected with membership of a trades union or political party, or with membership of a cultural association. Moreover, the most favourable age range is that preceding retirement, more especially 35 - 49, a stable and prosperous period in the life cycle.

Within the professional groups, middle range executives again are notable for their propensity for carrying out improvements, but are joined in this by tradespeople. This is surprising when we recall that this professional category was the least receptive to the idea of energy conservation and to the programmes. Those who were slowest in reacting favourably were civil servants or local authority employees, who identify most readily with actors/communicators (proximity effect). By contrast, people with independent professional status, though unreceptive to the programme at first, will take more actions in the end than the first group.

Among the characteristics of households which had an audit but did not and do not intend to take conservation actions after both programmes, we note in particular the age of the head of the household (>65 years) and that of the house (<5years), women living alone, female blue-collar workers and finally households with very low incomes. These households can, it seems, only take actions on condition that they receive some grants and perhaps also some other support. In this group there is of course a high proportion of tenants or people who are thinking of moving house in the near future.

### The diffusion process

One of the key results of our statistical analyses is the emergence of a consistent structuring of attitudes of households towards the programmes. In particular, these results show the existence of a real process by which households recognize, or fail to recognize, the offer made to them and identify, or fail to identify, with the objectives proposed; they also show a very wide range of types of attitude, from open opposition to active participation in a programme. We can also highlight the different grades of corresponding contextual factors; that is, we can list in order of importance different contextual variables explaining the same phenomenon, and hence propose an explanatory model.

Let us try, then, to re-construct our initial conceptual plan as it appears in the light of the results (see Figure 3.4). Recognition of a local programme for household energy conservation (Phase 1) is, in the final analysis, determined primarily by the residential context of the household. That is to say for example, that households who did not accept the proposal offered did not own their houses; they were even less receptive to the message when the house was terraced, and particularly when it was supplied with what is considered a cheap form of energy (town gas).

Secondly, it seems the idea of energy conservation is foreign to those households with the lowest educational background (blue collar workers, people with no higher qualifications) because it presupposes a certain way of thinking (good economic sense, forethought, optimization). Although it is not really possible to dissociate this from educational background, it does seem that the technical background of the household members (rather than of the whole household) reinforces the above phenomenon; hence a difference emerges between men and women.

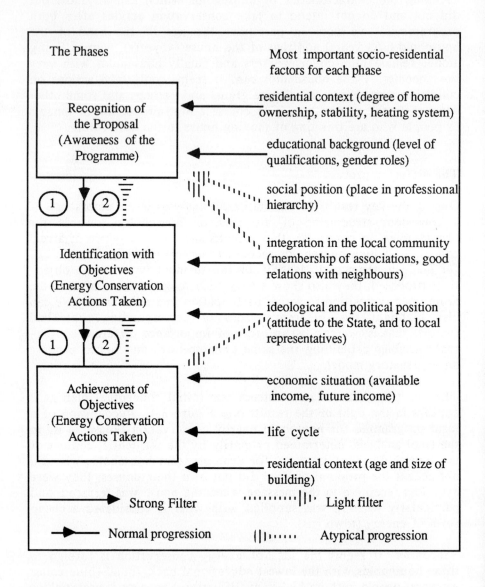

Figure 3.4 Social filters in the diffusion process

Several research teams are today trying to show the links between identity in the sphere of work and in the domestic sphere. The fact that very few blue-collar workers participated in the local programmes studied can largely be explained by the failure of the instruments set up to produce the proximity effect: the social relationships characterizing these programmes were those of domination, and were rejected by those who are 'dominated' at work.

The hypothesis of a positive correlation between the degree of integration in the local community and participation in the programme was also fully confirmed by our results. Local energy conservation programmes constitute therefore, in the same way as a music festival for example, a local event which produces a feeling of collective identity and can have a function of socialization (uniqueness effect). We will underline the importance of this result, which is also accompanied by a 'political effect'.

When we study the process as a whole, it appears that these last two phenomena were the cause of an atypical progression from one phase to the other (arrow 2 of Figure 3.4). Indeed in some sections of the public we found a refusal to recognize or a negative identification, and yet the final objectives (i.e. taking conservation actions) were still achieved: this was the case of the tradesmen and craftsmen.

With regard to this latter phase, we can end this summary of determining social factors by saying that taking energy-related home improvements depends on the household's economic situation, the life cycle of its members (pensioners, young couples as opposed to those between 35 and 49), but also, once again (but this time the size and the age of the house) its residential context.


### General conclusions and recommendations

*Comparison of the effects of the two programmes*

The programmes have been analysed as 'devices producing effects'. We are now able to assess the beneficial or negative effects of the two devices as a whole: unfortunately, the effectiveness of each of the instruments (taken separately) within these devices cannot be tested; we will simply be putting forward hypotheses in this respect.

The undeniable advantage of the marketing strategy used in La Rochelle is of course that of reaching the specific clientele at the lowest cost. The first announcement attracted those who were already interested and committed, typically the well-to-do. The major disadvantage of this low cost strategy is to reproduce the same social selectivity that is typical in national programmes. However, the trade fair brought in a new group, the opportunists, drawn mainly from the lower classes. This is the main lesson to be drawn from the evaluation of this programme, the use of the trade fair as the support channel made it possible to moderate this social selectivity. Indeed, the traditional audience of the trade fair is made up of those social groups which are difficult to reach: pensioners, less well-off households... and, in spite of the criticisms made earlier of the giving of prizes by drawing lots, this was a very attractive feature to these particular social groups.

The presentation of the La Rochelle programme had two merits from the point of view of effectiveness: it introduced a techno-scientific legitimacy (computers) and the results of the energy audits were always given with an explanation. On the other side of the coin, the inherent disadvantages of a programme of this type are firstly the fact that the impact on the local community is only superficial (i.e. no collective impetus is created), and secondly from the clients point of view there was no guarantee of a follow-up. It is known that such follow-up services are important.

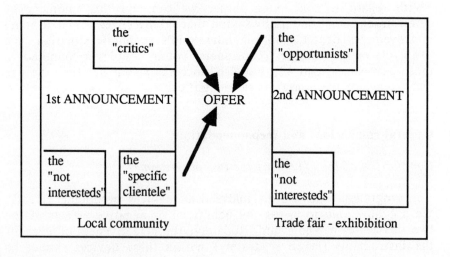

Figure 3.5 Diffusion of the Device in La Rochelle

As regards the programme designed and carried out at Conflans-Ste-Honorine, the most surprising result is that, in spite of its exhaustive and extensive character, it did not succeed in moderating the social selectivity mechanism. Here yet again is proof that a programme which does not precisely define its social target nor the methods used to fulfil its objectives, will be of most benefit to the most advantaged households. In Figure 3.6 the process in Conflans is depicted. The same pressures are put on all people in the community. Some social groups react in a positive way, others negatively.

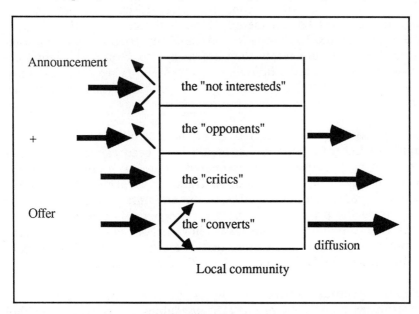

Figure 3.6 Diffusion of the device in Conflans

The comparative results of the two programmes can be explained by the factors referred to above, but they are also very probably due to what we call the 'suburban syndrome'. We have formed the hypothesis that the increase in (real or symbolic) ownership of individual houses among disadvantaged social groups has been accompanied by a reaction of withdrawal and rejection of any intervention which has not been solicited from within the domestic circle. The use of 'neutral territory' such as a trade fair perhaps helps to get over this fear of intrusion.

In addition to this fundamental question of selectivity, we must emphasize two very important implications of these results, namely that neither the intensity of the programme (its high cost) nor the fact that it was free to the participants are guarantees of greater social justice (the redistributive effects are more complex that at first appears). On the contrary, we would suggest that the impact in terms of conservation actions taken would have been greater if the people been expected to participate in someway, if not financially at least by expressing a demand for the programme.

*Cost effectiveness of the programmes*

To conclude this comparison, the cost effectiveness of the two programmes must be considered. Our calculations show that the relative impact of the La Rochelle and Conflans programmes was equal, although in absolute terms they are in a 1 to 3 ratio. The total cost for actions taken in the households where audits were done was 8.5 million francs in La Rochelle and 31.1 million francs in Conflans, taking into account intended improvements.

A figure should be deducted from these results, however, to account for improvements which would have been carried out if there had been no programme: an estimated figure of 2 million francs in La Rochelle and approx. 8 million francs in Conflans. These figures should of course be compared with the amounts invested by the organizers in the programme. These are respectively 0.6 million francs in La Rochelle and 5 million francs in Conflans. We should in reality be wary of such comparisons: these results are not directly comparable since they are based on very different situations.

Public spending nowadays cannot be justified to the French Government simply by proving its usefulness; it must also achieve the best possible 'multiplier coefficient'. This means the best ratio between the total cost of improvements carried out by household as a result of the programme and the cost of the programme. However, such a ratio does not take into account other beneficial social effects that were measured by our evaluation:

* the creation of economic activities for the implementation of the programme and for carrying out home improvements; development of a local market in particular (the proportion of improvements carried out by local tradesmen in La Rochelle increased from 19 percent for non-participants to 50 percent for participants);

* the improvement in the cohesiveness of the local community and in the perception of local councillors;

102

* the improvement of energy consumption behaviour (impossible to measure in our case, for lack of information about behaviours preceding the programme);

* the positive influence of the operation at regional level (positive influence on the residents of neighbouring towns or on local councillors, or in relation to public buildings).

*Some recommendations*

*Concerning the programme's organization:* without repeating here all the conclusions in the form of recommendations, reformulating them in practical terms may be of use to those designing and implementing programmes. Of course on the basis of the analysis of three programmes, we can only draw attention to some factors which may contribute to the smooth running of the programmes:

* In order of importance, we would firstly emphasize the need to provide a mediating system to help in the resolution of inevitable conflicts which arise between participating organizations.

* This precaution is all the more necessary when a programme is organized at local level, since as a result the structure tends to be very unstable. Close links with central administrative bodies are factors providing the greatest degree of stability.

* Equally the choice, quality and strength of their links with 'legitimizing bodies' are crucial for the successful operation of a programme. The more informal links that exist between those responsible in each organization, the more flexible the system will be.

*Concerning programme design:* our assessment of the effects produced by the programme studied suggest some practical lessons.

* Locally organized programmes certainly make it possible to reach a broader social spectrum than those organized nationally. However, in the absence of a precisely defined social target, social selectivity will operate.

* The principle of appeal by attraction enables the specific clientele to be reached at the lowest cost. In order to reach the 'difficult' social groups, props which are familiar to them must be used and

the programme adapted to the special nature of these props.

* The presentation should try to overcome the abstract nature of the idea of energy conservation by the use of material and visual aids such as infra-red pictures. Presentations should not assume that the participants are completely passive. Even minimal active participation is a necessary condition for their commitment which in turn contributes to the achievement of the objectives.

* Too much emphasis on an 'effect of persuasion' can lead to the programme being rejected by dominated social groups.

* Finally, a last lesson which can be drawn from this assessment is the importance of the dialogue between thermal experts and households. Householders, and especially their wives, must be listened to in order to win them over, and, moreover, they will only accept an expert report which confirms their preconceptions.

## References

Gaskell, G. and Pike, R. 1983, Residential energy use: an investigation of consumers and conservation strategies. *Journal of Consumer Policy*, 6, 285-302.

Lebart, L., Morineau, P., Pleuvret, P. Brian, E. and Aluja, T. (eds.) 1983, *Systeme portable l'analyse des donnees*. Cesta: Paris.

Leyral, R. 1984, Impacts sociaux de programmes locaux pour la maitrise de l'energie. Les cas de Veynes, La Rochelle, Conflans-Ste-Honorine Tome 1, *Analyse des programmes et des leurs contexts*. CSTB/AFME. Paris.

Monnier, E. 1984, Impacts sociaux de programmes locaux pour la maitrise de l'energie. Les cas de Veynes, La Rochelle, Conflans-Ste-Honorine Tome 2. *Evaluation des effects Induits*. CSTB/AFME, Paris.

[1] According to our colleagues J.C. Thoenig and F. Dupuy, authors of 'Sociologie de L'administration francaise' (Ed. A. Colin 1983) associations of high-ranking officials play an important role in the way in which the State functions; direct contact with a fellow member of the same Association often avoids long administative procedures.

This research was funded by the Agence Francaise de La Maitrise de L'Energie, the Conseil General de Charante Maritime and the Ministry for Research and Industry.

# 4 Competing energy advisory services in a German town

LUTZ HILDEBRANDT and BERNWARD JOERGES

## Background and rationale of the study

The study compares the structures, dynamics and impacts of four community-level energy conservation advisory programmes 'competing' within the same municipality – a South German university town. It is set in the context of West German energy policies directed at private households. We attempt to provide answers to a series of questions central to the public and policy debates on energy conservation strategies aimed at 'decoupling' economic growth and energy consumption, and at introducing changes in household energy technologies which are both environmentally sound and acceptable from the social and consumer policy perspectives. The most general focus of the study is thus an interest in the relationships, linkages and conflicts between energy, consumer and environmental policies, and the potential of energy conservation programmes for preventive (as opposed to reactive) environmental strategies as well as for equitable social conditions in the household sector.

For reasons set out in the introductory chapter of this book, the study focuses on local conservation programmes and here, in turn, on the particular issue of reaching and involving less advantaged consumer groups, particularly tenant and low income households. Before describing the study design and structure of analyses undertaken, a few remarks concerning the broader policy and research context may be useful for readers not familiar with the West German scene.

In the years before the study was undertaken, private households and small-scale consumers accounted for approximately 45 percent of final energy consumption in the Federal Republic of Germany. While official statistics do not separate private households and other small-scale commercial and agricultural users, it can be assumed that households account for approximately 65 percent of this figure. In turn, approximately 90 percent of household energy consumption is associated with space heating and hot water. Almost half of household energy consumption is based on oil. Between 1979 and 1982, energy consumption in this sector was reduced by about 15 percent, more than half of this reduction (in the first year after the energy crisis about 90 percent) can be attributed to conservation actions by consumers (Schiffer 1983). It is not possible to be certain about the proportions of energy conservation achieved by 'market forces', other factors operating somewhat independently of public policy, and policies and programmes aimed at bringing about energy conservation. However, the latter have undoubtedly contributed in good measure to the reduction in energy demand.

The policy framework developed by federal and state governments as a result of the second energy price crisis in 1978 and extended in 1981 as part of the so-called 'Bund-Laender-Programm' for the support of energy conservation investments, gave high priority to the exploitation of the conservation potential in the household sector (Luhmann 1981; Hildebrandt and Joerges 1983). In this programme, three general types of measures received funding (see the Federal Ministry for Economics 1977, 1981; 2nd and 3rd Extension of the Federal Government's Energy Programme):

* financial measures (taxation, subsidies)
* regulatory measures (statutes governing the operation of heating units)
* informational measures (social marketing type activities)

Beyond some rough estimates, little information is available about the ways in which regulatory measures have affected energy conservation (Horn et al. 1978; Scholz and Rammer 1982, pp. 313-494). By contrast, there is more precise information about financial measures, subsidies and income tax reliefs, at least concerning their undesired effects. Approximately 85 percent of the funds were invested in insulation, 75 percent of which was accounted for by double-glazing windows (Eisel 1982), the installation of which is controversial. The

106

programme has been criticized because it has tended to benefit better-off home owners and to leave out large parts of the population such as tenants and socially weaker groups, and because it had a number of undesirable side-effects such as rises in rents and building deterioration.

Information campaigns are generally considered more successful, especially in view of the adoption and effectiveness of legislative and financial measures. A number of programmes were designed and carried out in order to encourage the participation of the public in the Bund-Laender-Programm, including the introduction of direct communication measures, indirect channelling of information through the media, a network of advisory offices of the consumer organizations, and specialist information banks (Hildebrandt and Joerges 1983). However, little is known about the effects of information measures taken under the auspices of this programme. Quantitative estimates have been provided, for example, in a study for the ifo Institut (Scholz and Rammer 1982) for different instruments and programmes carried out by particular organizations, such as the Stiftung Warentest (the comparative product testing organization), which point to considerable conservation effects, at least for the years 1980 and 1981. However, such studies cannot determine the unique effects of information within the overall effects of other measures and 'spontaneous' conservation actions.

Given the relative stability of the energy market, the drop in energy prices and the more favourable economic climate since 1983 on the one hand, persistent high unemployment and increasing environmental pollution on the other, the priorities of government energy policy have since changed. Energy conservation policy is increasingly considered to be a vehicle of environmental and employment policy, the assumption being that investments made to promote the rational use of energy reduce environmental pollution and stimulate employment (Garnreiter et al. 1983).

It can be assumed that the objectives of the regulatory measures in the 2nd and 3rd extensions (1978, 1981) of federal energy programmes and the Bund-Laender-Programm have been achieved. Consequently, the emphasis has shifted towards information instruments. Consumer information programmes such as those carried out by consumer organizations continue to be considered highly significant, while some of the financial measures have been discontinued. Without doubt, the government is recognizing the results of empirical research indicating that, despite broad public discussion, the lack of specific information is one of the main obstacles to achieving energy conservation: consumers in general are not well equipped to manage their energy consumption efficiently under widely varying conditions of energy supply options and available technology (Sattler 1981; Gruber and Meyer 1982)

It is probably reasonable to speak of a genuine lack of information in the midst of a flood of information. There is evidence that the availability of scattered information, some of which is incompatible or contradictory, does increase general awareness regarding the need to conserve energy but does not change attitudes, let alone behaviour concerning relevant household routines. Garnreiter and his co-authors (1983) believe that the problem lies in the absence of relevant and practical information as well as in problems with people's receptiveness for information. Thus, energy advisory services have been given a key role in the implementation of conservation programmes initiated by energy utilities (Oesterwind 1983), the programme implemented by the federal government in liaison with the consumer unions (AgV) and a variety of programmes implemented by ecological organizations (Hildebrandt and Joerges 1983). In addition, many communities have begun to consolidate their information programmes by setting up positions for energy advisers or hiring independent energy consultants.

The issue of eliminating certain legal obstacles and concomitant conflicts between the interests of landlords and tenants which keep tenants from investing in measures to conserve energy, has received more attention of late (Federal Ministry for Economics 1982, pp. 12-13; Monse and Simon 1982, pp. 140-143; Garnreiter et al. 1983, pp. 60-70; Prognos 1983). Generally, the willingness of consumers to invest in energy conservation is considered to be high, provided legal and economic barriers can be overcome (Broeg and Wichmann 1982).

One of the more interesting developments since the establishment of federal and state level programmes has been the emergence of a variety of local energy conservation measures. However, with a few exceptions, detailed studies of the evolution, dynamics and impacts of such programmes are not available. What is completely missing are studies which link analyses of programme structure with analyses of programme use, and the factors making for consumer participation and impacts on consumers. Similarly, analyses of the personal and structural factors generally facilitating or impeding energy conservation actions, both within and outside of the context of public programmes in support of energy conservation, are conspicuously lacking. Our study of four local programmes directed at consumers in the same community aims at bridging these gaps.

## Conceptual approach and study design

In order to conduct a comparative analysis across four programmes, across programme-users and non-users, and across social categories, including disadvantaged groups, a site had to be selected where a variety of programmes was in operation, with sufficient numbers of clients to allow for statistical analysis, and where access to the agencies operating these programmes was assured. Additional criteria guiding the selection were:

* as much independence and 'dissimilarity' between programmes as possible, particularly the inclusion of an energy utility sponsored and an ecologically oriented programme, in order to generate variety across programmes;

* as high a level of public 'energy consciousness' as possible,
in the sense that community energy planning should figure prominently on the agenda of local politics, thus generating above average levels of energy awareness and controversy in citizenry at which programmes are directed.

Among about twenty municipalities in the Federal Republic of Germany which had active local/regional energy concepts or plans underway, the one community which fitted these criteria best was Tuebingen, a South German university town of approximately 70,000 inhabitants. In themselves, the selection criteria formulated exclude any general 'representativeness' of this community, and set it apart from most other communities with respect to energy conservation 'and environmental issues. And yet, being among the municipalities with the highest level of 'Green' voters (above 20 percent) and a high proportion of households with an academic background, the community may be regarded as representative of certain social trends at large, particularly strains on the party political system to accommodate growing numbers of, for want of a better term, 'post industrialist' voters not easily aligned along the traditional left/right political lines. More than for other western industrialized countries, this may be a typical pattern for the Federal Republic of Germany. Factors contributing to the success or failure of programmes in this overall setting therefore might help in revealing more general trends.

The four programmes in this community are:

* an energy advisory service operated by the local consumer organization similar to 60 local programmes implemented throughout the country by the national association of consumer unions and its regional (or state-level) subsidiaries;

* an energy advisory service established by the municipal council and administration as part of their energy plan;

* an energy advisory service established by the local utility company (for electricity, gas and water), partly as an extension of its traditional household services, now emphasizing the rational use of energy in heating and hot water consumption, but also as a response to municipal activities judged inadequate by the utility;

* finally, an energy advisory service established by a local group of ecologists, in critical response to both the energy plans and household directed initiatives of the municipality and the utility.

All households having made use of these services prior to our study were contacted through the four agencies and asked whether they would consent to being interviewed. A sample of 143 client households was achieved and a comparison group selected, matched on the criteria of ownership, housing type and family size. The total sample of 293 households was interviewed. In addition, 16 in-depth structured interviews with key personnel of the agencies implementing the four programmes and their legitimating organizations were performed, and available documentation concerning the four programmes evaluated.

Based on these two sets of data - programme related and household related - three types of analysis were performed, summarized in the following paragraphs.

* In the 'top-down' perspective, the four programmes were compared along the dimensions of a) organizational evolution and structure, basic policy goals, conservation objectives, implementation strategies and internal evaluation procedures; b) five overall organizational attributes considered important for programme success; flexibility, linkages, commitment, targeting, and comprehensiveness; c) overall programme effects at three levels of client penetration, that is programme awareness, programme use, and conservation actions induced.

110

* In the 'bottom-up' perspective, the four clienteles of the programmes were compared with regard to a series of contextual factors assumed to shape energy consumption behaviours and responses to conservation programmes. Here we focus on the way, a) personal context factors, such as the disposition to seek information, values and attitudes to energy conservation, and past conservation experience, and b) structural context factors, such as socio-economic position and status, and family life cycle stage mediate programme take-up.

* In a final 'bottom-up' perspective, we compare programme users and non-users, irrespective of the particular programme with regard to the factors mentioned above and a number of additional variables thought to be associated with programme take-up.

**Programme specific analyses: 'top-down'**

In this section, we present a short historical account of the development of the four services followed by a description of the main policy actors involved. Next a comparative evaluation of the four implementing agencies and their programmes is performed, considering their basic policy goals, specific programme objectives with regard to conservation, their strategies, implementation procedures, and finally, programme control. Next, an evaluation of the four services with respect to overall programme attributes (flexibility, etc.) is presented. We finally turn to a sequential analysis of programme response and 'penetration'.

*Historical background*

Until the end of the 1970s, the only energy advisory service that existed in the community was the utility company's general counselling activities. Turning this service into an energy advisory programme and the establishment of three other energy advisory services in the area can be traced back directly or indirectly to the provisions of the second extension of the Federal Energy Conservation Act.

The second extension has provided, since 1978, subsidies for communal utilities to invest in expanding the mains energy supply systems. Very quickly, the communal utility, Stadtwerke, developed a local supply plan to take full advantage of the investment aid offered through federal programmes. One of the things this plan involved

111

was priority use of natural gas and district heating in the inner city. District heating that had been provided by oil was henceforth to be produced in cogeneration plants using gas. To supply the surrounding areas, the electricity resulting from cogeneration was to be offered as so-called electrical district heating. To ensure efficient heating in households, the right to use the 'district-heating electricity' was to be granted only if households complied with certain stipulations concerning insulation.

It was the plan to use electricity for heating purposes that led to sharp controversies between the management of the utility company on the one hand, and ecologist groups and the Green Party faction in the city hall on the other. Ecologists and the Greens developed their own supply scenario, emphasizing greater use of renewable energy sources, coal powered cogeneration plants with fluidized bed combustion, and a stronger emphasis on insulation at the household level. Critics of the utility's supply plan also called for the establishment of a local energy advisory service that was to be part of the city administration, independent of the interests of the power industry and utilities. In 1980, strong public pressure resulted in the allocation of DM 60,000 for a municipal advisory office, but later, in a kind of barter transaction, advisory services were contracted out to a private engineering consultancy. These consultants conduct low-cost energy counselling for private households out of offices provided by the municipality and, at the same time, planning advice to other municipal projects related to energy conservation.

Both the ecologist groups and the utility found this to be an unsatisfactory solution. As a municipal company, the utility considered that it was responsible for all matters concerning energy advice. The ecologists criticized the type and substance of the service and increased their efforts to create their own advisory programme. At the time of our study, a small private company run co-operatively by a group of ecologists took the initiative.

As the public dispute about the municipal energy supply plan developed the advisory service of the local consumer union was invited by the federal union of consumer organizations to establish their own energy advisory service. With funds from the federal information programme administered by the Ministry of Economics, and channelled through the regional consumer union, a part-time consultant was hired to provide households with advice on energy matters from offices provided by the local consumer union.

Based on available publications and interviews with key personnel we have performed a rough structural analysis of formal and informal linkages between the main actors involved in these four programmes.

*The utility service* is autonomous in the sense that it forms an integral part of its corporate marketing programme. Legitimating agencies are, on the one hand, the municipality which owns the utility and, on the other, the Association of Communal Utilities (VKU). Large organizations like the Central Advisory Agency for Electrical Appliances (HEA) and the Association of German Power Producers (VDEW) provide training and information materials, and major manufacturers provide demonstration appliances (these are provided competitively as part of their general marketing strategies).

*The ecologists' programme* arises out of an extensive network of informal linkages, having been founded as a 'grassroots' or 'self-help' initiative not directly dependent on any other organization. It has strong links with the nation-wide organization of citizens initiatives (BUND) and a local group concerned with alternative energy issues (Arbeitskreis Alternative Energie). Two independent ecological research organizations and 'think tanks', the Okeo-Institut and the Institut fuer Energie und Umwelt (IFEU), provide informal support. There are strong links to ecological activists and concerned scientists within the university community and the local Green Party.

*The municipal advisory service* is formally part of the 'Hochbauamt' (building office), but operationally it is part of a privately run energy consultancy with few formal links to other agencies. Many groups participated in the debate about setting up this service, including 'Stadtwerke' (the utility) which was opposed to it.

*The local consumer organization* is an outlet of the regional consumer union (Verbraucher zentrale) which, in turn, is associated with the National Union of Consumer Organizations (AgV). Its activities are financed through these higher level organizations by the Federal Ministry for Economic Affairs (BMWi). The energy advisor of the local consumer organization is the only one among the four services who has established working contacts with (two of) the other local advisory services.

We find that a net of informal links have played an important role in establishing and situating the services of the municipality and the ecologists. The utility's service is, in contrast, formally and hierarchically incorporated in the utility company, while the formal incorporation of the consumer union's services is complex and relatively ambiguous. In particular, the formal links with the local and the regional consumer organizations remain relatively unclear. The services of the utility and the consumer union can be seen as generated 'top-down', while the municipal and the ecologists' service were initially generated 'bottom-up', through political mandate and citizens' initiatives. However, over time, if for different reasons, both these services have at best retained informal links with their initial constituencies.

*Comparative programme analysis*

Before evaluating the programmes it is necessary to highlight the similarities and differences between them.

*The basic policies of the sponsoring organizations* guaranteeing the financial and material viability of the services are considered first. It can be assumed that their goals and objectives in good measure determine the type and quality of services offered. As a criterion for formal links we have taken financial support and material dependence. This is the case for the utility's service and the service of the consumer organizations but the ecologists' service is only informally linked with other organizations such as the Federal Association for Citizens' Initiatives, and is financially independent. On the other hand, it has very close links to other ecological groups. The municipal service is difficult to appraise because it is a private consultancy with a commercial orientation having both political and economic guidelines and the material support of the municipal administration. Similarly, the energy service of the utility can be viewed as part of the marketing activities of the corporation with its underlying profit motive. The ecologists' service does not have explicit commercial objectives but must at least break even to continue to exist. A goal conflict between profitability and 'green' policy objectives can be assumed here. Only the energy service of the consumer union does not implicitly or explicitly pursue goals of organizational profitability.

*The centrality of energy conservation goals* relates to the link between general organizational goals and subsidiary conservation objectives derived from these. The utility has an explicit policy of driving oil from the market. Although replacing oil with other energy sources is part of the federal government's energy policy, it does not automatically lead to conservation if this merely substitutes electricity for oil. In contrast, the ecologists' service is based on a view of energy policy as an integral part of environmental protection policies and a hardline opposition to any use of electricity for heating purposes. The energy conservation objectives of the municipality's service can be inferred only with difficulty. On the one hand, the operating company has little intrinsic interest in conservation apart from responding to the concerns of its clientele, on the other hand the municipal mandate can be interpreted as an attempt to sparingly use tax revenues available for energy conservation measures. Similarly, energy conservation goals are subsidiary to the consumer organization, vaguely derived from the general objective of enabling households to function as 'rational economic actors'.

*Links with other supporting organizations:* All the services, except for the municipality's energy consultant, are linked with various regional and national organizations. The municipality's consultants however, are involved in the city's construction planning, and have close connections to various administrative bodies, giving them energy relevant expertise more or less compatible with the 'competing' energy planning of the utility.

*Consumer representation:* Concerning clients' representation in the services, the consumer union is the only one in which, almost by definition, the recipients of the services are formally represented in the sponsoring organization. However, at least initially, the ecologists' service may be looked at as self-organized by consumers having grown out of a strong grass-roots movement for environmental improvement.

*The specific objectives of the four services* are complex because one must differentiate between documented objectives and the objectives of the individual energy advisors. Our results indicate that beliefs and orientations of the energy advisors do not always coincide with those of the organization. In this regard, the extent to which advisers can deviate from the explicit objectives of a programme and the consequences this has for the relationship between the consultant and sponsoring organization of the advisory service itself must be considered. Apart from the municipal service, for which no objective is clearly stated, the objectives of the services studied as documented in official programme information are closely modelled on the policies of the organizations through which the services are provided.

all cases, it can be assumed that advisory services are meant, in the first place, to help people use energy more efficiently. However, the meaning of this varies with the dominant ideologies of sponsoring organizations: the concept of efficient household production in the case of the consumer union; promoting consumers' adaptation to pricing policies aimed at oil substitution in the case of the utility; a more comprehensive concept of resource protection and appropriate technological choices in the case of the ecologists.

*Information content:* In terms of information content, the utility's service has the least flexibility. It is also set apart by the stress placed on substituting other sources of energy in accordance with corporate strategy. All energy consultants proceed on the assumption that the most efficient approach to energy conservation is the introduction of 'packages' of measures, with characteristic differences concerning their respective mixes. It is notable that the consumer union's advisory service places strong emphasis on ecological issues, as of course does the ecologists' programme. By the same token, both programmes can be seen as pursuing, in a certain way, 'alternative' consumer policy objectives, emphasizing participatory and equity objectives. In the case of the consumer union's advisor this may be attributed to the personal enthusiasm of the advisor as much as to specific programme objectives. All advisors see home owners as their most relevant target group, and only the consumer organization's service considers tenant households to be a group requiring specific services, particularly in the context of complaints about heating bills.

*The programme strategies* used by these four advisory services inevitably focus on communicative instruments. Only the utility is legally empowered to resort to financial or regulatory measures in their own right, on the basis of the relevant decisions of the City Council. In this sense, observations concerning financial, regulatory and technical measures refer to the energy consultants' endorsement or non-endorsement of such measures. All advisors indicated that they put the technical context of households at the centre of their advice. As a rule, broad and general information about technical opportunities and their economic benefits is given. However, the way in which economic benefits are estimated differs greatly. Whereas the utility and the consumer union provide rough estimates of the impacts on energy consumption and conservation, the ecologists' service takes measurements in the households themselves and calculates economic costs and benefits. The municipal energy advisor does much the same, but relies heavily on plans provided by the clients themselves and does not make house calls as part of the service.

It is not easy to determine the extent to which the services try to persuade households to implement particular strategies. All advisors indicated that they provide neutral advice, as stated in their services' statutes. Asked for their personal stance, the consumer union's consultant emphasizes changes in the personal context of clients, that is awareness and know-how, which then would lead to conservation actions. The ecologists' advisors take a strong anti-electricity stand, thus excluding entire clusters of possible measures. The utility's advisor is constrained in his choices by the utility's supply plan. By contrast, the energy advisor working for the municipality argues dispassionately and remains, on request, open to advice on all kinds of technical measures, even those which may be judged meaningless in view of strict energy conservation criteria. Advisors' opinions on financial instruments differ somewhat, the utility and the municipal service leaning towards pricing strategies, the ecologists' and the consumer unions' towards financial incentives provided through the federal programmes. Both ecologists and consumer unions emphasize solar energy as an alternative technical option, provided it is economically efficient; the utility's advisor favours heat pump technology, while the municipal advisor heat storage technology.

*Programme implementation:* The organizational web through which the four services are implemented has been described. As for procedures, all advisors claim to work without a pre-determined programme, but rather to focus on the specific problems brought forward by their clients. Only the ecologists' service has developed a rough framework, cataloguing possible measures broken down according to effectiveness and financial cost. Some of the substance of the consumer union's service is prescribed in general terms in materials provided by the regional and national sponsoring organizations. As the energy advisors see it, the motive for a client seeking out a particular service stems almost always from some personal communication. At the same time, however, all advisors advertised their service publicly in various printed media such as the customer's magazine of the utility, the calendar of events published by the city gazette, or other local media. No definite figures were given for the costs of the programmes. As concerns funding sources, the utility service is financed as part of its public relations programme, and the consumer union's service is funded entirely through the government's energy programme. Funds for the municipal service come from the municipal administration, partially in form of payment of office rental, but also from fees collected from clients, subsidized in turn by the municipality. The ecologists' service is also financed through fees, and a considerable work input of the group of advisors running it. All of the advisors have an engineering/natural science background, none of them having formal training or extensive previous experience in advisory work.

*Programme control* in the sense of programme supervision or inbuilt evaluation is weak in all programmes. None of the services has developed a refined system of quality control, a record of the number of the clients being almost the only explicit indicator of programme success. The consumer union's service keeps a systematic file of the clients for future evaluation, provided of course the party counselled agreed. Thus, there is almost no routine information about the effect of the advice whether at the level of conservation actions taken nor obviously at the level of energy conserved. Only the ecologists' group prepared, at the time of the study, a programme of systematic post-advisory monitoring of their work, both in order to determine programme results and to test computer-aided service programmes under development. In sum, evaluation rests to a large degree on information and experience collected informally by the individual advisors rather than on explicit and systematic records.

*Programme appraisal*

Building on the programme descriptions in the previous sections and the results of our interviews with the energy advisors, the programmes are now evaluated according to five criteria: flexibility, the existence of 'linkages' or supporting ties with other organizations, the commitment of key personnel, the specificity of programme targeting, and the comprehensiveness of programmes in terms of objectives and instruments - all attributes considered to be major determinants of programme success. Our appraisal is performed by scoring programmes according to whether a given feature is 'present', 'present to a limited degree' or 'non-existent'. An attempt was made to appraise programmes in terms of actual performance at the time of the study, rather than in terms of potential. For each criterion, the four programmes are given a rank score. Table 4.1 summarizes results and speaks largely for itself. A few comments may be added.

Table 4.1
Overall evaluation of programmes

| Criteria | util. | ecol. | muni. | cons. org. |
|---|---|---|---|---|
| Programme in existence since | 1981 | 1983 | 1981 | 1979 |
| Flexibility | | | | |
| * freedom to distribute funds | x | - | - | - |
| * freedom to employ diff. instruments | x | x | - | - |
| * join coalitions with other agencies | - | (x) | - | x |
| * select target groups | x | x | - | (x) |
| * exemption from control | - | (x) | x | - |
| rank | 1 | 1 | 4 | 3 |
| ----> downward | - | x | - | x |
| linkages ----> upward | (x) | x | - | x |
| ----> horizontal | (x) | - | - | x |
| rank | 3 | 1 | 4 | 1 |
| Commitment | | | | |
| * to energy conservation issues | x | x | - | - |
| * to specific kind of groups | - | x | - | x |
| rank | 3 | 1 | 4 | 1 |
| Targeting: matching to target group requirements | x | x | (x) | x |
| rank | 1 | 1 | 4 | 1 |
| Comprehensiveness: | | | | |
| * regarding issues | - | (x) | - | x |
| * instruments applied | x | (x) | - | (x) |
| * contexts addressed | x | x | x | x |
| * channels used | - | x | - | - |
| * packaging | x | x | x | - |
| rank | 2 | 1 | 4 | 2 |

x   present
(x) present to a limited degree
-   non-existent

119

*Flexibility:* Only the utility has discretion in distributing their funds. It can negotiate pricing conditions or wage and salary structures. The municipal service and consumer organization service have discretion in employing instruments at their disposal but are limited on account of their poor equipment. The consumer organization's service has shown an ability to join in coalitions with a variety of other organizations, whereas public disputes around incompatible supply plans have created insurmountable barriers for co-operation between the utility and the ecologists on the one hand, the utility, the ecologists and consumer union's and the municipal services, on the other.

*Linkages:* In our view, the consumer union's service comes out first with regard to establishing a variety of 'downward', 'horizontal' and 'upward' linkages; it has established contacts between the different services, is affiliated with an 'independent' federation of consumers, and is supported both materially and financially by a powerful national organization. The utility's has no strong links to its clientele, except for the business relationships and market processes that exist between practically all households and the utility. The municipal service remains all but isolated having established working relationships only with parts of the municipal administration.

*Commitment:* Difficult as this particular criterion may be to assess, we conclude that the advisors of the consumer union's and the ecologists' services are more strongly committed to both the objective of energy conservation and to particular client groups. While all advisors claim to target their services to the specific conservation requirements of specific groups -- with the possible exception of the municipal service whose clientele as well as conservation orientation remains doubtful -- the advisors of these two services seem to have more genuinely embraced the goal of household energy conservation and established a stronger identification with their particular clienteles.

*Targeting:* While all the services must be rated generally 'weak' in this respect, only the municipality's advisor seems to lack it altogether, seeing 'households in general' as the potential clientele. The loose coupling of this service with the municipal administration makes it almost exempt from institutional control, too. By contrast, the ecologists' service is subject to a range of informal monitoring groups which effectively direct their work towards clients with an environmentalist orientation, cutting across conventional social categories. A more detailed analysis of the actual reach of the four services with regard to the social segmentation of their clientele will be given later.

*Comprehensiveness:* Again, the programmes and their advisors respectively, vary greatly from one another in this respect. This is partly due to the different technical backgrounds of the advisors and to the different degrees to which the services are materially equipped by their supporting agencies. As mentioned, the services concern themselves in principle with almost all aspects of household energy consumption, with a strong focus on technical measures. All services, with the exception of the consumer unions', attempt to offer 'package solutions', that is to propose some sort of integrated solution rather than one-off measures for given households.

As shown in Table 4.1, a rank ordering of the four programmes on the five criteria places the ecologists' service slightly ahead of the consumer organization's and the utility's services. These two are about 'even', with slight differences on some of the criteria. Further differentiation could be derived only by weighting these criteria, a procedure which is not warranted on the basis of our data. The municipal service comes out last in almost all respects, however. This is partially due to the lack of organizational affiliations and the half-hearted way in which this service is equipped by its sponsoring agency, and partially to the particular orientation of its personnel.

*A sequential analysis of programme penetration*

In order to relate the programme evaluation as presented in the previous sections to actual programme impacts, we will now draw on the main results of the households survey. Programme success can be measured as a sequence of 'hierarchical effects' (see for example Ewald and Rosenstiel 1980), using data indicating progressive penetration of a programme from mere acquaintance on the part of prospective users to satisfaction with services rendered.

The six indicators chosen for a comparison of programme-specific impacts are shown in Figure 4.1. In these indicators data from certain items in our household questionnaire are combined for the different subsamples of the entire sample (users and non-users) relevant to particular stages in programme penetration reached. In order to estimate programme impact, scores for these 'dependent variables' were calculated and the rank order of these scores interpreted as indicating the relative success of each of the four programmes.

121

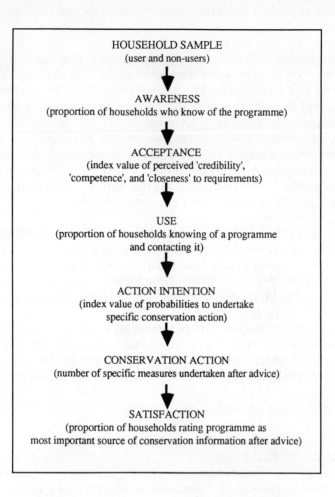

```
                  HOUSEHOLD SAMPLE
                   (user and non-users)

                            ↓

                      AWARENESS
     (proportion of households who know of the programme)

                            ↓

                     ACCEPTANCE
             (index value of perceived 'credibility',
         'competence', and 'closeness' to requirements)

                            ↓

                         USE
        (proportion of households knowing of a programme
                     and contacting it)

                            ↓

                   ACTION INTENTION
          (index value of probabilities to undertake
              specific conservation action)

                            ↓

                 CONSERVATION ACTION
      (number of specific measures undertaken after advice)

                            ↓

                    SATISFACTION
          (proportion of households rating programme as
 most important source of conservation information after advice)
```

Figure 4.1 Sequence hierarchy of programme impacts

As a first step we compare results regarding awareness, acceptance and programme use. Table 4.2 shows that the four programmes are quite similar on all these indicators. It emerges that the utility's service has the greatest chance of being contacted by the households, due to its high visibility. This is partially a straightforward effect of the utility's position in the community, each household necessarily entering into some relation with it via its electricity and/or gas consumption. Similarly, the consumer union enters the field with a high degree of visibility due to its general activities concerning consumer issues. Yet, high visibility does not result here in high acceptance and use, the utility and the ecologists' services rating higher than the consumer organization and the municipality's service.

Table 4.2

Sequential Programme Impact Analysis: Overview of Results

*Households knowing of programme Households using programme services*

| Programme | Knowers[1] | Awareness | Accept-<br>ance | Use | Action<br>intention | Conserv-<br>ation<br>actions | Satis-<br>faction |
|---|---|---|---|---|---|---|---|
| utility | 254 (122) | .87 (.81) | .62 (.50) | .43 | .38 | 1.41 | .44 |
| ecologist | 78 ( 28) | .26 (.19) | .58 (.53) | .33 | .40 | 1.53 | .63 |
| municipal-<br>ity | 50 ( 24) | .17 (.16) | .21 (.16) | .10 | .08 | .60 | .60[2] |
| consumer<br>organisation | 120 ( 55) | .41 (.37) | .48 (.36) | .24 | .54 | 1.59 | .56 |

1 In parantheses results from non–user subsample
2 Interpretation problematic due to size of subsample

We then move to action intentions, conservation actions taken and satisfaction with the programme. Again, results are shown in Table 4.2. We find that the readiness to undertake certain conservation measures is generally higher for users of the consumer union's service than users of the other services (and, we may add, non-users). The municipality's service shows the reverse effect, except for heat pump technology. Similarly, the clientele of the ecologists' service is in line with average levels of readiness to act, except for solar technology, and again, heat pumps. Interestingly, the users of the utility's service show little interest in these technologies.

Table 4.3

Likelihood of taking measures if 25% subsidy offered

| Action | util. | ecol. | mun- icip. | cons. org. | ave. | non- users |
|---|---|---|---|---|---|---|
| attic insulation | 27 | 25 | 13 | 32 | 25 | 24 |
| hot water retrofit | 33 | 29 | 07 | 35 | 29 | 24 |
| heat pump | 10 | 19 | 13 | 31 | 12 | 11 |
| solar | 06 | 17 | 0 | 14 | 08 | 06 |
| door/window insulation | 45 | 48 | 08 | 46 | 45 | 45 |
| thermostats | 42 | 45 | 07 | 48 | 39 | 38 |
| outer walls insulation | 36 | 31 | 20 | 36 | 34 | 33 |
| modernize heating | 37 | 37 | 07 | 39 | 33 | 30 |
| double paned windows | 42 | 46 | 0 | 42 | 40 | 38 |

Table 4.3 gives the results on a likelihood scale ranging from 0 to 100 for the intention to do certain measures not yet undertaken, provided a 25 percent subsidy of their costs were available.

If these measures are grouped according to their technical/economic scope - small, medium, and large measures - it appears that the clientele of the consumer organization shows the highest readiness to act for all three categories, followed by the ecologists' and utility's programmes (see Table 4.4).

Table 4.4
Likelihood of taking small, medium and large conservation measures

| Conservation Action | number of users | small | medium | large | overall average |
|---|---|---|---|---|---|
| *Programme* | | | | | |
| utility | 108 | 42 | 34 | 37 | 38 |
| ecologists | 25 | 42 | 38 | 41 | 40 |
| municipality | 4 | 25 | – | – | 08 |
| consumer organization | 25 | 67 | 41 | 55 | 54 |

The number of conservation actions undertaken after advice can be taken as a strong indicator of programme success. Table 4.5 shows the average number of conservation actions per household and per programme before and after advice.

Table 4.5
Conservation actions before and after programme use

| Users of | N | Ave. Before | Ave. After |
|---|---|---|---|
| utility | 113 | 1.55 | 1.41 |
| ecologists | 26 | 1.19 | 1.53 |
| municipality | 5 | 2.20 | 0.60 |
| consumer organization | 29 | 1.79 | 1.59 |
| all users | 143 | 1.47 | 1.38 |
| non users | 150 | 1.52 | – |

Key:
N = number of users
Ave. Before = average number of conservation actions before advice
Ave. After = .average number of actions after advice

Note that in this analysis equal weights are given to all measures. This shows that in general households having taken advantage of the programmes have already undertaken considerably more conservation actions than non-users. Correspondingly, the number of measures after advice tends to be smaller than before: households using a programme seem to have been active conservers in the past. Only the ecologists' clientele deviates from this trend, which maybe interpreted as a programme success. More detailed analysis of the data underlying these figures shows that before programme use the installation of double-glazed windows and other insulation measures dominate, whereas after advice the majority of measures concern improving heating systems, with a tendency in the ecologists' programme to experiment with new technologies.

Our last indicator of programme success summarizes users' evaluation of the importance and helpfulness of advice received. For each programme this index of satisfaction, as shown in the last column of Table 4.2, is based on the proportion of households judging its advice as most useful against a range of other advice sources. Neglecting the municipal service, the ecologists' programme, again, comes out first, followed by the consumer union's and the utility's.

*Overall Interpretation*

Summarizing the results of the programme impact analysis and programme structure analysis as presented in the previous sections, we arrive at the following interpretation.

The utility having local monopoly in energy supply can rely on an institutional framework comprising practically all households in the area. The relative success of its advisory service is therefore as much a consequence of this dominant position and systematic corporate marketing as of the superior technical facilities of its advisory programme. As a result, the utility's service has achieved the highest degrees of general awareness, acceptance and take up, as compared to the other services. Similarly, the consumer union's position in the community as an agency representing consumer interests at large and as part of a regional and national system of consumer protection gives its service a strong initial base. Its lack of institutionalized relations with its clientele may account for the fact that it rates lower on programme awareness. The ecologists on the other hand, lack both strong linkages to powerful organizations and, relative to the other services, financial and technical facilities. However, even though at the level of programme awareness they have a low rating, acceptance and use within the clientele reached are higher than for the consumer union's service.

Going on to the indicators closer to actual conservation behaviour, the utility rates relatively lower. This is, in part, accounted for by the utility's strategy to focus on high investment measures in the area of modernization of heating systems. On the whole, the clientele of the consumer union's service is strongest both at the stage of intention to undertake conservation measures and of measures undertaken after advice. The ecologists' service can boast an atypical ratio of measures undertaken before and after advice, together with the highest degree of satisfaction with services rendered. In view of our model of an hierarchy of effects we may conclude the following:

* the utility's service has achieved the strongest degree of penetration 'down to' the first stages of awareness, acceptance and use, loosing momentum at the stages of action intentions, conservation actions undertaken and satisfaction;

* the consumer union's service exhibits lower levels of initial penetration, but meets with the highest levels of action intentions and conservation actions undertaken;

* the ecologists' service, starting off with the lowest level of initial penetration, rises slowly with regard to acceptance, use and behavioural impact. It achieves a level of penetration, with its smaller group of adherents, lying somewhere between the consumer union's and the utility's reach, and produces the strongest degree of satisfaction;

* the activities of the municipality's service, having not even achieved a satisfactory degree of awareness of its programme, does not produce adequate values on any of the other indicators used.

The results from the evaluation of programme structures, based on available documentation and interviews with programme agents, are in keeping with the hierarchical analysis of informational and behavioural effects, based on the household survey. Of course, we must be careful about generalizations to local programmes in other communal contexts; however, a few points emerge nevertheless. Organizational 'weight' and flexibility as well as general credibility and perceived competence play an important role in attracting potential clienteles. The same applies to clear goal orientations, whatever the specific orientation. In order to 'carry through' a programme, commitment of personnel to the goal of energy conservation and identification with its particular clientele seems to be paramount. In the particular case of the ecologists' programme, a comprehensive goal orientation, (an integration of energy and environmental policy objectives) seems to have produced a strong 'bind', with a clientele predominantly composed of younger households with so-called 'postmaterialist' leanings. Diffuse and ambiguous goal structure, inadequate institutional support and technical facilities, uncompensated by strong personal commitment and prestige of programme agents, guarantee failure. Generally, services relying on part-time advisors seem to be at a disadvantage.

Finally, it clearly emerges that programme success is the result of an interactive process between programme build-up, attracting specific clienteles and adapting to their expectations. No single programme will carry its services through to a satisfactory completion of the measures it advocates irrespective of particular features of its clientele. Rather, programme structure is selective with regard to respondents, and in turn programme users, having opted for a particular scheme, provide it with coherence, momentum and legitimation. In this sense, it is not so much 'independent' features of programmes that help explain programme success with households seen as more or less passive recipients, but rather the 'fit' between the requirements and orientations of more or less circumscribed groups seeking to improve their energy situations, and the range and orientation of services offered by particular programmes.

**Programme-specific analyses: 'bottom-up'**

We will now change perspective from programme characteristics as they relate to outcomes, and look at programme outcomes as they relate to a range of contextual factors shaping consumers' responses. For any programme we assume that people's perception and awareness, the 'processing' of programme services and evaluation of suggested measures, forming action intentions, mobilizing resources, and finally the actual response in the sense of measures undertaken, are all related to what we have called personal and structural contexts.

*The personal context*

*The propensity to seek energy-related information*, and as a consequence level of energy knowledge, are assumed to be important
preconditions of programme use and subsequent conservation actions.
High information propensity is held to be characteristic of in-
novators and, on specific issues, of opinion leaders. It is grounded
motivationally either in a general personal predisposition to seek information, or it may be stimulated by problems occurring in the
household context and related decision making requirements. In this
latter case, immediate economic-technical problems and problem
awareness that has been mediated by communicating with others can
be distinguished.

The implication of these assumptions, that 'more' information
results in 'better' knowledge and decisions, has been questioned in
research on the phenomenon of information overload. Here, it is assumed that the effectiveness of information depends both on its
complexity and people's capacity to process it. Over-supply of information or information that is too complex leads to stress-like
situations and to poorer quality decisions (Jacoby 1983; Silberer 1979;
Raffe and Silberer 1981).

In order to ascertain the main reasons for contacting one of the advisory services, we asked four questions concerning economic-
technical problem situations and five questions concerning other
reasons or incentives for using a programme. Table 4.6. shows the
results, and it is easy to see that technical-economic considerations
predominate. More than one third say they were led to seek advice
by high energy costs or because of the purchase of heating equipment. Another important reason was plans to renovate apartments.
Interestingly, in programme contacts motivated through
'communication', information coming from the mass media and
equally information about the programme of national subsidies
played a very minor part. Where programme contact was not the
result of immediate household problems, personal communication
with friends, colleagues and acquaintances was the most important
source.

Table 4.6
Reasons for programme use
(in % of respective subsample, absolute numbers in parentheses)

| Reason | utility | ecologists | consumer | all users |
|---|---|---|---|---|
| modernization of house | 3.7 | 4 (1) | 8 (2) | 4 (5) |
| high energy costs | 39.8 | 42.3 (11) | 24 (6) | 41 (59) |
| purchase of heating equipment | 42.6 | 35 (9) | 32 (8) | 38 (54) |
| renovation of apartment | 15.7 | 32 (8) | 24 (6) | 18 (26) |
| advertisements in press/media | .9 (1) | – | – | 1 (1) |
| information about financial incentives | 2.8 (3) | 4 (1) | 4 (1) | 3 (4) |
| municipal energy concept | 2.8 (3) | 8 (2) | 8 (2) | 4 (5) |
| TV features on energy conservation | .9 (1) | – | – | 1 (1) |
| talking to friends, colleagues, acquaintances | 12 (13) | 32 (8) | 16 (4) | 15 (20) |
| others | 38 (41) | 56 (14) | 48 (12) | 41 (59) |
| number in sample | 108 | 25 | 25 | 143 |

The propensity to seek information was measured indirectly by determining the number of relevant sources known (indicator 1) and already used (indicator 2). Besides the four advisory services under study, five other information sources were included: the national organization for comparative product testing, the energy offices of national ministries, the national association of citizens initiatives, relevant local businesses, and relevant radio/TV features. Table 4.7 compares the users of the three programmes.

Table 4.7
Information propensity of programme users

|  | util. | ecol. | cons. |
|---|---|---|---|
| indicator 1: average number of sources known | 4.58 | 6.19 | 5.32 |
| indicator 2: average number of sources used | 1.87 | 2.73 | 2.68 |
| number in sample | 87 | 25 | 25 |

We find that users of the ecologists' programme rate highest on the indicators of information propensity. In contrast, users of the utility's service show relatively low propensity, while the clients of the consumer organization come closer to the ecologists' group.

To measure information overload we asked two questions about being given 'too much' information and 'too complicated' information in order to arrive at a clear decision. Since few of our respondents were able to answer, only a general trend can be detected. Values on both indicators of information load increase with the propensity to seek information. Thus on overload clients of the ecologists' programme rate high, the utility's programme low, with users of the consumer union's service somewhere in the middle.

*General value orientations and attitudinal factors* have in the past contributed little to the empirical explanation of actual conservation behaviours (Heberlein and Black 1976). Especially at the level of general attitudes to conservation and 'ecological' values, almost no significant direct relations with conservation actions have been found (Nietzel and Winett 1977; Lopreato and Merriweather 1976; Verhallen and van Raaij 1981; Newmann 1982). It has been shown, on the other hand, that highly specific attitudes can predict behaviour of similar specificity (Seligman et al. 1978, 1979, Ritsema et al. 1972).

Values and attitudes have been measured in two ways in the present study. One approach measures general orientations to energy conservation in the context of similarly general orientations to other central societal and policy issues. This allows us to measure the subjective importance given to energy conservation relative to other pressing social problems. A second approach operationalizes energy attitudes in the context of household management. Using a scale for positive and negative attitudes to nine household related implications of energy conservation, an overall measure of attitude to energy conservation was calculated and this is subsequently used in further analyses.

In the first approach, the 'energy crisis' as a societal problem was contrasted with the problems of 'unemployment', 'deterioration of urban quality' and 'environmental pollution'. We find that users of the three larger programmes are rather similar in their judgements. Unemployment is generally seen to be more important than the energy crisis, but the latter is seen as more important than urban quality, at least for users of the utility's and the consumer organization's programmes. There is almost total agreement that environmental pollution is equally important or even more important than the energy crisis. However, the main difference is that the ecologists' clientele put environmental pollution above unemployment, a judgement not shared by any other group. The scale for measuring specific attitudes toward energy conservation allows for a comparison across the entire sample (users and non-users) along a positive-negative continuum. It will be noted that, due to the small subsample of users of the municipal service, their results must be treated with extreme caution.

132

Table 4.8 shows the results, including the average of the entire sample as midpoint of the scale.

Table 4.8
Attitudes to household energy conservation:
Programme users and non-users

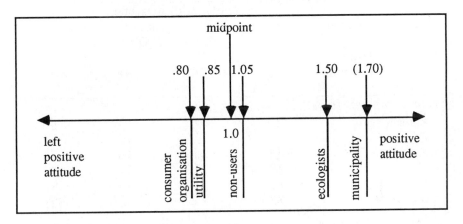

It turns out that, while all participants expressed positive answers throughout, users of the ecologists' service are more positive than any of the other groups. Across the clienteles of the three larger programmes we find highly homogeneous attitudes, particularly with regard to the environmental relevance of energy conservation and energy conservation as part of proper household management. Significant differences in attitudes concerning the relative importance of economic considerations only appear between the ecologist's and the utility's group. The utility's clientele tend to think of energy conservation as a household economic matter whereas the consumer union's group tend to see it as a series of technical issues.

*Structural contexts: socio-economic status and life cycle position*

Past research indicates that both informational activities (awareness, acceptance and use) and actual conservation behaviour vary with socio-economic status (Curtin 1976; Olsen and Goodnight 1976; Warren and Clifford 1975; Barnaby and Reizenstein 1975; Ester 1983). While it has been shown, on the other hand, that different types of families greatly differ in their energy consumption patterns (Van Raaij and Verhallen 1984; Fritzsche 1981) there is little known about the effects of family life cycle stage on conservation behaviour.

133

Table 4.9
Level of awareness as a function of socio-economic
status and life-cycle position
(users and non-users, N=293)

| Household segment | utility | Percentages of awareness | | |
|---|---|---|---|---|
| | | ecol-ogists | muni-cipality | consumer org. |
| sample percentage | 87% | 27% | 17% | 41% |
| *Socio-economic status* | | | | |
| 1 high | <u>91</u> | 27 | <u>27</u> | <u>46</u> |
| 2 | 85 | <u>31</u> | 19 | <u>50</u> |
| 3 | <u>89</u> | <u>35</u> | 16 | 43 |
| 4 | <u>89</u> | 11 | 21 | 37 |
| 5 | 85 | <u>31</u> | 14 | 37 |
| 6 low | 83 | 25 | 8 | 33 |
| *Family life cycle stage* | | | | |
| unmarried, no children, student | 82 | <u>63</u> | 4 | <u>48</u> |
| married, young children | 80 | 30 | 25 | 50 |
| married, grown-up children | 87 | 23 | 10 | 23 |
| unmarried, no children, employed | 87 | 28 | 17 | 46 |
| married, no children | 93 | 31 | 28 | 51 |
| married, retired | 84 | 7 | 11 | 25 |
| retired, living alone | 83 | 11 | 14 | 37 |
| Frequency in user sample | 254 | 78 | 50 | 120 |

Using an index of socio-economic status which combines disposable household income, educational level and the occupation of
the head of the household, giving six categories, and a typology of
seven household types to indicate life cycle, we have looked at the
differential impacts of these variables across the programmes.

## Table 4.10
### Level of use as a function of socio-economic status and life-cycle position
#### (users and non-users, N=293)

| Household segment | utility | Percentages of users ecol- ogists | muni- cipality | consumer org. |
|---|---|---|---|---|
| sample percentage | 75% | 17% | 3.6% | 17% |
| *Socio-economic status* | | | | |
| 1 high | 67 | – | <u>11</u> | <u>33</u> |
| 2 | <u>85</u> | 3 | <u>4</u> | <u>23</u> |
| 3 | <u>86</u> | 19 | 2 | 10 |
| 4 | <u>82</u> | 4 | 7 | <u>18</u> |
| 5 | 54 | <u>36</u> | – | <u>18</u> |
| 6 low | 20 | <u>40</u> | – | – |
| *Family life cycle stage* | | | | |
| unmarried, no children, student | 20 | <u>60</u> | – | <u>20</u> |
| married, young children | 73 | 9 | 18 | 17 |
| married, grown-up children | <u>86</u> | <u>29</u> | – | – |
| unmarried, no children, employed | 71 | 16 | 3 | <u>26</u> |
| married, no children | <u>89</u> | 8 | 6 | 6 |
| married, retired | <u>89</u> | 6 | – | 11 |
| retired, living alone | 73 | 9 | 4 | <u>18</u> |
| Frequency in user sample | 108 | 25 | 5 | 25 |

In Table 4.9 the proportion of households who are aware of the four programmes is shown (above-average levels are underlined). Generally, levels of awareness increase with status, and only the utility's and the ecologists' services achieve above-average awareness with middle and lower status groups. As for family life cycle position, the utility is best known in 'middle' stages, whereas the ecologists' service appeals more to 'younger' stages. We find that social status does not differentiate significantly between the four programmes however, while family life cycle does for the consumer union's and the ecologists' service.

Turning to use levels, as shown in Table 4.10 it emerges that the utility's clientele tends to be of higher socio-economic status than the other groups, while the ecologists' service attracts lower status groups - an effect of high proportion of student households in their clientele. Regarding family life cycle, no clear picture emerges, except for the generally high demand for energy services in the 'married, grown-up children' category. The effects of both socio-economic status and family life cycle position on programme use are statistically significant for the utility's and the ecologists' services but not for the remaining two programmes. Testing for income and age of head of household separately, supports this result: the utility's service tends to reach older and wealthier households, the ecologists' younger and poorer.

As regards programme take-up, an examination of the number and type of conservation actions undertaken does not reveal any systematic influence of socio-economic and life cycle context.

*Disadvantaged consumers*

We know that the energy crisis has hit poorer and otherwise disadvantaged consumer groups relatively harder. There are also findings which show that such groups are less prepared to seek and act upon energy conservation information (cf. Dillman et al. 1981; Rogers and Leonard-Barton 1980; Mettler-Meibom 1982). Our study has proceeded on the assumption that local programmes are better able to close this gap than central programmes. To investigate this we isolated three disadvantaged consumer segments: the lowest of the six status groups, pensioners and tenant households. These are not mutually exclusive categories. In order to determine whether disadvantaged consumer groups find it easier to respond to local rather than centrally administered programmes, we analyse awareness and programme take-up.

Table 4.11 Disadvantaged consumers: awareness and use of central and local conservation programmes

| Source | total sample | | all pensioners | | all low status | | all tenants | |
|---|---|---|---|---|---|---|---|---|
| | aware | used | aware | used | aware | used | aware | used |
| number of households | n = | 293 | n = | 79 | n = | 76 | n = | 156 |
| central: | | | | | | | | |
| comparative product testing organisation | 84 | 20.5 | 73 | 11 | 85 | 16 | 88 | 22 |
| ministries | 38 | 07 | 23 | 05 | 30 | 04 | 36 | 05 |
| national association of environmental initiatives | 49 | 06 | 19 | 04 | 53 | 01 | 49 | 06 |
| media | 74 | 36 | 67 | 34 | 68 | 30 | 76 | 38 |
| local: | | | | | | | | |
| utility | 87 | 37 | 84 | 32 | 84 | 21 | 83 | 34 |
| ecologists | 27 | 09 | 09 | 03 | 30 | 16 | 30 | 11 |
| municipality | 17 | 02 | 13 | 00 | 13 | 00 | 13 | 06 |
| consumer organisation | 41 | 09 | 30 | 05 | 37 | 07 | 40 | 06 |
| local businesses and crafts | 48 | 30 | 41 | 25 | 40 | 20 | 40 | 24 |

Again, the four regional/central programmes are selected for comparison: the national product testing organization, energy offices of federal level ministries, the national association of citizens initiatives and regular programmes on energy conservation in the media. In addition, we look at the degree of awareness and use of relevant services offered by regional and local business and crafts. Table 4.11 gives the results in percentages of the three categories and for the total sample, and two major trends emerge. The utility's service has, among the local programmes, the highest degree of visibility with disadvantaged groups, and among the central programmes only the organization for comparative product testing reaches similar levels, both for the entire sample and the disadvantaged segments. Media programmes, too, achieve quite high values. At the stage of use they even show the greatest reach of all the programmes on the list. Relative to the high awareness level of the national product testing service, its actual take-up among the disadvantaged groups is low. The ecologists' service, in turn , starts off with a much lower level of awareness, but ends up with similar levels of use. Low values emerge for the other central programmes as well as the local services of the consumer union and the municipality. In view of low awareness levels, local businesses and crafts exhibit relatively high use levels.

Generally, it can be concluded that, while central programmes can achieve high levels of awareness, actual take-up increases with spatial proximity. This applies not only to local energy conservation programmes but equally to (regionalized) radio and TV features and local/regional commercial services. Disadvantaged consumer groups generally rate lower on awareness and take-up of central programmes as compared with local programmes. However, the difference, as measured by the deviation from sample averages, is smaller than expected. Only the ecologists' service achieves above average levels of awareness and use in the disadvantaged categories. However, moving from the take-up stage to conservation actions implemented, more marked differences between the responses of the socially disadvantaged groups and average programme participants are apparent. Table 4.12 gives the figures for measures taken before and after programme use for the total sample and the disadvantaged segments. Excluding the small number of pensioners using the ecologists' and consumer union's services, only the pensioner group using the utility's service comes close to average levels (presumably because of generally higher income levels in the utility's clientele). All other segments fall off considerably. If these measures indicate real effects, it must be concluded that local programmes, too, if less so than central programmes, miss disadvantaged consumers.

Table 4.12 Disadvantaged consumers:
average number of conservation actions taken before and after advice

| conservation actions taken | utility | | | ecologists | | | consumer organisation | | | total sample |
|---|---|---|---|---|---|---|---|---|---|---|
| | low status | pension. | tenants | low status | pension. | tenants | low status | pension. | tenants | |
| before programme use | .93 | 1.17 | .87 | .91 | 2.0 | .72 | .60 | 2.0 | .75 | 1.47 |
| after programme use | 1.13 | 1.34 | 1.11 | .83 | 2.5 | .94 | .60 | 1.75 | .87 | 1.38 |
| number of households | 17 | 23 | 47 | 12 | 2 | 18 | 5 | 4 | 8 | 143 |

We will now briefly present results from analyses of the multiple relationships between the major personal and structural context variables on the one hand, and consumer responses to programmes on the other. Results and interpretations reported in previous sections are based on the analysis of bivariate relationships, taking pairs of variables at a time. Their validity is limited in the sense that these analyses do not 'control' for major intervening factors and therefore do not lend themselves to causal interpretation.

A first attempt at causal modelling used path analysis. This tested a series of hypotheses regarding the personal context (particularly normative orientations, attitudes to and past experience with energy conservation) as a major factor intervening between structural variables (socio-economic status, economic context) and actual response to the programme. The role of attitudinal factors in 'moderating' structural effects has been shown in past research (Stern et al. 1982; Hildebrandt 1984). Specifically, the following hypotheses were tested:

* the number of conservation actions undertaken in the past has a positive effect on intentions to undertake further actions;

* conservation attitudes and normative expectations positively influence conservation action intentions;

* relative heating costs positively influence energy conservation attitudes and action intentions;

* socio-economic status positively affects energy conservation attitudes and action intentions.

Testing these hypotheses for the three larger programmes and for low, medium and high investment conservation actions, no clear results emerge. None of the hypotheses holds across the clienteles of the programmes under study. The second and fourth hypotheses must, on the basis of our data, be rejected. Finally , the analysis shows that conservation intentions are generally related to past conservation behaviour in the sense that households who have undertaken little or nothing before programme use tend to do little or nothing afterwards and vice versa.

In an earlier section we used a hierarchy of effects model to describe programme response as a function of - looking 'bottom-up' - action intentions, programme use, programme awareness, and programme structure. What follows is a brief description of the results of a causal model relating 'programme acceptance', a variable intervening between programme awareness and programme use, to programme use and energy conservation actions taken, on the one hand, and to socio-economic and legal status as well as past behaviour, on the other. The causal structure of the model reflects the following set of hypotheses:

* the greater the acceptance of a programme, the more likely it is to be used;

* the greater the use of programme information, the greater the effect in terms of conservation measures undertaken;

* programme use and resulting conservation actions depend on past conservation behaviour;

* programme acceptance and past conservation behaviour are determined by the socio-economic context of energy consumption.

Without going into technical details, we used the LISREL V programme with a ULS method for estimating coefficients (Joreskog and Sorbom 1985; Hildebrandt 1983).

The main conclusions of these analyses are as follows. For the utility's programme, educational level is the one main determinant of all three variables measuring programme impacts: acceptance, use and conservation actions. The effects of other variables are not as strong; there is a positive effect of income on programme acceptance and a negative effect for legal context (tenant/home owner). The assumption of hierarchical effects in the process from acceptance through use to conservation actions is supported by the model. However, as indicated by previous results, programme use is only weakly connected to conservation actions taken.

The ecologists' programme, again, has its main 'entrance' through educational level. Nevertheless, there are a number of peculiarities. Income has positive effects on programme acceptance, but negative effects on the level of use. Again, legal status (tenant versus home owner) negatively influences programme acceptance. Past energy conservation behaviour does not produce better acceptance, nor programme use. In turn, programme use is negatively related to conservation measures taken.

Finally the consumer organization's programme attracts in the first place households with high educational level, and shows a strong influence of occupation on programme use. Income positively relates to programme acceptance, while past energy conservation behaviour tends to reduce programme use. Again, the hierarchical relation between communicative and behavioural stages of programme response holds.

In sum, we find that for the programmes and the community under study, educational level is the most important factor determining responses to programmes and that high income levels are generally a precondition for programme acceptance.

## Programme non-specific analyses: users versus non-users

In the previous sections, we have implicitly compared users and non-users of conservation programmes by referring programme specific data either to the total sample or to the non-user comparison samples. In the following paragraphs results on the influence of economic, technical, legal and community contexts on energy conservation are reported by contrasting all users and non-users. Inspection of the data for programme-specific effects did not yield significant differences between programme clienteles for these factors.

### Economic, technical and legal contexts

Next to socio-economic status variables which 'summarize' the economic position and situation of households, the structure of household expenditures can be assumed to indicate a household's economic context. In order to appreciate the economic utility of energy conservation investments, one should not choose absolute costs as the only criterion, but relative costs, that is, costs in relation to disposable household income.

Assuming that the readiness to invest in energy conservation varies with the proportion of disposable income taken up by energy costs, we have chosen as a criterion the percentage of household income allocated to heating. Testing relative and absolute heating costs against the number of conservation measures taken by programme users and non-users, it emerges that for users the determining factor is absolute costs while for non-users relative costs predict level of energy conservation measures. This could be an effect of greater awareness concerning energy problems in the user sample, it could also be the result of a more favourable ratio between heating costs and yearly income in this group.

Regarding the technical context of household energy consumption, we asked about the type of heating system and the number and type of other energy consuming household appliances. Interestingly, we did not find any relationship between heating system and socio-economic position; however, the number of appliances varies greatly with socio-demographic level. Similarly, type of heating system bears little relationship to decisions to use energy advisory programmes and to implement conservation measures.

*The community context*

There is some empirical evidence that various aspects of community structure, particularly the existence of informal communication networks and the position and role of 'opinion leaders', are highly conducive to diffusing the message and stabilizing results of energy conservation programmes (Darley and Beniger 1981; Rogers and Kincaid 1980; Rogers and Shoemaker 1971). Since the direct measurement of such structures in the community is beyond the scope of the present study, we chose two self-reported indicators: the willingness to join others in taking action concerning energy conservation (mobilization), and an index based on the two items of 'intensity of communication with other persons about the subject of energy conservation' and 'propensity to seek energy information' (opinion leadership).

On the first indicator we found that mobilization was very low, only eight households had been involved in collective action, a further nine said they planned to do so in the future, but the majority of people interviewed rejected the idea. Nearly all persons who took or planned joint action concerning energy conservation measures were clients of the ecologists' service.

Cross-Tabulating measurements of mobilization and opinion leadership, respectively, with three measures of conservation behaviour - conservation action taken in the past, conservation programme used and number of conservation measures after programme use, significant relationships between energy conservation behaviour and mobilization/opinion leadership were found. We may conclude that the existence and the degree of involvement in communal communication structures constitute important intervening factors for the effectiveness of conservation programmes.

## Summary and conclusions

This study was devoted to a comparative analysis of the factors making for the relative success of four different local conservation programmes in a community. While we find that local programmes achieve high levels of programme use and consequent conservation actions among private family households, the overall level of penetration remains unsatisfactory. This is particularly true in the case of disadvantaged consumer groups such as low-income and tenant householders.

Generally, conservation programmes of the type studied here cater to the requirements of upper-middle class households, particularly the highly educated, financially secure in the middle stages of the life-cycle. In addition, programme involvement is strongly associated with previous commitment to energy conservation. There are also indications that participation in energy conservation programmes is part of a general involvement in local communication networks.

Beyond these general features, the four programmes differ markedly with respect to the particular clientele they attract or select. Equally they differ in the process of penetration, from making prospective users aware and responsive to their particular services, through establishing contact, inducing conservation measures in the home to achieving satisfaction with services rendered. These differences can be traced to characteristic programme features.

The local utility's service, on the one hand, achieves superior levels of penetration at the initial stages of programme awareness, acceptance and contact with clients, loosing momentum somewhat at the later stages of people actually planning and carrying out conservation measures. The utility's visibility, long-standing relations with customers, technical and marketing competence among other advantages, guarantee that it is relatively successful overall.

The ecologists' service in contrast, starting out with much lower levels of initial awareness and number of clients, achieves remarkable results in terms of conservation measures induced and client satisfaction. More comprehensive goal-orientation, high commitment and innovative drive seem to compensate for lack of technical and financial resources and appeal to a clientele which is distinctly different from the middle of the road bourgeois clientele of the other services.

The consumer union's service achieves levels of participation somewhere between these two programmes, profiting again from relatively good visibility and general communal trust, its more inclusive consumer-protection services and a committed, co-operative approach to energy advice.

The municipality's service falls short on all stages of programme penetration, probably due to its diffuse and ambiguous policy orientation, inadequate technical facilities and institutional support, uncompensated by strong personal commitment to consumer energy conservation.

Seen in perspective, the three larger programmes have built up and adapted their services to the expectations of different groups of clients. One can assume that these groups might not have been reached by any one programme, even if the range of services offered had been more comprehensive. This selectiveness of programmes, both regarding orientation and capability to act on the part of clients and with respect to taking clients through the processes of acquiring information and implementing their own plans, may be the central finding of this study. The implication for local energy policy is to allow and more consciously provide for pluralistic approaches to energy conservation.

All the programmes studied show a series of deficiencies. Advice given tends to remain restricted, possibly with the exception of the ecologists' service, to measures endorsed and subsidized by central programmes. Novel measures, particularly those justified on ecological as opposed to immediately cost-effectiveness grounds, remain outside the purview of the programmes. Similarly, they are limited to advice, and additional financial, legal and technical services are not offered as part and parcel of programme services. Another limitation has to do with continuity of service in that they tend to remain one-off, not providing for follow-ups and, by the same token, evaluation of the effectiveness of measures undertaken. Finally, none of the services is equipped in terms of personnel and organizational technique to perform systematic targeting and directional marketing of

145

conservation services in order to reach difficult groups not coming forward to actively seek advice on their own account.

The most critical net result of these deficiencies is the unsatisfactory record of all services with respect to passive and socio-economically disadvantaged segments of the population who tend to be progressively lost to public programmes as one moves from awareness to action. Finally a major finding is that the programmes under study are not sufficiently integrated with more comprehensive communal planning and relevant policy as well as administrative structures. While the results achieved are to a large extent due to the embeddedness of the three larger services in, albeit very different, organizational and political structures, they lack both mutual co-ordination and alignment with overall municipal planning, particularly in the areas of environmental protection, housing and urban development.

## References

Barnaby, D.J., and Reizenstein, R.C. 1975, Perspectives on the energy crisis: gasoline prices and the southeastern consumer. *Survey of Business*, 2, 28-31.

Brog, W. and Wichmann, B. 1982, Sparpotential und die Grenzen ihrer Ausschopfung In *Schriftenreihe der Forschungstelle fur Energiewirtschaft, Band 15, Ienflusse des Verbraucherverhaltens auf den Energiebedarf privater Haushalte*. Berlin, 89-108.

Bundesministerium fur Wirtschaft 1982, Daten zur Entwichlung der Energiewirtschaft in der Bundes republik Deutschland im Jahre 1982. BMWi, III D3.

Bundesministerium fur Wirtschaft 1977, Energieprogramm der Bundesregierung, zweite Fortschreibung vom 14. 12. 1977.

Bundesministerium fur Wirtschaft 1981, Energieprogramm der Bundesreigierung, dritte Fortschreibung vom 5. 11. 1981.

Cunningham, W.H. and Lopreato, S.C. 1977, Energy Use and Conservation Incentives: A Study of the Southwestern United States. New York.

Curtin, R. 1976, Consumer adaption to energy shortages. *Journal of Energy and Development*, 2, 38-59.

Darley, J.M. and Beniger, J.R. 1981, Diffusion of energy conserving innovations. *Journal of Social Issues*, 37, 150-171.

Dillmann, D.S. Rosa, E.A. and Dillman, J.J. 1983, Lifestyle and home energy conservation in the United States: The poor accept lifestyle cutbacks while the wealthy invest in conservation. *Journal of Economic Psychology*, 299-315.

Eisel, R. 1981, Zahlen zur Modernisierung und deren Forderung nach dem ModEng. *Bundesbaublatt*, 3, 154-158.

Ester, P. 1983, *Consumer Behaviour and Energy Conservation.* Dortrecht: Nijhoff

Ester, P., Gaskell, G., Joerges, B., Midden, C., Van Raaij, W.F. and De Vries, T., (eds.), 1984, *Consumer Behaviour and Energy Conservation.* North-Holland, Amsterdam.

Fritzsche, D.J. 1981, An analysis of energy consumption by stage of family life cycle. *Journal of Marketing Research*, XVIII, 227-232.

Garnreiter, F., Jochem, E., Gruber, E., Hohmeyer, D., Mannsbart, W. and Mentzel, Th. 1983, Auswirkungen verstarkter Massnahmen zum rationallen Energieeinsatz auf Umwelt, Beschaftigung und Einkommen. Fraunhofer-Institut fur Systemtechnik und Innovationsforschung (ISI), Forschungsbericht 101 03 076, UBA-FB 83-032, Berlin.

Gruber, E., and Meyer, T. 1982, Demonstrationsprojekt Landstuhl: Energieeinsparung und Solarenergienutzung in Eigenheimen. Energeisparende Innovation im Eigenheim aus der Sicht des Bauherren und Bauexperten. Karlsruhe.

Heberlein, T.A., and Black, J.S. 1976, Attitudinal specifity and the prediction of behavior in a field setting. *Journal of Personality and Social Psychology*, 33, 474-479

Heberlein, T.A., and Warriner, G.K. 1983, The influence of price and attitude on shifting residential electricity consumption from on to off peak periods. *Journal of Economic Psychology*, 4, 107-130.

Hildebrandt, L. 1983, Kausalmodelle in der Konsumentenver- halteusforschung. In Irle, M. (Hrsg) Enzyklopadie der Psychologie, Band 12, Methoden und Auvendungen in der Marktpsychologie, Gottingen.

Hildebrandt, L. 1984, Attitudes and values as predictors of energy information behavior patterns. In Kinnear T.C. *Advances of Consumer Research*, Vol IX, Provo .

Hildebrandt, L., and Joerges, B. 1983, Consumer Energy Policies in the Federal Republic of Germany. Internationales Institut fur Umwelt und Gesellschaft, Wissenschaftszentrum, Berlin.

Horn, M., Rammer, P. and Scholz, L. 1978, Eimflup der Tarifgestaltung auf die Stromnachfrage unter besonderer Beruckshichtijung der Abnahmestruhtur und der Stromverwendungsarten in der Bundesrepulbik Deutschland, Ifo-studien zur Energiewirtschaft 1. Munchen.

Jacobi, I. et al. 1974, Brand Choice Behavior as a Function of Information Load. In *Journal of Marketing Research* 11, 63-69.

Joreskog, K.G. and Sorbom, D. 1981, LISREL V - Analysis of

Linear Structural Relationships by Maximum Likelihood and Least Squares Methods. Research Report 81-8, University of Uppsala.

Lopreato, S.C. and Merriweather, M.W. 1976, Energy Attitudinal Surveys: Summary, Annotations, Research, Recommendations. Center for Energy Studies, University of Texas, Austin.

Lavidge, R.J. and Steiner, G.A. 1961, A model for predictive measurement of advertising effectiveness. *Journal of Marketing*, 25, Oct, 1961, 59-62.

Luhmann, H.J. 1981, Energieeinsparung durch Verstarkung dezentraler Kapitalallokation. Wirtshcaftspolitische Vorschlage zum Abbau von Wettbewerbsnachteilen fur die Energieeinsparung im Bereich der Haushalte und Abschatzung des Energiesparpotentials. Frankfurt/Bern.

McDougall, G.H.G., Claxton, J.D., Ritshcie, B.J.R. and Anderson, D.C. 1981, Consumer energy research: a review. *Journal of Consumer Research 8*, 343-354.

Mettler-Meibom, B. 1982, Soziale und okonomische Bestimmungsgrossen fur das Verbraucherverhalten. Schriftenreihe der Forschungsstelle fur Energiewirtschaft, Band 15: Einflusse des Verbraucherverhaltens auf den Energiebedarf privater Haushalte. Berlin, 37-72.

Monse, K. and Simon, L. 1982, Energiepolitische Handlungsfelder fur Verbraucherorganisationen. Gesamthochschule Wuppertal, Fachbereich Wirtschaftswissenschaften, Arbeitsgruppe fur Verbraucherforschung und Verbraucherpolitik. Wuppertal.

Newman, K.A. 1982, Human values: Do they make a difference in individuals commitment to energy conservation? University of California. Paper presented at the International Conference on Consumer Behaviour and Energy Policy, Noordwijkerhout (NL).

Nitezel, M.T. and Winett, R.A. 1977, Demographics, attitudes and behavioral responses to important environmental events. *American Journal of Community Psychology*, 5, 195-206.

Oesterwind, D. 1983, Energieberatung im Wandel, *Der Stadtetag*, 10, 688-689.

Olsen, M.E. and Goodnight, J.E. 1977, Social aspects of energy conservation. Northwest Energy Policy Project, Study Module 1-B, Final report.

Prognos, 1983, Beeinflussung der Energienachfrage durch organisatorische und insititutionelle Innovation. Basel.

Raffee, H. and Silberer, G. 1981, Informationsverhalten des Konsumenten. Ergebnisse empirischer studien. Wiesbaden.

Ritsema, B.S.M., Midden, C.J.H. and Heijden, P.G.M. van der 1982, Energiebesparing in gezinshuishoudingen: attitudes, normen in gedradingen, een landekijk ondezoek, Werkgroep Energie - en

Milieuonderzoek, Rijksuniversiteit Leiden/Energie Studie Centrum - Energieondezoek Cantrum, Nederland.

Rogers, E.M. and Leonard Barton, D. 1979, Adoption of Energy Conservation among California Homeowners. Working paper. Stanford University Institute for Communication Research.

Rogers, E.M. and Kincaid, D. 1980, *Communications Networks: A New Paradigm for Research*. New York.

Rogers, E.M. and Shoemaker, F.F. 1971, *Communication of Innovations. A Cross-cultural Approach*. New York.

Rosensteil, L. and Elwald, G. 1979, Marktpsychologie, Band I; Konsumerverhalten und Kaufentscheidung, Stuttgart.

Sattler, M. 1981, Energiebesparatung. Bestimmung des Bedarfs an Energieberatung und der beruflichen Qualifikation von Energieberatern. Munchen.

Schiffer, H.W. 1983, Entwicklung und struktureller Wandel im Energieverbrauch der Bundesrepublik Deutschland seit 1979. *Zeitschrift fur Energiewirtschaft 3*, 224-238.

Scholz, P.and Ramner, P. 1982, Quantitative Wirkungen der Energiesparpolitik in der Bundesrepublik Deutschland. Ifo-Insitut: Ifo-Studien zur Energiewirtschaft 3/2.

Seligman, C., Kriss, M., Darley, J.M., Fazio, R.H., Becker, L.J. and Pryor, J.B. 1978, Predicting residential energy consumption from home owners' attitudes'. *Journal of Applied Psychology*, 9, 70-90.

Silberer, G. and Raffee, H. Hrsg, 1984, Warentest und Konsument Nutzung, Wirkungen und Beurteihung des vergleichenden Warentests im Konsumentenbereich, Frankfurt.

Silberer, G. 1979, Warentest-Informationsmarketing vobraucherverhalten. Die Verbreitung von Gutertestinformationen und duren verwendung im Konsumentenbereich, Berlin.

Stern, P.C., Black, J.S. and Elworth, J.T. 1982, Personal and contextual influences on household energy adaptions. National Academy of Sciences, University of Illinois USA. Paper presented at the International Conference on Consumer Behaviour and Energy Policy, Noordwijkherout, (NL), Umweltbundesamt 11983, Berlin.

Verhallen, Th.M.M. and van Raaij, F. 1981, Household behavior and the use of natural gas for home heating. *Journal of Consumer Research*, 8, 253-257.

Warren, D.I., and Clifford, D.L. 1975, Local neigbourhood social structure and response to the energy crisis of 1973-75. Institute of Labor and Industrial Relations, University of Michigan, Ann Arbor.

Woodward, A. 1986, Municipal Responses to the Energy Challenge: Metz France and Saarbrucke/FRG. The Political Angle on Energy Economy, IIES, Wissenschaftszentrum, Berlin.

# 5 A community insulation programme for tenants in the Netherlands

JOOP VAN DER LINDEN and THEO VAN EIJK

## Introduction

An important aspect of energy policy in the Netherlands is the diversification of energy sources. A further issue of current concern is energy conservation. The latter is clearly illustrated by a proposed national conservation programme. The primary goal is an overall efficiency improvement of 40 percent in total domestic energy consumption by the year 2000 (as compared to 1973). For residential space heating the target is an energy efficiency improvement of 60 percent (De Boer et al. 1982). The National Insulation Programme (NIP) is designed to stimulate, co-ordinate and support the insulation of existing dwellings. The major instruments of the NIP are providing information and financial support (for a detailed discussion of Dutch energy conservation policy see: De Boer et al. 1982). In 1984 about four percent of all dwellings were fully insulated, while 37 percent had had no additional insulation since being constructed. Homes in the owner occupied sector appeared to be much better insulated than those occupied by tenants (Minderhout and Zwetsloot 1984). The participation of tenants in the introduction of insulation measures in existing dwellings is considered to be one of the main problems in reaching the goal of energy conservation in residential space heating (NWR 1983).

From an inventory and analysis of consumer energy conservation programmes in The Netherlands (De Boer et al. 1982), it was concluded that little is known about how consumers respond to energy conservation programmes, hence the acknowledged need for thorough evaluation studies. Another finding was that tenants and low income groups were not being reached by the traditional (centralized) programmes. These findings based on the Dutch situation are in line with findings from research conducted elsewhere (McDougall et al. 1981; Ester 1985; McDougall and Ritchie 1984; Stern et al. 1981). The objective of this study is to contribute to the understanding of the ways in which energy conservation programmes at the local or community level affect private households. The study focuses on the adoption decisions of households when they are confronted with an energy conservation programme (in this case an insulation programme) in their neighbourhood. In order to investigate the nature of their decision-making, we chose an adoption-decision theoretical approach. As conceived in the conceptual framework guiding this multinational project, energy consumption behaviour is not only a product of the personal characteristics of the consumer but also of the technical, legal, economic and socio-cultural contexts. Therefore, promoting energy conservation requires the introduction of changes at the macro (or structural) and the micro (or personal) levels. In other words, an adoption-decision approach, taking the perspective of the consumer, illuminates only a segment of the total process. For a more complete understanding we will also look at the process from the perspective of policy enactment.

The insulation project in Zutphen was selected for this case study. There were several reasons for the selection of this project. It was a local community programme making use of existing higher level (national) programmes. The programme was directed at tenants and it offered additional (non-specialist) insulation measures. The financial aspects of the scheme were tailored to the needs of low income consumers and tried to overcome economic barriers for tenants to adopt insulation measures. It was not a one-shot programme: residents were informed about the programme, they could accept or refuse the offer. In addition they were able to discuss the programme with neighbours and to observe how the insulation works were carried out in other houses. This made it possible for us to study a programme at work, when some residents had adopted the insulation programme, while others had not (yet) adopted it. Moreover, the implementation of similar programmes in other communities was considered.

151

## Research strategy

The decision of a household to accept an offer of having insulation measures taken in their home can be seen as an instance of the adoption of an innovation. Analytically speaking, the decision-making process may be considered as a process comprising the following phases (Engel and Blackwell 1982; Van Raaij 1981; Rogers and Shoemaker 1971).

*Problem recognition:* if the household is happy about its present energy situation and is not concerned about, for example, comfort levels or costs, then it is unlikely that they will recognize that they have a problem. However, if the situation is judged unsatisfactory, perhaps the bills are too high, or it is not warm enough in winter, then they will be likely to define the situation as a problem and be motivated to change it.

*Awareness:* having recognized that there is a problem they must then become aware of the innovation (in this case insulation) as a possible solution to the problem.

*Perceptions and attitudes:* Awareness of the innovation will lead to more knowledge about the possibilities and potential consequences of accepting it. The understanding obtained leads to the pros and cons of accepting the innovation being weighed up. In this way an attitude will be developed to the innovation.

*Adoption-decision:* Eventually a decision will be made to accept the innovation or to reject it (perhaps provisionally).

After acceptance, the new situation will be assessed. In the case of rejection, later information may modify the result of one of the phases in the decision-making process, rendering possible acceptance at a later date.

The householder's course through the various phases of this decision-making process may be affected by the energy conservation programme, as well as by the existing personal, household and structural contexts. These influences may be direct but often they are the outcome of a communication process. We will consider communication processes within the household within the neighbourhood and between the programme and the residents.

These considerations led to a number of variables or clusters of variables being incorporated into the investigation. These are shown in Figure 5.1.

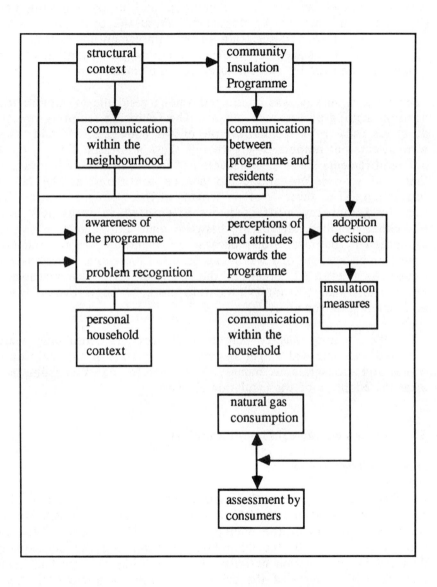

Figure 5.1 A model of the adoption process

## Research methods

Several methods were used to assess the community insulation programme and its influence on consumers. Firstly, interviews with persons involved in the implementation and in participating organizations and analyses of documents about the programme were used. This led to a description of the implementing agency and linkages with other agencies, their basic policy goals, content of the programme and the instruments used for implementation.

Secondly, a survey was conducted among residents to explore the decision making processes of tenants. The following sampling procedure was used. From a total sample of 482 addresses, 254 addresses were selected at random. Forty-two of these addresses did not meet our requirements since the residents had moved into their homes less than one year before and could not be considered as the target population. Also, there were no tenants at three other addresses. Of the 209 remaining addresses, we attempted to interview one household member, alternating between male and female. We were unsuccessful 70 times, either because co-operation was refused (48 times) or because no one was home on three successive occasions (22 times). As a result 67 percent of the 209 interviews were successful. For the analysis, 127 interviews were used; 11 home-owners were eliminated from the analysis.

Thirdly, natural gas consumption figures of households were gathered and analysed to get an impression of one of the main outcomes of the programme, namely the change in energy consumption after the adoption of the insulation measures.

## The Zutphen energy conservation project

### Historical background

In 1981 increasing unemployment levels and rising heating bills moved the Town Council of Zutphen to consider the possibility of calling in the help of the unemployed to tackle the task of energy conservation. Due to the economic recession and the subsequent decrease in construction activity, many building workers had been laid off in the course of the crisis. In Zutphen a number of these workers organized themselves into the 'Zutphen Jobless Group', and approached the Provincial Steering Party on Unemployment. This agency, which receives a grant from the provincial authorities and which includes representatives of the Chamber of Commerce, trade unions and employers, was set up with the aim of advancing employment in the province by, among other things, subsidizing local initiatives, supporting employment schemes and building up a favourable climate for new entrepreneurs. The contact between these two groups led to the idea of setting up a trial project for energy conservation. The aim they had in mind was to set up a housing insulation project for a number of jobless people, possibly with the initial support of grants and other government schemes, but with the explicit aim of becoming an independent and wage-paying business, with practical training opportunities for the unemployed. A working party comprising representatives of Zutphen Council, Zutphen Housing Association, the provincial gas board 'Gamog' and others was set up to develop this plan. These developments eventually resulted in the establishment of the Zutphen Foundation for Employment Schemes, referred to further by its Dutch abbreviation WPZ. The first task of the foundation was the insulation scheme discussed here.

*Goals and objectives*

As can be inferred from the initial history of the project, the primary aim of WPZ is to create employment, train the jobless and eventually become an independent business. This central policy aim is laid down in the statutes of the Foundation. Involvement with energy saving activities was considered a realistic possibility for creating a reasonable number of jobs. Working on the basis of these aims, it was possible to take advantage of several facilities set up by the national government to stimulate employment. Provincial and local authorities, too, provided financial support out of funds specifically intended for employment opportunities. In addition, the idealistic approach of the group was instrumental in gaining the co-operation and support of various other agencies. These are discussed in the following paragraphs.

*Linkages with other agencies*

The implementing agency (WPZ) obtained the support and co-operation of a number of agencies at an early stage in its development. The Provincial Steering Party on Unemployment played an important role in the initial stages of the WPZ Foundation's creation. This agency provided starting capital. This was in the form of a grant, made available by the provincial authorities and used to finance the initial costs of materials, tools and training. Technical training was provided by Zutphen Housing Association. The co-operation of Zutphen Council also included a financial contribution in the initial phase. Several other agencies were instrumental in the initial phase of WPZ. The district labour exchange approved the appointment of two unemployed persons in the project for a period of one year. The associated expenses were paid for by government subsidies. Additionally, a laid-off building worker was appointed to carry out insulation work in the first year of the Foundation's existence, working while retaining his unemployment benefit - approved by the social security authorities - so that wage costs did not put pressure on the budget of WPZ.

The district's Chamber of Commerce, one of whose aims is to protect the interests of tradespeople and shopkeepers, was prepared to give its seal of approval to the project, under certain conditions. These conditions put a number of restrictions on the Foundation's activities and its acquisition policy. The restrictions imposed by the Chamber of Commerce related to the nature of the work to be performed. There were to be no specialist jobs undertaken because local building contractors were afraid of unfair competition. For this reason it was insisted that the Foundation should not try to sell the insulation measures to private houseowners, but limit itself to working for tenants of dwellings rented from the local housing association. The co-operation of the labour exchange and use of national unemployment scheme grants meant that the Foundation had to employ young jobless people who could thus gain some professional experience. The local housing association set the requirement that insulation and possibly fitting of skylights were the only permitted jobs. All other work, in particular maintenance activities, were to be performed by the housing association.

The local housing association played an important role by giving support to the scheme. Thus it was possible to obtain an inventory of the houses under the management of this housing association, earmarking those eligible for insulation. The housing association made a calculation of the rent increase required to cover the work to be carried out, making use of a national grant scheme for existing houses. Initially, the bill made out by WPZ for the insulation work was paid by the housing association, who applied for the national insulation grant. This grant, amounting to about 25 percent of the cost of insulation, was deducted from the total investment. The remaining sum was then passed on by the housing association to the tenants in the form of a supplementary rent charge. This rent supplement is calculated using the dynamic cost price method. A basic principle here was that future housing expenses should not place an unnecessarily high burden on present tenants, but that the housing association should break even at the end of the house's exploitation period. A consequence of this policy is that the housing association did not break even in the first years of the insulation programme.

With regard to the Zutphen Housing Association, the project was financed from their capital reserves. Furthermore, the national grants, which are often paid out only one to two years later, were advanced by the housing association. Another agency involved in the activities of the WPZ foundation is the Energy Conservation Centre consultants' bureau. The Centre gave advice on the insulation to be carried out, on materials and costs and on the eventual savings to be achieved. This consultation was paid for by WPZ, the costs later being passed on. During execution of a trial run on 30 dwellings, it was found that the figures had to be modified somewhat: the Energy Conservation Centre had underestimated expenses and overestimated savings. The (re)calculated savings on the heating bill were subsequently checked by the provincial gas supplier, Gamog. This utility agreed with the estimated saving figures and was prepared to make a deduction on the residents monthly bills, to a level corresponding to the anticipated lower gas consumption. This deduction on the advance bill made it more attractive for tenants to have their homes insulated.

*The target group*

Given the restrictions outlined above, WPZ decided to direct their attention towards two tenanted housing estates in the Moesmate and Tichelkuilen neighbourhoods of Zutphen. These 7-to-8 year old houses had already been provided with cavity-wall insulation and double glazing. They were heated by a gas-fired central heating system. Additional (non-specialist) insulation could therefore be added to achieve maximum efficiency. More recently WPZ has started insulating houses in other neighbourhoods with packages of measures tailored to the specific housing situation.

*Technical instruments*

On the basis of the trial project in a neighbourhood covering 30 dwellings of 4 types and the advice of the Energy Conservation Centre, two packages of supplementary insulation measures were drawn up. Both packages comprised floor insulation, insulation of central heating pipes, installation of a pump switch in the central heating unit, broadening of window-sills, application of aluminium foil behind the radiators and fitting of an attic door. One of the packages comprised roof insulation as an additional measure. Residents were free to choose between the two options. The reason for the double option was that roof insulation is fairly expensive, thus involving a larger rise in rent.

Materials for the works were purchased by the Foundation. In the initial phase the housing association set certain requirements concerning the materials used. The only respect in which WPZ deviated from the standards set was that quality was better than specified and the price for residents was kept as low as possible. The Foundation's prices were within the normal market range. As a supplementary activity to the insulation scheme, WPZ is considering the sale of standard packs of insulation material to owner-occupiers who want to insulate their homes.

*Costs to clients*

In terms of the costs based on the rent increase minus the reduction on their future energy bill, the residents paid nothing for the fitting of insulation in their homes. Their aggregate fixed charges of rent plus the heating bill remained the same. However, the effect of these energy-saving measures could turn out to be greater or less than estimated, and at the end of the seasonal heating period the gas board either gives a return on excess payments or issues an additional bill. Obviously, the increased domestic comfort created by provisions of this nature should be taken into consideration (see section on outcomes of the programme).

*Communication instruments*

The WPZ Foundation takes care of information and acquisition. Expenses made in this respect are passed on in the charges for work done. To attract clients, the Foundation proceeded as follows. Residents of houses on the target estates were sent letters with objective information on the cost of the insulation measures, the necessary procedures and the anticipated savings on energy bills. Many residents reacted almost immediately, telephoning the Foundation for more information. After a house call by one of the staff, tenants often agreed to having the proposed insulation fitted. WPZ suspects that a large part is also played by the community grapevine. Another factor in attracting clients is the fact that they can see for themselves, in the homes of neighbours or acquaintances, the insulation measures that have been implemented. At the moment however, after a busy start requests from clients are not running as smoothly as before. As a result workers at the Foundation intend to pursue a more active approach, distributing pamphlets, making telephone calls to residents and trying to solicit orders from residents in their homes in the evening hours (after appointments). At these an explanation will be given of the proposed measures and an objective assessment offered of the energy savings and improved domestic comfort. The local press has also given coverage to the project. As yet, no use has been made of the possibility of holding public meetings to provide the community with more information on the project. The group intends to start doing so in order to maintain continuity of work. On their part, the housing association occasionally provided the Foundation with a job, in cases where uninsulated houses became available through residents moving from the estate. In such cases new tenants are given the option of signing an agreement to have their home provided with insulation.

*Implementation*

There are three building workers employed full-time on the WPZ Foundation's insulation scheme. In addition, 2 part-time staff members have been appointed for marketing, job preparation and general co-ordination. Financially, the project reached a breakeven point after six months. At present, there is no requirement to make use of grants of any kind. The Foundation is housed in premises used by various new enterprises, WPZ renting space to the insulation project and to other small businesses. The WPZ Foundation now offers other services such as office work, marketing, economic, legal and technical advice to the enterprises in the building. To date (May 1984), 200 of the 500 dwellings in the Moesmate and Tichelkuilen neighbourhoods have been provided with additional insulation by the Foundation.

*Assessment*

The insulation project has not yet been assessed by the Foundation. The group are not able to say whether the energy savings had been estimated correctly. Consequently, it is still assumed that annual savings amount to 700 m3 of natural gas (about 30 percent savings) and 300 kWh (about 8 percent savings). The two winters since the project's initiation have been rather mild, which makes it difficult to assess actual conservation effects. An additional factor that is likely to cloud the picture for the residents is the recent rise in the price of gas, approximately 6 percent in the years 1983-4 and 1984-5.

The housing association, with whom the Foundation has a good relationship - although it is seen by WPZ to be one of dependence - would very much like an evaluation of the project. Their interest is motivated by the fact that they have implemented a reduction on the annual price-index-linked rent increase. Up to 1984, this practice meant that rents were raised by at least 6 percent a year. As of 1984, this rent increase was lowered to 3 percent. This has moved the housing association to reconsider its co-operation with the project. The housing association has to make considerable investments on the basis of a cost-price calculation that is relatively unfavourable to them. With the annual rent increase of 6 percent implemented in previous years, this was still a feasible proposition, but now the housing association wants to review the results of the insulation scheme so as to be able to justify continuation.

## Outcomes of the programme

The following questions will be dealt with in this section: how many people in the neighbourhood concerned were aware of the insulation project?; how many people participated in the programme?, how do adopters evaluate the new situation?; and how much energy is saved as a consequence of the programme? From our survey data it can be concluded that the programme appeared to be well known in the neighbourhood. Furthermore, a considerable number of residents accepted the programme's offer of home insulation. Of all residents, only 13 percent were not aware of the programme, so the majority of the residents had received at least some information about it. Forty one percent of the residents can be considered as adopters of the retrofit programme since they had their homes insulated under the scheme. Forty six percent of the residents were familiar with the programme but had not had their homes retrofitted, but some of them were considering adoption. The programme's retrofitting certainly had an effect on comfort levels. Of all persons living in homes that were retrofitted by the scheme 65 percent thought that the measures taken had made their home more comfortable in winter. Increased problems with condensation were reported by 16 percent of the residents, while 84 percent had experienced no change in this respect or had indicated fewer problems than before. Forty one percent said they had set the thermostat in the living room to a lower temperature than before, 57 percent reported no change. Almost 60 percent had less trouble with draughts after the insulation. Some residents (8 percent) said that the insulation had led to a more frequent use of certain rooms in the house (the use of the attic).

Three out of four residents thought they had saved on their energy bills because of the insulation measures, the rest did not think so. However, of those who thought they had saved money most had no idea of the amount involved. Approximately one-third thought that costs and benefits of the retrofit were in equal, 46 percent felt that the advantages were greater that the costs and 19 percent thought the costs were greater that the advantages. Given a situation in which they had to make a new decision, the greater majority said they would take the same decision again and have the home insulated, 10 percent would not, while 6 percent did not know. It can be concluded that residents whose houses were retrofitted by the scheme, had a rather positive evaluation of the measures taken.

To answer the question of resulting energy savings, the consumption figures of the residents in the homes insulated by the programme were compared with the consumption figures of others. We considered the period from June, 1979 to June, 1984. Using the 'degree-days method', the figures were corrected for differences in temperature during this period, so the consumption figures for the different years can be validly compared. Fig. 5.2 shows that, during the period June, 1979 - June, 1980 (before the start of the programme) there was a difference in gas consumption between those who subsequently accepted the insulation programme and those who did not. The average consumption of adopters was lighter, indicating a higher level of participation in the programme among heavy energy users. The general trend in energy consumption was clearly downward until 1982. Since then, consumption rates have been constant. In the period 1982-1983, when some of the adopters dwellings were provided with insulation, the average consumption of this group was about equal to the consumption of other households of the same type. When more and more homes in the adopters group were insulated, their average consumption went down, while the average consumption of the homes that were not insulated under the scheme remained relatively constant. On the basis of the individual consumption figures for the period before the start of the programme and the general trend for households in similar homes not insulated under the scheme, it was possible to calculate an expected consumption figure for the period June, 1983 - June, 1984. For this analysis, only respondents who had lived in the same house during the whole period were used. The expected figures calculated were compared to the real figures in the situation with insulation provisions. It is concluded that 88 percent of the residents living in one-family homes insulated by the scheme, consumed less natural gas than was expected from the general trend.

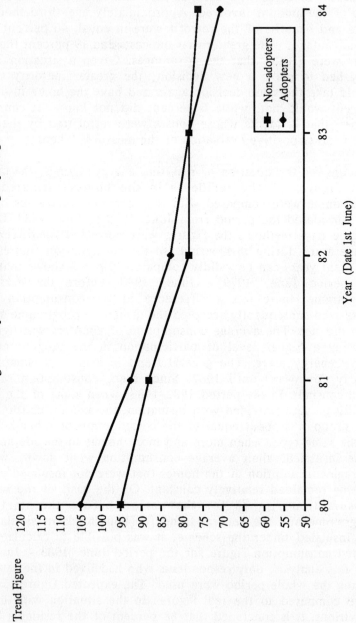

Note: Trend figures generated between 1-6-1979 and 1-6-1984
Average consumption in 1979/80 for total group being 100.

Figure 5.2 Natural gas consumption

162

It can thus be concluded that the insulation measures of the programme resulted in energy savings. Although there were considerable differences among individual residents, the mean savings for a household in a one-family home was 398 m3 natural gas; thus the average consumption is 16 percent less than expected consumption.

**Consumer analyses**

*Awareness of the programme*

Only a small percentage, 13 percent, of the residents had never heard of the programme; 87 percent knew about it. Assuming that perceiving a situation as non-optimal makes people more sensitive to information relevant to changing this situation, we expected a relationship between 'problem recognition' and 'awareness of the programme'. As an indicator of problem recognition we used a question in which people were asked to assess the construction of their house with regard to the possibility of heating it to comfortable temperatures without using excessive amounts of natural gas. It appeared that this questioning did not differentiate between residents who were aware of the programme and residents who were not aware of it. This may be explained by the way residents were approached with information. An active search for it was not necessary for residents.

Personal and household context variables (that is sex, social-economic status) were also of minor importance in explaining differential awareness of the programme. The main factor explaining the lack of awareness of the programme was a lower frequency of social contacts in the neighbourhood. None of the residents who were unaware of the programme had frequent contacts with neighbours (once a day or more), while 55 percent of the residents who were aware of the programme had frequent contacts with neighbours. Thus the existing social networks appear to play an important additional role in the creation of awareness.

*Participation in the programme*

Of the 127 respondents, 52 (41 percent) could be classified as adopters of the retrofit programme since they have had their homes insulated under the scheme. Two other respondents lived in retrofitted houses, but had moved in after the retrofit and thus are not considered as adopters. The remaining 73 respondents, were not (yet) adopters of the programme, but 9 (7 percent) were considering it; 47

163

(39 percent) could be considered as 'real' non-adopters: they were familiar with the programme, but had not had their homes retrofitted nor were they considering it. How can these decisions be explained? In this section we will explore the factors that may explain the outcome of the adoption-decision process of the residents.

*Communication between the programme and the residents:* Table 5.1 indicates how residents who were aware of the programme had received information about it and how they first hear of the scheme. The majority said they had been informed by a letter from the scheme itself and that this was the best source of information (see Table 5.2).

Table 5.1
Information channels for first hearing about the scheme
and getting information about it

| Channels | % awareness | % information |
|---|---|---|
| letter from scheme | 41 | 67 |
| housing association | 24 | 42 |
| newspaper | 2 | 30 |
| housecall | 2 | 29 |
| from others in the neighbourhood | 9 | 26 |
| phonecall from scheme | 1 | 10 |
| do not know/cannot remember | 21 | – |

Table 5.2
The best channel of communication

| Channels | % |
|---|---|
| letter from scheme | 48 |
| housing association | 20 |
| newspaper | 2 |
| housecall | 22 |
| from others in the neighbourhood | 9 |
| phonecall from scheme | 5 |

The amount of information coming from the scheme to residents did not differ between adopters and non-adopters. One exception was housecalls which were more frequently mentioned as a source of information by adopters; however these housecalls were typically a result of resident's prior interest in the programme. There were, however, differences in the perception of the information received. Adopters generally felt that they had received sufficient information to make a proper decision. Only 10 percent in this group thought the information was inadequate, while 31 percent of the non-adopters and 34 percent of these considering adoption thought that more information was needed to make a proper decision. More adopters than non-adopters or those considering adoption said that the received information gave them a good idea of what the insulation measures were going to involve. They more often reported that they had got a good idea of the costs and of the savings that could be achieved. The groups were also quite different in their assessment of the reliability of the information supplied. Only very few residents thought of the information as definitely unreliable, but many residents indicated some uncertainty as to whether the information supplied was reliable or not. Most of the non-adopters (66 percent) belonged to this group.

*Personal and household context variables:* Educational background and social economic status did not differentiate between adopters and non-adopters. Neither did residential characteristics. The groups were equally satisfied with their homes and neighbourhood and intentions to move were similar in the different groups. In the non-adopters group more people indicated that the majority of their friends and acquaintances lived in the same neighbourhood or town, while the adopters more frequently reported that the majority of their friends and acquaintances lived elsewhere. This may indicate that the adopters were a more cosmopolitan group, a variable frequently found to be related to early adoption (Rogers and Shoemaker 1971).

With regard to the micro-economic context of the households 38 percent said they had problems making ends meet with their current incomes but there were no differences between the groups. However, when asked about their past and future income, some differences appeared. Non-adopters had experienced more income reductions during the last three years than adopters had and they were more pessimistic about their future income position.

*Adoption and other energy-related behaviours:* Respondents were asked at what temperature they were most comfortable in the living room, on a winter evening. The mean temperature reported was 20.6 C. There were no differences between the groups. The mean actual temperature on the thermostat during the daytime when respondents were at home, was 19.7 C, if not at home in the daytime, 13.9 C, and at night, 12.0 C. Again, no differences between the groups were found. The temperature reported on the thermostat at night showed a slight difference, with non-adopters reporting lower temperatures than adopters (9.0 C versus 12.6 C respectively). There were no differences between the groups in the percentages of households who indicated that arrangements were made about the thermostat setting (40 percent). Neither were differences found in the percentages of respondents in each group who indicated that during summer months the pilot light of the boiler was turned off. In 32 percent of the households, the gas meter reading was checked and recorded in a booklet or on a card. This was true for adopters as well as non-adopters. It seems that the adoption of the retrofit programme is a form of behaviour that is rather independent of the other energy- related behaviours.

*Household dynamics:* While for many consumer products and services the individual consumer is the decision taker, in case of energy conservation decision making may involve the family (Shama, 1983). In almost 90 percent of the families the programme had been discussed. In most of them (76 percent) the final decision was a joint one. In the group of adopters, the opinions of the household members were apparently quite different to those reported in the group of non-adopters. Very few cohabitants of adopters had a negative attitude towards the programme, while 80 percent of the cohabitants of non-adopters had a negative attitude. Again, those considering adoption showed scores in-between.

*Perceptions of the programme:* In line with the findings on programme awareness it appeared that participation in and initial attitudes towards the programme were not related to our indicator of problem recognition. However when the adopters decided to have their homes retrofitted, they generally had different perceptions of the programme than those of the non-adopters or those considering adoption. In the adopters group, respondents expected more comfort in their homes, less draughts and greater savings on energy bills, as a result of the insulation programme. In the non-adopters group, more respondents expected increased dampness and condensation to result from the programme. So, there was a clear relationship between the expected outcomes of the retrofit with the decision taken. Non-adopters had less positive expectations than adopters. Those consider-

166

ing adoption scored in between. However, even in the non-adopters group, 46 percent expected savings on the heating bill, 42 percent expected less draughts and 39 percent expected the retrofit to make their house more comfortable. Many of the non-adopters expected at least some positive consequences of the programme.

Twelve factors residents might have considered were presented and they were asked to indicate which of these had played a role in their decision-making. The most important considerations appeared to be:

* the expected savings on the energy bill
* the improved comfort/better housing quality
* the additional rent sum charged

Job creation, saving energy for future generations and environmental considerations were of only minor importance.

Table 5.3
Considerations in decision-making

|  | mean ranks | | | |
|---|---|---|---|---|
|  | A | C | N | |
| Additional rent sum charged | 65.7 | 57.3 | 38.2 | ** |
| Comfort/housing quality improvement | 45.5 | 43.5 | 64.2 | ** |
| Nuisance of having the job carried out | 53.5 | 54.5 | 53.4 | n.s |
| Draught problems | 40.4 | 59.8 | 67.2 | ** |
| Expected savings | 38.2 | 52.5 | 70.9 | ** |
| Dampness/condensation trouble | 50.1 | 56.3 | 56.8 | n.s. |
| Creation of employment | 48.7 | 45.1 | 60.4 | * |
| Going along with others in the neighbourhood | 53.5 | 48.9 | 56.1 | n.s. |
| Difficult to say no | 54.5 | 47.9 | 53.4 | n.s. |
| Helping to save energy for future generations | 51.7 | 49.8 | 56.1 | n.s. |
| Contribute to a cleaner environment | 51.3 | 54.9 | 55.7 | n.s. |
| Insulation work already carried out in the house | 59.9 | 52.8 | 46.4 | * |

* $p = <.05$, ** $p = < .001$ Lower score denotes high levels of importance
Key: A = adopters; C = those considering adoption N = non-adopters

As would be expected, there were clear differences in the importance of some considerations for adopters, those considering adoption and non-adopters. Table 5.3 presents a comparison of the three groups on the twelve considerations using a Kruskal-Wallis one-way analysis of variance. For adopters the expected savings and the comfort improvements were most important, while non-adopters paid more attention to the additional rent sum charged.

When asked for the most important consideration, 29 percent replied 'expected savings', 31 percent 'the costs' and 18 percent 'comfort'. The same differences among the groups were found as before. For adopters, savings and comfort were most important, while for non-adopters costs played a major role.

*The Community Context:* Social contacts may be of importance in the decision making process. Most residents reported having social contacts in the neighbourhood. However there were no differences between adopters and non-adopters in their frequency of local, social contacts. Adopters, however, had more frequently discussed the programme with neighbours than had non-adopters. Those who talked about the programme with other people in the neighbourhood reported hearing mainly positive opinions about it. Few residents (7 percent) said that opinions of neighbours had some influence on their own decisions. Almost half of the respondents (45 percent) had seen work already carried out under the insulation scheme in other homes in the neighbourhood and adopters and non-adopters did not differ in this respect. However, of those who had seen work being done, 22 percent indicated that this had some influence on their own decision. For the adopters group this percentage was 38 as opposed to only 5 percent in the non-adopters group.

## Conclusions and recommendations

The present study evaluated an existing local energy conservation programme in the Netherlands. Results of our research indicated that almost all of the intended target group were aware of the programme, moreover a considerable number of people (41 percent) decided to have their homes insulated. This level of involvement is much higher than that of most centralized programmes (Gaskell and Pike 1983), indicating that the relatively poor penetration of programmes at the national level (for example mass information campaigns, the provisions of grants) can be substantially increased by programmes operating at the local level.

The major effects of the insulation were (a) increased comfort, and (b) an average saving of approximately 400 m natural gas per household per year, this constitutes a reduction of 16 percent. The success of the programme points out the necessity for national programmes to incorporate the specific needs of the various target groups (Olsen and Joerges 1981). The present project managed to tailor the programme to the existing local situation. This was activated by designing a complete package of insulation measures adapted to the specific circumstances, and by making the financial arrangements attractive to the renters.

The financial aspects of the programme, including an energy bill reduction and an equal increase in rent to cover programme costs would not have been possible without inter-agency co-operation.

The description of the project also demonstrates however that this process of programme development needs appropriate organizational structures. The co-operation and support of many organizations had to be fostered (for example local housing association, the gas supplier) and the potential opposition of organizations had to be dealt with (for example the chamber of commerce). This requires a high level of organizational competence and substantial involvement and perseverance on the part of the initiators. Such a complex organizational task could obstruct the initiation of similar projects. A national organization that stimulates and supports local projects, like Neighbourhood Energy Action in Britain (see Chapter 2), would be very useful in this respect.

The second major purpose of the project concerned creating employment opportunities. This aspect enabled the project to use several facilities specifically set up to stimulate employment. This is another example of existing linkages contributing to the programme's success. The combination of goals, however, may also have negative consequences. The priority for job creation may lead to the search for other employment opportunities instead of the initiation of neighbourhood-oriented energy conservation programmes. Thus, from the perspective of energy conservation there may be a problem of longer-term continuity. Another weakness, perhaps a result of the combination of different goals, was the restricted nature of the programme in respect of energy conservation. For instance, information about other energy related behaviour changes, - a cheap way of promoting energy conservation - was not included in the programme.

The findings of our survey indicate that the adoption decision is a decision of the household as a whole and not a decision that is taken by one person alone. Very few cohabitants of adopters had a negative attitude towards the programme, while 80 percent of the cohabitants of the non-adopters had a negative attitude towards the programme. The implication of this for energy conservation programmes is that information about the programme must be in the form that is accessible, or at least communicable to, all household members. Our results further indicate that the adopters of the programme and the non-adopters did not differ in either socio-economic status or educational background. An unusual finding was that the people who expected to move within the next few years participated in the programme to the same extent as those who did not expect to move. The method of payment for the insulation measures (an increase of the rent) could be an important factor in explaining this finding.

An unexpected finding from the innovation decision research perspective was that the perception of the existing thermal quality of the house as insufficient (used as an indicator of 'problem recognition') was not an essential precondition for the adoption decision. This finding can be explained by the active way in which residents were approached by the project, as well as by the comprehensiveness of the insulation programme. An active search for information was unnecessary for residents. This finding confirms the suggestion that approaches through readily accessible information channels may fulfil many steps in the decision process at the same time, thereby expediting the entire process (Winett and Kagel 1984). Adopting the programme did not appear to be related to other energy conservation behaviours (for example thermostat setting, gasmeter recordings, turning of the pilot light of the boiler). In other words, the programme did not lead to changes in other energy saving behaviours. This confirms our suggestion that specificity of information is crucial and that it is unrealistic to expect a generalized effect spreading to other forms of energy conservation. In the non-adopters group many respondents were not convinced of the reliability of the information provided. This may explain the lack of participation of some residents.

As suggested by Leonard-Barton (1980), social networks may be important in the adoption of energy conservation behaviour. Our results confirm this view and show that social contacts in the community played an important role in creating programme awareness. Social contacts were important for the decision process by (a) offering opportunities for discussing the programme with neighbours, and (b) making it possible for residents to observe how the insulation measures were carried out in other houses.

The adoption of a new product is partly a function of the characteristics of the product. Relative advantage, compatibility, complexity, comprehensiveness, communicability, and trialability are keywords in this respect (Rogers and Shoemaker 1971; Darley 1978; Van Raaij 1979; Engel and Blackwell 1982; Dickerson and Gentry 1983; Shama 1983). Finally, we will discuss the insulation programme from this perspective. The programme in Zutphen was specifically tailored to the existing local situation. The project managed to offer residents a complete package of insulation measures, adapted to their specific circumstances. As a consequence the idea of home insulation could be presented in such a way that people understood the costs and benefits not only in general terms but also at a concrete level. It is easier to get an idea of costs and benefits of a package of measures than of a number of separate measures. Our results show that most residents felt sufficiently informed to make the right decision. However, one third of those who did not adopt the programme indicated that they were not sufficiently informed to make a proper decision. This underlines the importance of comprehensiveness. The increased comprehensiveness and communicability by packaging the set of insulation measures could result in a loss of trialability. the packaging makes it impossible to adopt one or two insulation measures and then, after assessing the effects, to adopt other aspects of the programme. For many of the non-adopters the costs appeared to play a major role, suggesting that the offer of a smaller, cheaper, and therefore more trialable package could have been attractive to them. This could be a first step in the adoption of the complete package. The programme in the present form, however, does contain some element of trialability. The possibility of observing how insulation measures were carried out in other houses and of discussing these matters with neighbours can be seen as a form of trialability. Not surprisingly, the perceptions of the relative advantage of adoption were a major factor explaining the outcome of the adoption decision process. Adopters expected more comfort in their homes and savings on their energy bill as a result of the programme. onadopters were less convinced of these consequences, and for them the financial costs played an important role in the decision making process. Thus, reliable information about the costs and benefits is of crucial importance in an insulation programme.

## Footnotes

In contrast to many other countries, where the Foundation is exclusively used by charities and allied organizations, in the Netherlands this legal form is also often adopted by small-scale non-profit organizations operating as local businesses.

## References

Boer, J. de, P. Ester, C. Mindell and M. Schopman 1982. *Consumer Energy Conservation Policies in the Netherlands*. Institute for Environmental Studies, Free University of Amsterdam and Foundation for Consumer Research (SWOKA), Amsterdam, The Hague.

Darley, J.M. 1978. Energy Conservation Techniques as Innovations and their diffusion. In: Socolow, R.H. (ed.), *Saving Energy in the Home, Princeton's Experiments at Twin Rivers*, Cambridge, Massachusetts.

Dickerson, M.D. and J.W. Gentry 1983. Characteristics of Adopters and Non-Adopters of Home Computers. *Journal of Consumer Research*, 10 225-235.

Engel, J.F. and R.D. Blackwell 1982. *Consumer Behavior*, 4th edition, Holt Saunders, New York.

Ester, P., *Consumer Behavior and Energy Conservation* 1985. Nijhoff Publishing Company, Dordrecht.

Gaskell, G. and R. Pike 1983. Residential Energy Use: An Investigation of Consumers and Conservation Strategies. *Journal of Consumer Policy*, 6, 285-302.

Leonard-Barton, D. 1980. *The role of interpersonal communication networks in the diffusion of energy conserving practices and technologies*, presented at the Banff-Conference on Consumer Behaviour and Energy, Banff.

McDougall, G.H.G., J.D. Claxton, J.R.B. Ritchie and C.D. Anderson 1981. Consumer Energy Research: A Review. *Journal of Consumer Research*, 8, 343-354.

McDougall, G.H.G. and J.R.B. Ritchie 1984. Consumer Energy Conservation Policy, an Analytical Approach. *Energy Policy*, 201-212.

Minderhout, P.A. and M.G.F. Zwetsloot 1984. Basisonderzoek Aardgas Kleinverbruik. In: *Gas*, 4, 198-205

N.W.R. 1983. *Derde enquete warmte-isolatie van woningen in het bezit van woningcorporaties*, Almere.

Olsen, M.E. and B. Joerges 1981. *The Process of Consumer Energy Conservation, an international perspective*, presented at the Conference on Societal Responses to the 'Energy Crisis', Dubrovnic.

Raaij, W.F. van, 1981. Verspreiding van energiebesparende innovaties onder huishoudens. In: P. Ester en F. Leeuw (eds). *Energie als maatschappelijk probleem*, Assen.

Rogers, E.M. and F.F. Shoemaker 1971. Communication of Innovations, *A Cross-Cultural Approach*. The Free Press, New York, London.

Shama, A. 1983. Energy Conservation in US Buildings. *Energy Policy*, 148-167.

Stern, P.C., J.S. Black and J.T. Elworth 1981. *Home Energy Conservation, Programs and Strategies for the 1980's*. The Institute for Consumer Policy Research, Consumers Union Foundation, Mount Vernon, New York.

Winett, R.A. and J.H. Kagel 1984. Effects of Information Presentation Format on Resource Use in Field Studies. *Journal of Consumer Research*, 11, 655-667.

This research was supported by the Directorate General for Environmental Management of the Dutch Ministry of Public Housing, Physical Planning and Environmental Management and by the Netherlands Foundation for Consumer Research (SWOKA) and the Directorate General for Science Policy of the Dutch Ministry of Education and Science.

# 6 Implementing energy policies in Swedish municipalities

TAGE KLINGBERG

## Introduction

The final use of energy in Sweden is approximately 1.300 pJ/year, of which some 37 percent is used for industrial purposes, 20 percent for transport and about 43 percent in the building sector (also called the 'other' sector). Residential buildings (single family houses and apartment buildings) use about two thirds of the energy in the building sector, or about 30 percent of the total energy used in the country. In this chapter some of the experiences from the national programme to promote energy conservation in the residential sector are discussed.

The most important energy conservation programmes for buildings in Sweden are nationwide, established by the national government. These are implemented at the local level by the 284 municipalities. The manner and intensity of this implementation differs - and so does the impact on the property owners and the residents (owners or tenants). This study focuses on the municipal implementation and on the effects on the property owners and tenants of the loans and grants system and the advisory programme. Before discussing these programmes a brief overview of the national energy policy since the last world war is presented.

## Old goals revived

The disruption of energy supply from foreign countries during the Second World War left its marks on Swedish energy policy during the 1940s and 1950s. Development of domestic energy sources became an important goal. This was to be achieved largely through hydroelectric energy and nuclear power. However, the abundant and inexpensive supply of oil during the 1950s and 1960s and the unforeseen increase in overall energy demand led to an unplanned increase in oil dependence. For a short time the Suez-crisis revived the fear of a cut-off from supplies, but by and large, the goal of independent energy supply was not maintained. A tax on oil products was not enough to curb the increasing demand. However, the concern about vulnerable imports still existed. When the Arab oil embargo struck Sweden in 1973/74 there was an immediate revival at national level of the goal of decreased dependency on imported energy. The state (national) government instituted a gasoline rationing scheme. Information on energy conservation was widely disseminated. A loans and grants programme to enhance energy conservation in existing buildings went into effect in July, 1974. Additional insulation to walls, installation of thermostatic radiator valves, and improvements to heating or ventilation systems are examples of measures eligible for support. A grant of up to SKr. 2000 and a loan of up to SKr. 4000 could be obtained for each dwelling. Later the limits were raised. To date, over 8 billion SKr have been distributed as grants or subsidized loans. In 1978 an extensive programme of home audits was launched. In almost every municipality householders could get an audit performed and advice given free of charge.

At the municipal level energy was not considered to be an important issue. Rather it was seen as a problem for the national government, which chose to use the municipal administration for implementation of the programme, this being the normal procedure for Swedish policy implementation in many fields, for example social care or housing. In this way loans and grants for energy conservation were channelled through the same agencies as housing loans, and followed the same administrative routines. In addition implementation of more stringent energy codes that came into force in 1977 became a natural part of the supervisory work of the local building committees - of which there is one in each municipality. The national energy conservation policy instruments (programmes) were aimed at the whole building sector. By taking advantage of the existing municipal bureaucracy the programmes were implemented with little delay. There was one exception: a scheme of local energy advisers started in 1978. In most municipalities they were organized separately in a rather ad hoc way, at some efficiency costs, at least during the first years. The energy advisers are employed by the municipalities, which, are refunded by the state with some 150 million SKr/year.

## What happened?

It is apparent from the national energy statistics that the use of energy in the building sector (the 'other' sector, which means all activities outside industry and transports) has decreased. But what is not clear is by how much, because statistics and definitions still leave much to be desired. The National Energy Conservation Plan adopted in 1981 called for the use of energy in the stock of existing buildings in 1978 to be reduced by 30 percent by 1988. (Engebeck and Wickman 1982). This implied a yearly reduction in these buildings of about 3 percent. Taking new construction into account the resulting annual reduction in energy use in the building sector should be about 1.6 percent.

During 1983/84 attempts were made to assess the results achieved. The Swedish Council for Building Research estimated that about half of the goal had been achieved. Thus the Council concluded that Sweden was well on the way to fulfilling the 10-year goal (BFR 1984). However the National Board of Energy (1984) considered that these figures may have been too optimistic, and estimated that only about a third of the goal had been reached. No one disputes, however, that important achievements have been made, and that they can largely be attributed to greater energy efficiency in buildings (see Table 6.1). This is due to increased insulation, weatherproofing of doors and windows and improved heating and ventilation systems, in more general terms to improved operation of buildings and investments in energy conservation measures. These investments have been made by the property owners frequently with financial support from the government.

For the purpose of this discussion it is sufficient to accept that considerable results have been achieved. The exact amounts are not at issue here. Experts agree that the results have largely been obtained in the residential sector (amounting to about two thirds of the energy use in the building sector) which is the focus of interest in this discussion. The net consumption of energy use for heating and hot water has changed over the period 1970-83 as shown in Table 6.1.

## Table 6.1

Development of energy efficiency in residential buildings. Net use of energy for heating water and household appliances. kWh/M2 per year. (National Board of Energy 1984, pp. 68, based on Carlsson).

### Annual energy use in kWh/m2

| Year | Single-family dwellings | Multi-family dwellings |
|------|-------------------------|------------------------|
| 1970 | 190 | 240 |
| 1975 | 166 | 237 |
| 1980 | 150 | 204 |
| 1983 | 125 | 183 |

As can be seen from the table, energy efficiency in single-family dwellings started to improve earlier than in the multi-family buildings. Furthermore their reduction in consumption was greater over the period considered (34 percent versus 24 percent).

It is the explanation of these improvements that is the focus of this chapter. What is the relative importance of the government conservation programmes for the results achieved in comparison to other factors, such as the price of energy? Furthermore to the extent that the government programmes have had the desired effect, what can be concluded about the efficiency of different ways of organizing and operating the programmes at the local government level?

**Why did it happen?**

The fundamental question concerns the extent to which government interventions, such as advisory systems and loans and grants triggered the energy conservation results achieved? The problem in answering this question lies in the fact that action taken by householders may not be caused by the government's programmes even if it follows advice given and is financed by loans and grants. Several studies find evidence of a considerable number of 'free riders'. Another problem is that even if owners of dwellings have actually been influenced, it may only result in actions taken a few years earlier than would have been the case even if no government support had been available. Thus, it is tempting to exaggerate the effects of government programmes when trying to analyse the whys and wherefore's.

To strictly determine the effects of government support programmes - be they advisory or economic - is, in fact, very difficult. It can never be proved people would have done the same thing to their houses in the absence of financial support. They may say when interviewed, that they would, but hypothetical questions of this kind are generally held to be most unreliable. Instead, we have done the following: we have tried to assess the real penetration of the government programmes, to get a picture of the extent to which actions have been taken completely independently of these programmes. This at least gives some indication of the importance of other factors, primarily the raised prices of energy. In addition we looked at information on differences between participants, those who have used the programmes and non-participants, those who have not.

One approach to assessing programme impacts is to compare programme penetration (utilisation of government loans and grants) with the actual frequency of conservation actions. If a large number of owners are taking conservation actions but without government support this is an indication (even though no proof) of weak programme impact.

*Loans and grants*

By 1982 in about 62 percent of the single family houses some energy conservation actions had been taken. In the event a little less than one third of these had taken advantage of government loans and grants. Of this third some could have done so even without support. These are what we call the 'free riders'. We have estimated that a modest 10-20 percent of all conservation measures were actually directly caused by subsidies. In addition, the incentive system has certainly had informational and 'propaganda' effects, contributing to increased awareness and interest in energy conservation. (Klingberg and Simila 1984a). An econometric analysis of these effects of the loans and grants system indicates that they were largest in the mid-seventies and declined after this, one reason being the substantial oil price increases in 1978-90. (Klingberg and Wickman 1984). Another reason for the decline may be diminishing 'propaganda' effects. In multi-family residential buildings loans and grants were used more often. Almost two thirds (64 percent) of property owners in this category taking conservation actions had used government loans and grants at least once and most of them used the subsidies every time. (Alfredson 1984). Since the energy loans to multi-family buildings are more heavily subsidized than those to houses it is safe to conclude that the government subsidies accounted for more of the investments in these buildings than in the single family sector. Both behavioural activities and investments to use energy more efficiently have increased in recent years in the multi-family sector. One reason may be that the buildings have received more favoured treatment from the incentive system than the single-family houses during these years. Another reason may be that in larger and more complex buildings, with the additional complication of the landlord-tenant relationship, more time is required for organization, negotiating, planning of activities, and implementation. It may take a couple of years to change the priorities of large property-owning organizations.

Even though higher energy prices appear to explain most of the conservation activities the loans and grants system has certainly contributed significantly especially in apartment buildings. However, there are costs related to these benefits: the incentive system entails administrative costs, both on the government and on clients. More important is the tendency of the subsidies to encourage builders to choose technical solutions which may not be optimal from a 'societal point of view'. This means that the solution requiring least total resources (looking at all actors - thus the term 'societal') may be rejected in favour of a solution giving greater benefits to the property owners. Thus they may find it advantageous to invest in a subsidized heat pump or heat exchanger even though low-cost heat may be delivered from a large municipal heat pump through the district heating network. The extra cost is carried by the tax-payers who have to fund the subsidies to the property owners. (Engebeck 1983).

*Municipal energy advisers*

The municipal energy advisers help owners to act more 'rationally' by disseminating information, answering questions and conducting home audits. Since the beginning of the programme in 1978 some 15 percent of home owners have called upon the advisory services. Those using loans and grants are also more likely to use the advisers (30 percent of the loan-users had obtained advice) than other active, that is energy-conserving, house-owners. The 'real' effects, that is as different from actions that would have been taken anyway - if advisers had not been available, are limited, since people frequently use advisers to check plans which are already developed. Here again, the effects in the multi-family sector may have been larger. Our research indicates that knowledge of the existence of the advisory programme is not as widespread as knowledge of the incentive system. The later starting date of the advisory programme may account for this. There is, according to our interviews, a latent demand for advisers. About one third of the house-owners say that they would like help, and most of them want assistance on a number of occasions. They want help with planning the conservation measures as well as with procurement of contractor services and with the control of work carried out. This is much more than the normal procedure operating today, in which the advisers normally visit just once.

## Economic and technical contexts

The different municipalities implement the government programme in different ways, because the technical and economic contexts in the areas vary. Other contextual factors may vary which also influences programme impacts. These issues will now be considered.

### Varying municipal involvement

By relying on the municipal apparatus, a uniform implementation could not be expected in contrast to a situation in which state agencies had been established for the purpose. Swedish municipalities have in many ways considerable discretion over their activities. Implementation of the national energy policy has thus varied. One major explanation for this is that municipal energy utilities have varied structures. Some (often the larger municipalities) are heavily involved in the supply of electricity and district heating; others have no district heating but supply electricity; still others have no involvement in energy supply at all, leaving it to private or state-owned power companies. Depending on the type of involvement and the situation on the local energy market, the municipality's interest in energy conservation has come to be very different in different municipalities.

Are the municipalities ideally suited to promoting energy conservation? Normally not, sad to say. Efficient operation of buildings has seldom been a concern of the municipalities. There may be exceptions: if for example a municipal energy utility company is under expansion it may want to ensure that energy consumption levels

180

in the existing buildings are brought down to its 'future economic level' in order to avoid investing in a supply system (for example district heating) creating over-capacity. This appears to be the case in the city of Uppsala, which has an efficient combination of energy conservation and supply (Woodward 1984a). However, in other cities this is not the case. If a system is already existing and designed for a large capacity a successful conservation programme leads to poorly utilised district heating facilities, and thus poor economic returns for the municipal utility company. This may be the case in Gothenburg, which is not growing any more (Woodward 1984b). The municipal authorities of Uppsala and Gothenburg, very logically, have organized their advisory services differently, and they also show different attitudes toward some energy conservation measures. In Gothenburg to give one example, some property owners have been denied electricity to supply heat pumps because these pumps would decrease the demand for hot water from the district heating system.

The varying municipal interest in promoting energy conservation is, of course, a reflection of different economic consequences of reduced energy use. In other words, the economic benefit of reduced consumption varies because the marginal cost of supply is different. Therefore it is rational for different municipalities to promote conservation with different intensity. Conservation is just not urgent in areas where supply of energy is cheap.

*Technical status and economic advantage*

It is not only the municipalities that show varying degrees of interest in energy conservation; so do the property owners. This is partly for very good reasons, since the technical status of buildings and the economic advantage of conservation varies. This will briefly be illustrated here.

This discussion is based on a survey in 1982 of 508 single-family homes. 322 of these were selected at random from house owners in general while 186 were sampled from householders who had been granted a conservation subsidy. The survey included details of household characteristics, technical qualities of the home, conservation measures taken, investment cost, government subsidy (if any), reasons for taking conservation actions and savings achieved.

In Sweden the technical qualities of a building are normally related to the year (or decade) of erection. Over the years the quality measured in U-values has improved successively. If we look at the proportion of home-owners undertaking conservation action we find, not surprisingly, that older houses are more often subject to retrofit than new ones (see Figure 6.1). In particular we find that houses built after 1977 - which are known to have good U-values (see Engebeck 1984) - are rarely retrofitted.

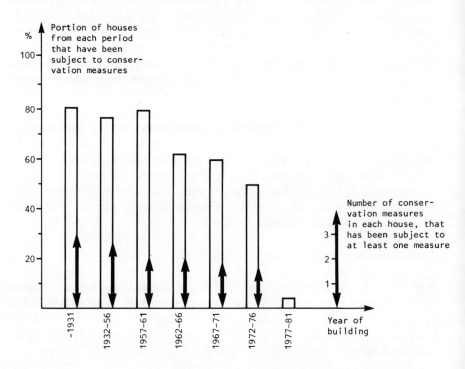

Figure 6.1    Portion of single-family houses subject to energy conservation measures related to period of construction. The figure also shows the number of conservation measures taken.
N=320. (Source: Klingberg and Simila 1984a)

The figure shows more conservation activities in the older houses, which indicates rational behaviour on the part of home owners. Results from our study show a distribution of subsidies and advisory services which approximates to a similar pattern. The larger need for upgrading older houses is reflected in the fact that loan users have been found on the average, to live in older houses than non-loan users. Also, we found that those carrying out a major renovation of their house were more likely to use government loans and grants than others. A factor adding to this tendency may be that major renovations are often financed by subsidized housing loans, modified to renovation situations. When applying for such a loan it is easy to apply for an energy loan and grant at the same time.

It seems beyond doubt that economic factors are of prime importance to decisions concerning energy conservation measures (see Klingberg and Simila 1984a and Klingberg and Wickman 1984). As a logical consequence the economics of a particular programme should influence the rate of adoption. This is illustrated by the drop in number of loans/grants to single-family houses after the abolition of the grant of 3,000 SKr per dwelling on July 1 1981 , although loans were still available (see Wickman 1984). Several shifts in the rate of applications for loans/grants have been clearly associated with changes in the financial conditions of the programmes. Furthermore, the penetration of information may be dependent on the economic situation. Furubo (1984) studied the Energy Conservation Committee's information campaigns and concluded that information on energy conservation is effective only if there are economic incentives for the receiver to take action. In other words, an economic advantage is of crucial importance for the realization of energy conservation.

*Single-family houses*

In Table 6.2 we contrast the types of conservation measures taken by house-owners using and not using government incentives.

Table 6.2
Percentages (%) of active owners who have taken various energy conservation measures (Klingberg and Simila 1984) ('active' = who have retrofitted their home)

| Type of measure | L (N=185) | A (N=196) |
|---|---|---|
| Insulated attic | 47.0 | 41.6 |
| Insulated walls | 38.4 | 35.0 |
| Insulated floors | 17.3 | 11.2 |
| Installed new windows | 18.9 | 13.2 |
| Installed thermostatic valves | 38.4 | 24.4 |
| Installed new furnace | 22.7 | 12.7 |
| Installed new burner head | 7.0 | 9.7 |
| Installed motor shunt | 17.3 | 6.6 |
| Installed heat exchanger | 8.6 | 3.0 |
| Made agreement to service furnace | 3.2 | 4.1 |
| Weather-stripped doors and windows | 37.8 | 52.8 |

Key:
L = Loan Users
A = Active owners in random population sample

As expected, for most energy conservation measures, the frequency is higher among the loan users. The differences are largest for the more expensive measures, such as insulation of the building envelope. However, the most striking aspect of the table is the rather

184

small overall difference between loan users and non-users. This indicates that a considerable percentage of 'free riders' are included in the loan user group. The term 'free rider' refers to those beneficiaries, who would have improved their homes even if state subsidies were not available. They take advantage of the subsidy without really changing their conservation investments.

The greater frequency of more expensive measures among loan users may in part be due to effect of the loans and grants system. But the reverse may also apply. Those who have decided to take action may be more likely to apply for government money if the measures are costly. If we look at the small measures, that is installation of thermostatic radiator valves and motor shunts, we find them to be much more frequent among loan users. This might be explained by the novelty of these measures: they are not well known, and loan users may have learnt about them only through the loan-application process. This is in line with the hypothesis that new measures are promoted by the loans and grants system. The figures for installation of heat exchangers support this. Let us now look at the take up of loans and grants across different energy conservation measures taken among all (both retrofitted and non-retrofitted) one-family houses in a random sample from middle Sweden. See Table 6.3.

It can be seen that the ratio of subsidized and unsubsidized measures taken varies from 0.01 (1 percent) for weatherstripping (normally not eligible for support) to over 0.60 (60 percent) for motor shunts and heat exchangers. For larger insulation measures and 3-pane windows the ratio ranges from 0.28 to 0.39. The total average based on these numbers is 0.25 that is 25 percent of the number of all energy conservation measures taken are wholly or partly financed by government loans and/or grants. If we exclude weatherstripping and service-agreements (both non-eligible measures) the figure is 0.34 or 34 percent. These 34 percent are an estimate of the maximum possible direct impact of the government support system on decisions to take conservation measures in owner-occupied one-family houses. It should be remembered that this 34 percent does not mean that 34 percent of all conservation measures were triggered by government support. Many measures may legitimately be assumed to have been taken anyway, but with a subsidy available many people choose to apply for it and use it; perfectly legally.

Table 6.3
Takeup of government loans/grants for different measures
(Klingberg and Simila 1984).

Percentage of owners

| | who took measure | used loan/ grant | Col 2 div by Col 1 |
|---|---|---|---|
| *Type of measure* | | | |
| Insulated attic | 25.6 | 10.1 | 0.39 |
| Insulated walls | 21.6 | 8.4 | 0.39 |
| Insulated floors | 6.9 | 1.9 | 0.28 |
| Installed 3-pane windows | 5.9 | 2.2 | 0.37 |
| Installed thermostatic valves | 15.0 | 3.0 | 0.21 |
| Installed new furnace | 7.8 | 2.5 | 0.32 |
| Installed new burner head | 6.0 | 0.3 | 0.05 |
| Installed motor shunt | 4.1 | 2.5 | 0.61 |
| Installed heat exchanger | 1.9 | 1.2 | 0.63 |
| Made agreement to service furnace | 2.5 | 0.3[*] | 0.12 |
| Weather-stripped doors and windows | 32.5 | 0.3[*] | 0.01 |
| Sum of measures above | 129.8 | 32.8 | 0.25 (ave) |

*(Note: 129.8 works out to 1.3 measure per house)*

Total random sample (N=319 one-family houses)
(* = measure normally not eligible for loan/grant)

186

## Multi-family and non-residential buildings

Unfortunately, we have little similar data for apartment and commercial buildings. We know that home-owners were quicker to take advantage of loans/grants as well as the advisory services than were owners of apartment buildings. It is argued that this is because home-owners can gain more from the programme services than larger property owners.

There is, in the rented buildings sector in Sweden, a problem of the division of incentives between tenants and landlords, causing the resulting incentive to be less than in owner-occupied houses. If the energy bill is the tenant's responsibility, they have an incentive for energy conserving behaviour, but the landlord may have little incentive to invest in insulation. If, on the other hand, the cost of energy is included in the rent ('total rent'), the tenants have little incentive to behave in an energy conserving way, while the landlord has a greater incentive to make investments. Thus, under either system the incentives to save are in principle smaller than for an owner-occupied home with the same energy conservation potential (Klingberg et al. 1984). This can be expected to cause a lower, or at least slower, take-up of energy conservation activities in rental property than in owner-occupied homes. Observations of actual activities tend to confirm this.

Earlier types of rental contracts often gave the tenants the benefits of reduced energy costs. The newer type of contracts, where energy costs are included in the rent ('total rent'), may have increased the incentive for landlords to take action and to use government loans and grants. There has been increased use of programme services in larger buildings since about 1978 (Klingberg et al. 1984). Another factor that may explain the slower start of energy conservation in apartment buildings is its complexity. It is likely that it takes a few years to establish and implement an energy conservation programme in a building that is technically complex and, in addition, may require an organizational change.

## Contextual factors

Programme take up and impact differ not only as a result on the technical and economic contexts but also because of differing consumer contexts and preferences.

### Inter-household communication

It has been argued that greater inter-household communication may lead to more energy-conscious behaviour than otherwise. This seems particularly relevant to multi-family buildings, where metering of heat and tap water is collective, giving little incentive to save, unless, each tenant knows that everybody else is equally committed and involved. This may work in 'small collectivities' according to Hamler (1984). Thus, the successful energy conservation in an apartment building in Skogas south of Stockholm seems to have relied on inter-household communication to a great extent (Byggforskningsradet 1979). It may also be the case that greater communication between households promotes take-up of government programme. We asked house-owners about the most important source of information concerning the two programmes (see Table 6.4)

Table 6.4
Most important source of information for those knowing about the two programmes (Klingberg and Simila 1984a)

|  | Prime source of information about | |
|---|---|---|
|  | loans/grants | advisors |
|  | % | % |
| Information from gov't agency | 25 | 32 |
| TV or radio | 17 | 13 |
| Newspapers | 29 | 25 |
| Friends and neighbours | 11 | 9 |
| Other | 18 | 21 |
| Total | 100 | 100 |
| Number of informed house-owners | 307 | 203 |
| (as % of all house owners) | 95% | 63% |

Judging from Table 6.4 information from friends and neighbours is not very important. However, we do not know whether the information level or the impact of the programme would have been better if inter-household communication had been greater.

*Household mobility*

It is also argued that those who are less mobile and have lived in a house longer, are more likely to improve it. In our study of home-owners, those who had taken conservation measures had lived in their homes for more than 11 years (median value) while the figure for non-active owners was only six years. This supports the hypothesis. But another reason for the difference may be that those with new homes (say built after 1977), do not need to bother about retrofitting or just have not had time to live there more than maximum five years (at the time of the study in 1982). If we look at homes built prior to 1977 the number of years lived in the home does not differentiate between active and passive owners. (Klingberg and Simila 1984a).

If we change perspective and look to the future we find that those who have been active, that is who have taken conservation measures, are more often certain that they will live at least another five years in the house than are passive owners.

Thus overall our findings indicate that for a certain age of the house, the number of years the owners have lived in it does not predict whether they will retrofit it or not. But plans for the future are more relevant: those planning to stay have a greater propensity to improve their homes than those planning to move within a few years.

*Economic situation and social status*

According to social diffusion theory people with higher socio-economic status (income, education etc.) are more likely to be well informed, to utilise government programmes and to be innovative and active. Some data on the characteristics of loan users will be reported but it must be noted that much of the data comes from the owner-occupied sector, which is a restricted sample of people. The average home-owner is better off, economically and educationally, that the average renter. In our study of home-owners in middle Sweden 34 percent were classified as belonging to social group 1 (the highest), which contrasts with 14 percent for the total population in the same geographical area.

If we look at the characteristics of those utilising the loans and grants programme ('loan-users') we find that they have on the average a slightly better education level than the 'non-users'. Also, they have a slightly higher average social class. The 'loan-users' had almost 15 percent higher declared median income (Klingberg and Simila 1984b). Thus, we may conclude that those taking advantage of loans/grants are better off than others. The social differences between loan-users and non-users are larger than between those who are active and passive in relation to energy conservation actions. This is probably a result of the fact that better off people are more likely to contact and negotiate with the authorities, and to make use of financial advantages.

We have also looked at the year of application for loans/grants, in order to see if there is support for the diffusion theory hypothesis that better off people react faster. We find no such tendencies in our material. People applying for loans/grants in 1974 and 1975 show the same socio-economic profiles as those applying later. Looking at the take-up of advisory services the hypothesis of well-off people being in the forefront gets some support in our material: younger home-owners take advantage of the advisers more frequently than older. People from social group 1 (the better off) use the advisers more, but the tendency is weak, and education by itself shows no correlation to use of advisory service.

## Some policy implications

Looking back over the ten years since the oil embargo we can see that the government acted rapidly by - among other things - implementing a loans and grants system in mid-1974. By several subsequent decisions in the Riksdag (the Swedish Parliament) the scheme of policy instruments had been widened and revised. At the municipal level, the response to the 'oil crisis' was much slower. It was not until 1977-78 that energy became a political issue of importance at the local level. This is surprising since most municipalities had for some time been involved in energy supply, for example with public utilities. Equally although they had to implement the loans and grants programme it took some four years to get energy on the political agenda in the municipalities. It is possible that, as a general rule, it takes a few years for the local political and administrative machineries to focus on a new problem, while the national government is more apt to react quickly. If this is the case, it follows that

190

when the country is suddenly confronted with a 'new' and urgent problem (an issue at least perceived as new) the national government should act because failing such action, the municipalities will remain passive. As time goes by and the municipal machineries become busy tackling the problem, the national government can start preparing for the longer term steady state, dismantling temporary agencies and programmes and establishing those needed on a permanent basis.

*The subsidy system*

Our studies indicate that the loans and grants to energy conservation in existing buildings have added to the number and extent of energy conservation activities taken by owner-occupiers - especially during the first years of the programmes. Perhaps the most important effects of the subsidies have been to 'get the ball rolling'. There is a considerable time-lag involved in adapting to new price-levels. One function of government programmes is to shorten this time-lag, to act as an accelerator. As practical experiences are won and disseminated, and energy conservation is integrated in the more routine programmes for maintenance and upgrading, the justification for a subsidy becomes successively weaker. But when is it reasonable to do away with the subsidies? Without going into any theoretical or empirical detail, we make some suggestions.

The more active and well-informed house owners and managers of larger properties have adjusted their operations and investment planning to the new price levels. But probably a considerable percentage have still to be reached. A study of the activities of owners with identical houses showed that - according to interviews and on site visits - 10 of 36 houses (28 percent) were not improved while the rest were already retrofitted (Hanstorp and Norman 1982). Klingberg and Simila found 39 percent of passive owners, of which probably the majority ought to be doing something. We estimate that about one house-owner out of every four is still to be activated. And this figure may be even larger among owners of larger buildings. These observations argue the case for better targeting of the subsidies. The broad 'spray of subsidies' is costly - and maybe not effective any more. There may be other, more specific, arguments for subsidies, such as promotion of new technology or promotion of flexible heating systems, that is systems that can use different energy sources.

## Information and advice

General information about energy conservation has very limited effects, at least according to an evaluation of the activities of the National Energy Saving Committee. The information should be concentrated on such measures that have a good potential and where there is a good chance of finding a receptive audience (Furubo 1984). According to our survey of 500 home-owners in middle Sweden only about 13 percent (19 percent of those who had taken conservation measures) had used the service of an energy adviser. 30 percent of the home-owners say that they would like to have help from an adviser (Klingberg and Simila 1984b). This indicates poor targeting and may explain the limited effectiveness of the advisory services. Another indication is that many house-owners need help at several stages of the process (planning, procurement, control) and not - as is offered to them today - only once, which is in the planning stage, and not later in the process. Many multi-family property owners have not taken any conservation actions to their buildings although they probably ought to have done so in their own self-interest. To the extent that this is correct advisory services may be warranted. But studies and observations discussed in this chapter indicate that the present services do not necessarily reach the property owners in greatest need. Also the advisers' modus operandi may need to be changed to a more active, 'field oriented' approach including follow-ups and evaluations. More use of existing local connections such as associations of property managers and home-owners might be more effective. Reaching those who today are passive should be a central objective.

## Targeting and co-ordination

We have found arguments for better targeting of subsidies as well as of the advisory services. This requires better integration of the programme implementation in the municipal organization to obtain stronger backing. Local conservation efforts - including the work of the advisers - should be better co-ordinated with the supply side, that is with the local utility, to avoid a situation such as in Gothenburg, where the advisers promote conservation measures that the utility attempts to block (Woodward 1984b). One step toward improving the targeting of subsidies and at the same time probably enhancing the impact of the advice is to involve the advisers in the administration of loans and grants. The advisers could help property owners to plan their energy conservation investments at the same time as they - together - fill out the loan application. In this way

192

property owners could see the economic consequences of the planned technical solution. And the adviser can get a feel for what is causing resistance on the part of owners. A model for this type of combined advice and administration of subsidies is found in the agricultural and forestry sector.

*Toward a steady state*

As interest, knowledge and energy conservation activities are successively spread to the currently passive owners - helped by more targeted programmes - a situation is approaching in which adaptation (from a private-economic point of view) to a higher price level of energy is not far from complete. In that situation the state and municipal governments would need to have the organization and the programmes adapted for a permanent situation or a situation of gradual and steady change. An advisory service may be required as a permanent institution - as Sweden already has concerning traditional building technology. The local building committees (each municipality has one) are well suited as hosts to the energy advisers, or the present building inspectors could be involved in giving advice concerning energy conservation. Integration of the ad hoc advisory services into the building committees seems to be a logical progression.

Economically, a steady state solution, does not call for a subsidy programme of loans and grants unless special arguments appear. Otherwise, the aim can be to dismantle the subsidy programme after a phase of targeted subsidies to the passive owners.

The energy conservation issue is successively approaching a 'steady state'. Energy concerns are being included in the normal operating and planning procedures. In other words, energy conservation per se was once an outstanding political issue but is now 'retreating' to a question of lesser political concern as other issues attract growing attention. Recently, however, energy has been coupled to demands for a more integrated policy approach, where many factors are considered together such as energy supply, energy conservation, general economic activity, urban renewal and maintenance of buildings and environmental protection. Thus the future of energy conservation will be seen it its linkages with other issues on the political agenda.

# References

Alfredson, H. 1984. *Kunskap om energisparatgarder.* (Knowledge of energy conservation measures). Byggforskningsradet. R 142:84, Stockholm

BFR. (Byggforskningsradet). 1979. *Sa har gjorde vi* (We did it this way). T25:1979, Stockholm.

BFR. (Byggforskningsradet). *ENERGI 85* (Energy 85). National Council for Building Research, Stockholm.

Carlsson, L.G. 1984. *Energianvandningen i bostader och lokaler 1970-82* (Energy use in dwellings and other buildings 1970-82). National Council for Building Research, R 132:84, Stockholm.

Engebeck, L. 1984. *Are building codes effective tools for reducing energy use in new residential buildings? Some Swedish experiences.* Paper presented at the ACEEE Summer Study in Santa Cruz, California.

Engebeck, L. 1983. *Ekonomisk analys av varmeatervinning* (Economic analysis of heat recovery). Report to the city of Stockholm. National Swedish Institute for Building Research, Gaevle.

Furubo, J. 1984. Information on energy conservation, in *Effects of energy conservation programmes*, Klingberg et.al. National Swedish Institute for Building Research, Bulletin M84:2, Gaevle.

Gaunt, L. 1984. Household, life style and energy conservation in Klingberg, T. (ed.) *Energy conservation in rented buildings.* National Swedish Institute for Building Research, Bulletin M84:11, Gaevle.

Hanstorp, S. and Norman, B. 1982. *Smahusagares energisparatgarder - en studie av tva hustyper* (Single-family home-owners' energy conservation measures - a study of two types of houses). The Department of Building Economics at the Royal Institute of Technology, Report no 141, Stockholm.

Hamler, J. 1984. Problems and possibilities connected with individual metering and invoicing of heating and hot water in Klingberg, T. et.al. *Energy conservation in rented buildings.* National Swedish Institute for Building Research, Bulletin M84:11, Gaevle.

Klingberg, T. and Lindahl, C. 1982. *Kommunerna och energin. En studie av energiplanering och energuhushallning i tre mellansvenska kommuner* (The 'Kommuns' and energy. A study of energy planning and conservation in three Swedish municipalities). National Swedish Institute for Building Research, Bulletin M82:19, Gaevle.

Klingberg, T. ed. 1984. *Energy Conservation in Rented Buildings.* National Swedish Institute for Building Research, Bulletin M84:11, Gaevle.

Klingberg, T. and Simila, M. 1984a. *Energisparstod till smahusagare* (Energy conservation support to house-owners). National Swedish Institute for Building Research, Bulletin M84:6, Gaevle.

Klingberg, T. and Simila M. 1984b. Energy loans and grants to house-owners - a survey in Klingberg et.al. *Effects of Energy Conservation Programmes.* National Swedish Institute for Building Research, Bulletin M84:2, Gaevle.

Klingberg, T. and Wickman, K. 1984. *Energy trends and policy impact.* CECP Technical Report III, IIUG. Wissenschaftszentrum, Berlin.

National Board of Energy. 1984. *Energihushallningsprogrammets effekter*, (The Effects of the Energy Conservation Programme), Stockholm.

Woodward, A.E. 1984a. *Uppsala: the utility as energy integrator.* Department of Sociology, University of Uppsala.

Woodward, A.E. 1984b. *Gothenburg: conservation conflicts and supply in Sweden.* Department of Sociology, University of Uppsala.

# 7 Consumer responses to a highly subsidized home insulation scheme in Eugene, Oregon, USA

MARVIN E. OLSEN and VALENCIA A. FONSECA

**Policy and research background**

Conserving energy has become a major concern of increasing numbers of US citizens since 1974, despite the fact that the federal government has never adopted energy conservation as a major national goal. The general concern of the study described in this chapter is why consumers in the US have increasingly been responding to community level energy conservation programmes.

*Federal policy*

The United States federal government does not have any kind of comprehensive energy conservation policy, and has never treated conservation as a high priority goal. During the Carter Administration, Congress did enact a series of energy conservation laws aimed primarily at the individual states, but they were never integrated into a comprehensive policy to conserve energy. Moreover, the conservation programmes created by that legislation were not very ambitious in their goals nor very extensive in the scope of their activities, and they received rather limited funding.

The Reagan Administration strongly emphasizes energy production over conservation. Its National Energy Policy Plan of 1981 and 1983 (USDOE 1981 and 1983) states that conservation of energy is to be achieved primarily in the marketplace by allowing energy prices to rise. This policy has resulted in nearly total abandonment of all efforts by the US Government to promote energy conservation. Basically, the present position of the United States Government toward energy conservation is that

* the federal government has little or no responsibility for promoting energy conservation;

* this is a proper concern for local governments if they wish to undertake it, but they must fund all such efforts themselves;

* primary responsibility for promoting energy conservation lies with private utilities, oil companies, and firms providing conservation goods and services; and

* the decision of whether or not to conserve energy must ultimately rest with each individual consumer acting in the marketplace.

*Pacific northwest regional policy*

Although the United States lacks a comprehensive national energy policy, in 1980 Congress established such a policy for the Pacific Northwest Region, consisting of the states of Washington, Oregon, Idaho, and Montana. The enabling legislation, the Pacific Northwest Electric Power Planning and Conservation Act, deals only with electricity. By necessity, nevertheless, it created a broad policy framework for all energy planning and conservation in the region. The basic purposes of the Act are to (BPA 1981):

* encourage conservation and efficiency in the use of electric power, and renewable resources development in the Pacific Northwest.

* assure an adequate, efficient, economical, and reliable regional power supply.

* provide for widespread public, governmental, and user participation and consultation in (a) developing effective plans and programmes for energy conservation, renewables, other resources, and fish and wildlife protection, mitigation, and enhancement, (b) facilitating orderly regional power planning, and (c) providing environmental quality.

197

To achieve these goals, the Regional Energy Act created the Pacific Northwest Electric Power and Conservation Planning Council. This body - composed of two representatives from each of the four states - prepared a comprehensive Regional Electric Power and Conservation Plan, which was adopted in 1983. The Plan's most novel and significant feature, mandated by the Act, is that highest priority is given to conservation as a source of power to meet regional electrical needs. All cost-effective conservation measures (as well as renewable energy resources and cogeneration processes) must be utilised before any additional thermal (coal or nuclear) generating plants are constructed.

The Regional Conservation Plan specifies guidelines for conservation programmes to be conducted by the Bonneville Power Administration (the federal agency that controls all federally funded electricity generation and transmission in the region), state and local governments, and utilities. As an inducement for utilities to implement such programmes, BPA is authorized to give billing credits to utilities for all reductions in electricity consumption below specified levels. BPA can also impose a surcharge on the power costs of utilities that fail to enact adequate conservation programmes. Extensive research (Synergic Resources Corporation 1982) has demonstrated that such programmes can have tremendous economic benefits for both utilities and consumers in the residential as well as all other sectors of energy use. From the perspective of utilities, virtually all household weatherization improvements cost less than 3.5 cents per kilowatt hour, compared to the current estimated cost of about 8.0 cents for new thermal generating plants. From the perspective of households, most common weatherization actions pay for themselves in five or less years through reduced electricity bills.

*Previous research*

Since 1974, several hundred studies have been conducted on people's attitudes toward energy conservation and the extent to which they are taking conservation actions in their homes (Anderson and McDougall 1980; Olsen and Joerges 1983). In addition, a few studies have directly measured the amount of energy being saved by such actions (Pease 1982). None of that previous research tells us very much, however, about why consumers respond or fail to respond to community conservation programmes. How do household members perceive conservation programmes? How do they communicate with one another about saving energy? How do they manage their use of energy in the household? How do they decide whether or not to participate in energy conservation programmes? For what reasons do they make those decisions? We presently have few answers to such questions.

Three previous studies are relevant to the concern of this study. The first study was an evaluation of the Washington Water Power Company's 'Home Weatherization Programme' conducted by Rosa, Olsen, and others (1983). That research examined a wide variety of factors to identify the best predictors of interest in home weatherization, having a home energy audit, taking home weatherization actions, and accepting a no-interest weatherization loan from WWP. The strongest predictors of having participated in the WWP weatherization loan programme were the following factors: amount of education; size of the household; family members approve of weatherization; a belief that borrowing money to weatherize one's home is acceptable; a belief that having a lien on one's house to secure the loan is acceptable; and a clear and convincing presentation of the loan programme by the utility. The relevance of most of these variables is fairly self-evident, but they provide only limited insight into why households did or did not take part in the WWP programme.

Second, the Bonneville Power Administration conducted a Residential Weatherization Pilot Programme in the service areas of eleven small public utilities in the Pacific Northwest in 1980-1982. That programme provided free home energy audits to more than 6000 electrically heated homes, and no-interest loans for weatherization actions to almost 4000 of those homes. The programme was evaluated by Hirst et al. (1983), who compared three samples of households: (1) no audit or loan: (2) audit but no loan; and (3) audit and loan. They found no important differences between the first two samples, but households in the third sample had significantly higher education and income levels and were larger in size. Having an audit but not taking a loan produced no energy savings, but households which did weatherize with a loan reduced their electricity consumption by an average of approximately 4130 kilowatts per year. No attention was given in this research to the dynamic processes that determine why households did or did not respond to BPA's Residential Weatherization Pilot Programme.

Third, a study by Wilk and Wilhite (1983) focused explicitly on 'Household Energy Decision Making.' They conducted 'open-ended loosely structured' personal interviews with 30 households in Santa Cruz County, California, who had spent at least $100 on home weatherization actions, plus 30 households that had not taken any weatherization actions. These researchers tentatively concluded that 'external' factors such as informational campaigns or community programmes have little or no influence on the actual decision to invest in weatherization, and rational calculations about saving money do not affect the decision-making process in any direct way. They suggest that the decision to take weatherization actions is often sparked by an event that is totally unrelated to energy use, such as the birth of a child, a decision to remodel the house, or the last child leaving home. In other words, something has to occur in the household to move energy conservation from a 'latent' to an 'active' state.

**The study**

Because of the lack of relevant previous research, and also because this study was restricted to a single community in the United States that is quite atypical in its pervasive concern with conserving energy, the study reported here must be viewed as exploratory in nature.

*Purpose of the study*

This research focuses on the processes within households that determine how and why they respond or fail to respond to community energy conservation programmes. The purpose of the study is to explore the nature and dynamics of the linkages between energy conservation programmes and household conservation actions and energy savings. Two broad types of such linkages are examined: the various contexts that shape household energy consumption and conservation; and the manner in which households function as energy management systems.

The specific objectives of the study are to:

* discover which aspects of various household energy consumption contexts influence their participation or non-participation in a weatherization programme

* explore the ways in which households function as energy management systems and how those practices influence their decision to participate or not participate in a weatherization programme.

200

* determine the kinds and extent of household weatherization actions taken by participants and non-participants in the weatherization programme.

* measure the amount of energy savings achieved by households that have participated in the weatherization programme.

*Methodological procedures*

Eugene, Oregon, was selected as the site for this study because of the very extensive and innovative set of household conservation programmes that are presently being conducted in this community. An additional consideration was the willingness of the municipal utility – the Eugene Water and Electric Board (EWEB) – to make its conservation programme files and consumer electricity consumption records available for the research. EWEB provides electricity and water to approximately 125,000 residents in the City of Eugene and adjacent areas.

The study was limited to households that had already had a Home Energy Analysis performed by EWEB. To be selected for the study, a household also had to satisfy all the following requirements: a single-family residence; heated by electricity (entirely or primarily); continuous residency of the same occupants since 1 January 1981 and need at least three major weatherization improvements, as revealed by the Home Energy Analysis.

Two separate samples of EWEB customers were drawn randomly from company records, stratified by education and income levels to ensure considerable variation on those factors. Sample I consisted of 150 households that had received a Home Energy Analysis but at the time of the study had not weatherized their houses through the 'Buy Back' financial grant programme offered by EWEB. Sample II consisted of 150 households that had received a Home Energy Analysis and then had weatherized their house through the Buy Back Programme. Since all of the households in both samples were interested enough in conserving energy to have Home Energy Analysis, this sampling procedure held constant the variable of concern with energy conservation, so that the study could focus directly on programme participation. The two samples were also quite similar on many other characteristics. They paid the same rate for electricity, were subject to a legal mandate to weatherize their houses, held similar environmental values, had similar socioeconomic status, knew what weatherization improvements were needed in their houses, and had all taken simple conservation actions such as turning down the furnace thermostat.

All households in both samples were asked to do two things: to complete a written questionnaire consisting entirely of closed questions that was mailed to them; and take part in an hour long semi-structured personal interview with entirely open-ended questions that was conducted by a professional interviewer. In the approximately two thirds of the households that contained two opposite sex adults (72 percent in Sample I and 66 percent in Sample II), both adults were asked to complete a questionnaire separately and then to participate together in the interview. Their separate questionnaire responses were later combined with their joint interview data, so that the unit of analysis for the study was the household, not individual respondents.

Although several follow-up letters and personal telephone calls urged people to participate in the study, many of the households that completed the questionnaire said that they could not take the time to be interviewed. Consequently, complete data were obtained from only 29 households in Sample I, for a 19 percent completion rate, and from 57 households in Sample II, for a 38 percent completion rate. Given these low levels of response, neither sample can be considered statistically representative of all households in Eugene that have or have not participated in the utility's Buy Back Weatherization Programme. The purpose of this study, however, was not to generalize to the entire population of Eugene, but rather to examine in considerable depth the factors that affect household responses to energy conservation programmes.

Two kinds of information were also obtained from EWEB concerning all the households in both samples. All of the weatherization actions recommended by the Home Energy Analysis, as well as the actions taken by Sample II households through the Buy Back Programme, were recorded. With the permission of the households, their electricity consumption records were obtained for the period from January 1981 through August 1983. Since all of these homes are heated with electricity, those consumption data represent virtually their entire energy use (except for wood stoves or fireplaces).

## Programme description and analysis

Six types of instruments have generally been used by utilities and communities in the United States to promote household energy conservation: information dissemination, energy audits, low-interest or no-interest weatherization loans, partial-payment weatherization grants, full-payment grants, and mandatory energy efficiency building standards. The current conservation efforts in Eugene include all of these instruments except weatherization loans. (A previous loan programme was replaced in 1981 by the Buy Back Grant Programme.) In addition to very extensive dissemination of conservation information through all means of communication by the municipal utility, the city government, local neighbourhood associations, and Oregon State University, these efforts include the five programmes described below. The first four of these are conducted by the Eugene Water and Electric Board, while the fifth is a joint endeavour by EWEB and the City.

*Programme features*

* *Home Energy Analysis Programme:* This free residential energy inspection provides a computerized heat loss analysis of one's house; a detailed list of all the weatherization actions needed on the house to satisfy city, state, and BPA energy efficiency standards; the estimated cost of each recommended action; the estimated first-year kilowatt-hour savings of each action; and the cost-effectiveness of each action.

* *Residential Water Heater Wrap Programme:* EWEB installs insulation wraps on all electric water heaters in its service area at no charge. This is done routinely when a Home Energy analysis is performed. In addition, installation teams periodically go door-to-door through all residential sections of the community, offering to install a water heater wrap.

* *Buy Back Weatherization Programme:* To participate in this programme, a household must first have a Home Energy Analysis. At the time of that analysis the Buy Back Programme is explained to the household members. If the house is entirely or partially heated with electricity (which is the case in over half of all Eugene residences), the owner signs an agreement with EWEB specifying which weatherization improvements are approved by the utility and their maximum allowable cost (125 percent of the Analysis estimate). The work can be done by any licensed con-

tractor or by the owner. When the improvements are completed, EWEB inspects them to make sure that they have been done properly. EWEB then pays a large portion of the total cost of those weatherization actions. The exact amount of this payment is determined by a formula that provides 29.2 cents for each kilowatt hour of electricity that is expected to be saved by the weatherization actions during the first year. The utility is in effect 'buying back' the electricity that the household is expected to avoid consuming during that year. The average total cost of actions per household taken under this programme has been about $1750, of which the programme has paid on the average about $1350, or 77 percent. Thus, an average household has paid about $400 for all its weatherization actions.

* *Low Income Weatherization Programme:* This supplement to the Buy Back Programme provides additional funds for weatherization improvements to low income households. Households are eligible for this assistance if their total income is no more than 125 percent of the Federal poverty guideline. For these households, EWEB pays the entire cost of all recommended weatherization actions.

* *Residential Weatherization Ordinance:* This city ordinance is the first of its kind in the US. It specifies a number of energy weatherization standards that all existing single family to four family residences must satisfy. Those standards pertain to attic insulation and ventilation, floor insulation and vapour barriers, insulation of water heaters and heating ducts, and caulking and weatherstripping of exterior windows and doors. Beginning in 1985 the ordinance imposes a $500 fine for non-compliance, but it will be enforced only when a residence changes its utility service as a result of a sale or remodeling.

*Programme analysis*

Because all of the above energy conservation efforts are co-ordinated and integrated by EWEB, they can be analysed as a single programme, which for convenience we shall call the Eugene Residential Weatherization Programme.

*Goals and objectives:* The eventual goal of the Eugene Residential Weatherization Programme is to weatherize all residences in the EWEB service area so that they are as energy efficient as possible. This should significantly reduce residential electricity consumption

204

and thus reduce the amount of electricity the utility must provide. Its more explicit objectives are to weatherize one half of all homes in the service area by 1988; and ensure that all Eugene residences meet minimum energy efficiency standards at time of sale. The programme is limited to residences that are entirely or partially heated with electricity, which is about half the residences in the service area. Homes that are heated with gas or oil are excluded from the programme. It focuses entirely on improving the energy efficiency of residences, and does not attempt to alter the ways in which households use energy, their appliances (except wrapping water heaters), their overall life-styles, or the sources from which they obtain electricity. With the exception of additional financial assistance provided to low income households, the programme is not specifically targeted toward groups in the community. In particular, it is not adequate for renters. They can obtain a Home Energy Analysis, but only building owners can participate in the Buy Back Programme at the present time.

*Organization and implementation:* The Eugene Residential Weatherization Programme is conducted entirely at the level of the local community, although it follows guidelines established by the US Department of Energy, the Bonneville Power Administration, the Pacific Northwest Power Planning Council, and the State of Oregon. EWEB also co-operates closely with the Lane County Government (which includes Eugene) and the Eugene City Government. Responsibility for carrying out the programme rests with EWEB's Energy Conservation Centre. This Centre has a staff of about 50 people, including programme planners and co-ordinators, Home Energy Analysis technicians, customer service representatives, financial specialists, and clerical personnel. There is no direct citizen input into EWEB programme development or implementation, although the elected City Council approves EWEB's basic policies and adopted the Residential Weatherization Ordinance.

The Eugene City Council, the City Manager, the Director of EWEB, the Director of the Energy Conservation Centre, and the staff of the Centre are all highly committed to the importance of conserving energy. That commitment also pervades many community and neighbourhood organizations in Eugene, the local media, and a large proportion of the citizens. It is not an exaggeration to say that Eugene is one of the most conservation-minded communities in the United States.

All energy conservation programmes conducted in the Pacific Northwest must conform to the general guidelines specified in the Regional Power Plan and to detailed rules established by the Bonneville Power Administration. The Plan encourages utilities to adopt very comprehensive but flexible approaches to conservation. While the BPA rules are somewhat restrictive concerning the kinds of residences that can be included in the Eugene programme, EWEB has been able to overcome many of those restrictions by supplementing BPA financing with its own funds. And the Energy Conservation Centre has considerable latitude and flexibility in implementing the programme.

The Centre explains its programme to Eugene residents in a variety of ways, including announcements on radio and television, pamphlets included with utility bills, articles in the local newspaper, and talks given at meetings of local organizations. In addition, at the time a household has a Home Energy Analysis, the inspector thoroughly explains the Buy Back Programme and gives the household a pamphlet that tells how to participate. Interested customers can also come into the Centre for a personal meeting with a Customer Representative who will describe the programme and answer all questions. These communication procedures are very effective, as evidenced by the fact that there is always a long waiting list of households who want a Home Energy Analysis.

*Funding and costs:* In 1982, the Eugene Residential Weatherization Programme cost approximately $2,200,000, including both reimbursements to households and administrative expenses. The programme expanded during 1983, however, so that by May of that year (when this study began) the total cost for the first five months of 1983 had already been about $1,600,000. In both years, BPA provided about three quarters of those funds. The remaining programme costs are borne by EWEB, with supplements for low income households from state and federal funds. During the first five months of 1983, the average cost of weatherizing a residence was $1757, of which the Buy Back Programme paid $1343 and the consumer paid the remaining $414.

*Evaluations and accomplishments:* The Energy Conservation Centre continuously monitors the Residential Weatherization Programme to determine how well it is functioning. It does a 'process evaluation' of the programme to determine programme participation and costs. It also does an 'outcome evaluation' of the programme to ascertain the weatherization actions taken by households and their estimated electricity savings. Prior to this study, however, it had not made any effort to measure actual energy savings or other impacts on consumers. Therefore, its calculations of the cost effectiveness of the programme were based only on engineering estimates of how much electricity should theoretically be saved by the weatherization actions taken and not on the energy savings actually being achieved by participants.

By the time of this study in May 1983, approximately 6000 Eugene households had received a Home Energy Analysis. During the first five months of 1983, there were 3325 requests for Home Energy Analyses, 2172 analyses were conducted, and 5918 households were waiting for an analysis. Of the roughly 40,000 households in the EWEB service area, approximately 2500 had weatherized their house through the Buy Back Programme. During the first five months of 1983, 1341 residences were weatherized through the programme, of which 25 received low income funding. The weatherization improvements made through the programme as of May 1983 were estimated to be saving about 4600 kilowatt hours of electricity per house per year. (Average total household use of electricity is approximately 17,000 KWH per year.) Again, however, these figures are only engineering estimates, not direct measurements of actual energy savings.

**Programme participation**

Why do some households decide to participate in EWEB's Buy Back Weatherization Programme, while others do not? To discover what characteristics distinguish households in Sample I that had not participated (at the time of the study) from those in Sample II that had participated, two sets of data were obtained. These pertained to the contexts of household energy consumption (technical, macroeconomic, legal, community, and household) and to the dynamics of household management (maintenance, financial, energy, and decision making).

Table 7.1 reports the distributions of responses concerning energy consumption contexts taken from the written questionnaire. Data are given first for all respondents and then separately for programme non-participants and participants. Since these are not randomly selected samples, the percentages must be viewed with considerable caution. For simplicity, the following paragraphs discuss the principal findings in non-quantitative terms.

## Table 7.1
### Energy consumption contexts findings

*Note: All numbers are percentages (%)*

|  | All Respon-dents | Non Partici-pants | Partici-pants |
|---|---|---|---|
| **Technical Context** | | | |
| Age of house | | | |
| Less than 10 years | 12 | 17 | 7 |
| 10-24 years | 40 | 47 | 35 |
| 25-49 years | 39 | 35 | 43 |
| 50 or more years | 9 | 0 | 15 |
| Size of house | | | |
| Less than 1000 sq. feet | 14 | 10 | 17 |
| 1000 to 1499 sq. feet | 43 | 34 | 50 |
| 1500 to 1999 sq. feet | 24 | 34 | 17 |
| 2000 or more sq. feet | 19 | 22 | 16 |
| **Macro-Economic Context** | | | |
| Know current electricity rate | 29 | 32 | 26 |
| Know electricity rate has doubled in last 5 years | 30 | 28 | 33 |
| Understand the Buy Back Programme of cash grants | 82 | 82 | 82 |
| Know average total cost of weatherization per house | 21 | 22 | 20 |
| Know average cost of weatherization to households | 16 | 15 | 17 |

Table 7.1 continued

## Legal Context

| | | | |
|---|---|---|---|
| Understand the city's Weatherization Ordinance | 18 | 17 | 19 |
| Understand the Regional Power Plan | 8 | 5 | 10 |
| View city utility (EWEB) as more serious about conservation than city government state government, BPA, or the federal government | 60 | 60 | 60 |
| View city utility (EWEB) as more able to implement conservation than city government, state government, BPA, or the federal government | 47 | 49 | 46 |

## Community Context

| | | | |
|---|---|---|---|
| Length of residency in present house | | | |
|   Five or fewer years | 37 | 44 | 31 |
|   six to twelve years | 36 | 25 | 44 |
|   Thirteen or more years | 27 | 32 | 24 |
| Number of friends, neighbours, and relatives who have weatherized | | | |
|   None, one, or two | 18 | 19 | 17 |
|   Three or more | 80 | 78 | 81 |
| Discuss saving energy with friends, neighbours, or relatives | | | |
|   Few times a year or less | 54 | 41 | 64 |
|   Once a month or more often | 47 | 59 | 37 |
| Other people think weatherization is wise | | | |
|   Close friends think so | 85 | 78 | 90 |
|   Close relatives think so | 92 | 93 | 92 |
|   Immediate neighbours think so | 64 | 46 | 78 |

Table 7.1 continued

Number of local organizations attended regularly

| | | | |
|---|---|---|---|
| None | 44 | 51 | 38 |
| One or two | 47 | 37 | 56 |
| Three or more | 9 | 12 | 6 |

| | | | |
|---|---|---|---|
| If belong to an organization, it has promoted conservation | 25 | 18 | 31 |

Household Context

Age of oldest person in the household

| | | | |
|---|---|---|---|
| Under 30 years | 11 | 15 | 7 |
| 30-39 years | 32 | 34 | 30 |
| 40-49 years | 21 | 17 | 24 |
| 50-59 years | 15 | 20 | 11 |
| 60 or more years | 22 | 15 | 28 |

Marital status

| | | | |
|---|---|---|---|
| Single living alone | 22 | 10 | 31 |
| Single living with another adult | 7 | 10 | 6 |
| Married living alone | 2 | 3 | 2 |
| Married couple living together | 68 | 78 | 61 |

Number of people living in the household

| | | | |
|---|---|---|---|
| One person | 15 | 12 | 17 |
| Two people | 34 | 22 | 43 |
| Three people | 35 | 29 | 22 |
| Four or more people | 26 | 36 | 18 |

Education of best educated person in
the household

| | | | |
|---|---|---|---|
| Less than high school graduate | 6 | 8 | 6 |
| High school graduate | 15 | 13 | 17 |
| Some college | 35 | 35 | 35 |
| College graduate | 16 | 15 | 17 |
| Graduate study or degree | 28 | 30 | 26 |

Total annual household income

| | | | |
|---|---|---|---|
| Less than $15,000 | 22 | 21 | 24 |
| $15,000 to $24,999 | 33 | 29 | 35 |
| $25,000 to $34,999 | 30 | 37 | 26 |
| $35,000 or more | 15 | 13 | 16 |

Table 7.1 continued

Total monthly housing costs

| | | | |
|---|---|---|---|
| Less than $200 | 20 | 15 | 24 |
| $200 to $399 | 38 | 38 | 38 |
| $400 to $599 | 29 | 38 | 23 |
| $600 or more | 13 | 10 | 16 |

Household financial condition during last
5 years

| | | | |
|---|---|---|---|
| Declined | 50 | 67 | 37 |
| Remained about the same | 9 | 8 | 9 |
| Improved | 41 | 26 | 52 |

Areas in which the household reduced
expenditures during last 5 years

| | | | |
|---|---|---|---|
| New appliances | 34 | 48 | 24 |
| New furniture | 34 | 48 | 24 |
| New car | 26 | 32 | 20 |
| Clothing | 23 | 25 | 22 |
| Food | 14 | 15 | 13 |
| Home improvements | 40 | 50 | 33 |
| New house | 21 | 32 | 13 |
| Leisure | 37 | 45 | 32 |
| Vacations | 43 | 52 | 35 |
| Education | 13 | 22 | 6 |
| Medical care | 16 | 20 | 13 |

Household financial condition at present

| | | | |
|---|---|---|---|
| Serious problems or some difficulty | 15 | 23 | 9 |
| Managing adequately | 45 | 46 | 44 |
| Fairly or quite comfortable | 40 | 38 | 46 |

Amount household could spend for
weatherization

| | | | |
|---|---|---|---|
| Less than $250 | 14 | 20 | 10 |
| $250 to $500 | 19 | 15 | 23 |
| $501 to $750 | 35 | 23 | 45 |
| More than $750 | 14 | 25 | 6 |

Table 7.1 continued

Presently able to or did pay cash for
weatherization

| | | | |
|---|---|---|---|
| Able to or did pay cash | 65 | 47 | 79 |
| Would have to or did borrow money | 24 | 30 | 19 |
| Couldn't pay case and wouldn't borrow | 7 | 15 | 0 |

Desired payback period for weatherization

| | | | |
|---|---|---|---|
| Less than three years | 26 | 35 | 19 |
| Three to five years | 34 | 23 | 43 |
| Five to seven years | 19 | 20 | 19 |
| More than seven years | 15 | 10 | 18 |

Expected household financial condition during
next 5 years

| | | | |
|---|---|---|---|
| Will decline | 24 | 23 | 25 |
| Will remain about the same | 34 | 41 | 28 |
| Will improve | 40 | 33 | 45 |

Agree with pro-environmental values

| | | | |
|---|---|---|---|
| Earth has limited room and resources | 82 | 84 | 81 |
| We must live in harmony with nature | 78 | 85 | 72 |
| Environment should be preserved | 49 | 47 | 51 |

Approve of governmental growth limitations

| | | | |
|---|---|---|---|
| Economic growth should be limited | 47 | 35 | 57 |
| Population growth should be limited | 51 | 41 | 58 |

General attitudes toward energy conservation

| | | | |
|---|---|---|---|
| Favour conservation over production | 79 | 77 | 80 |
| Conservation should be national policy | 84 | 84 | 85 |

Specific attitudes toward energy conservation

| | | | |
|---|---|---|---|
| Place great personal importance on it | 60 | 51 | 66 |
| Feel personal responsibility for it | 32 | 25 | 38 |

*Technical context*

For households, the most important features of the technical context affecting their energy consumption pertain to the physical characteristics of the dwelling unit. This study is limited to single-family houses that are entirely or largely heated with electricity, so that the two critical factors of type of dwelling and type of heating are held constant. Two important characteristics on which these houses vary considerably are age and size. Many more non-participants live in houses that are less than 25 years old, while more participants live in houses older than that. And non-participants tend to live in somewhat larger houses (2000 or more square feet), while participants are more likely to live in smaller houses.

*Macro-economic context*

Since all of the households in the study purchase their electricity from the Eugene Water and Electricity Board at the same rate of $0.26 per kilowatt hour plus a flat service charge, there is no variation in that aspect of their macro-economic context. There are no noteworthy differences between the two samples in their knowledge of that rate, its increase during recent years, the purpose of the Buy Back Programme, the total average cost of weatherizing a typical Eugene house, or the cost of that weatherization to a typical household through the Programme. In short, the macro-economic context does not appear to influence participation in the EWEB Programme.

*Legal context*

Objectively, the legal context of energy consumption is the same for most of the respondents in the study. Except for the small proportion of them who live outside the City of Eugene or are tenants, all of these people are subject to the Eugene Residential Weatherization Ordinance, although relatively few of them correctly understand it. More broadly, all of them are also covered by the Pacific Northwest Regional Power Plan that gives highest priority to energy conservation. Again, very few people are aware of these provisions. Subjectively, the Eugene Water and Electric Board is viewed by a large proportion of the respondents in both samples as the agency that is most serious about promoting energy conservation and is best able to , implement conservation programmes. No aspects of the legal context therefore appear to influence participation in the programme.

## Community context

A moderate length of residency in one's present house (six to twelve years) is most common among programme participants, while non-participants are more likely to have either shorter or longer residency.

Programme participants are no more likely than non-participants to know other people who have weatherized their homes. However, participants tend to discuss energy conservation less often with friends, neighbours, and relatives than do non-participants. Participants are more likely, however, to believe that their friends and neighbours (although not their relatives) think that weatherization is a wise action.

Membership and regular attendance in local clubs and organizations (excluding a church or synagogue) is considerably more common among programme participants than non-participants. Moreover, among those people who are active in a local club or organization, many more participants than non-participants say that it has recently done something to promote energy conservation.

## Household context

On the average, programme participants are about six years older than non-participants. Participants are especially likely to be age 60 or older. More participants than non-participants are single persons living alone, while more non-participants are married couples living together. Households of participants frequently consist of just one or two people (often one adult and a child), whereas those of non-participants more often contain three or four people. On the average, participating households are slightly smaller (2.7 persons) than non-participating households (2.9 persons). These respondents are considerably better educated than the general population, but the two samples do not differ in their average educational attainment. In terms of annual total household income, programme participants are underrepresented in the $25,000-$34,999 bracket, but overall the median incomes of the two samples are almost identical, at about $24,000. A similar pattern is observed with total monthly housing costs. Participants are underrepresented in the $400-$599 category, but the median amounts for both samples are very similar, at about $430.

Dramatic differences are observed between the samples, however, in regard to their household financial condition during the past five years. Non-participants are twice as likely as participants to say that their financial condition has declined, whereas participants are twice as likely to say that it has improved. When the respondents were asked if they had reduced their expenditures for eleven kinds of goods and services during the past five years - appliances, furniture, a car, clothing, food, home improvements, a new house, leisure, vacations, education, and medical care - programme participants were less likely to report reduced expenditures in each of these categories. A similar pattern can be seen in the current financial conditions of these people. Non-participants are more than twice as likely as participants to say that they are having serious financial problems or some difficulty making ends meet financially. In contrast, many more programme participants say that they are living either fairly or quite comfortably. This condition has direct consequences for household weatherization. Almost twice as many participants as non-participants state they could afford to spend $750 or more for weatherization improvements at the present time. Moreover, when non-participants were asked if they were presently able to pay cash and participants were asked if they had paid cash for their portion of weatherization costs through the Buy Back Programme, the participants gave a positive response almost twice as often as the non-participants. Non-participants were much more likely to say that they would have to borrow the money or could not pay cash and would not consider borrowing the necessary funds. Another aspect of household finances relevant to weatherization actions is the length of the payback period desired for such investments. Non-participating households are more likely to want a very short payback period of three years or less, while most of the participating households are willing to wait five or more years for weatherization investments to pay for themselves. A final indicator of the extent to which households feel financially secure is their expectations concerning their financial condition during the next five years. Programme participants are considerably more likely to believe that their financial condition will improve, while non-participants expect theirs to remain about the same.

A large proportion of the respondents in both samples hold strong pro-environmental values, which may help to explain why they all requested a Home Energy Analysis. However, participating households more often approve of governmental policies and programmes to protect environment by limiting economic and population growth. The majority of non-participating households disapprove of such policies and programmes. When the idea of conserving energy is discussed in general terms, it is as strongly favoured by non-participants as by programme participants. When this topic is discussed in more specific and personal terms, however, participants are more likely to say that conservation is of great importance to them personally and that they feel a personal responsibility to help alleviate the energy problem.

*Household management dynamics:* Most of the questions about households management were asked in the personal interviews and recorded verbatim, and hence could not be easily quantified. The following paragraphs present these findings thematically (with the exception of one table), emphasizing differences between programme participants and non-participants.

*Household roles:* The manner in which various roles and responsibilities are divided among the members of a household is a basic aspect of all household dynamics. The following discussion is limited to households containing two adults. Primary responsibility for physical maintenance tasks is taken by the man in two-thirds of the non-participating households, but in only slightly more than one-third of the participating households. Conversely, shared responsibility for these tasks is more common among programme participants. The role of initiating ideas about doing new or different things concerning the house is more frequently assumed by the woman in non-participating households, while this role is more commonly shared among participants. Decisions about major expenditures for the household are made jointly by both partners in nine-tenths of all households. Joint decision making is slightly more common in participating households. Both partners are equally interested in taking home conservation actions in only about half the households. This is considerably more common among programme participants, however. In contrast, men in non-participating households are twice as likely as those in participating households to be the person most interested in conservation actions. Simple energy-saving tasks - such as turning off unwanted lights, setting the thermostat, and closing curtains at night - are done by both partners in two-thirds of all households. There are no differences between the two samples in this regard.

*Energy communication:* A second fundamental aspect of all household dynamics is the manner in which members communicate about the functioning of the household, including energy consumption and conservation. Again, only two-adult households are

216

described here. Equal knowledge by the partners about energy use in the home and ways of reducing energy consumption is considerably more frequent in participating households. In non-participating households, the man is much more likely to be more knowledgeable about energy use. Only about one-third of the couples discuss energy issues and problems at least once a week, while about two-fifths of them say that these topics are discussed approximately once a month. Quite interestingly, couples who have not participated in the Buy Back Programme report having these discussions somewhat more frequently than those who have participated in the programme. When households talk about energy issues and problems, men often dominate these discussions in both samples. A large proportion of those discussions about energy matters result in one or both of the partners suggesting that the household take some conservation actions. The two samples are also similar in this pattern.

*Energy Decision Making:* A third fundamental aspect of all two-person household dynamics is the process through which the members reach decisions about matters such as taking home weatherization actions. The initial decision to request a Home Energy Analysis was made jointly by both partners in two-thirds of these households, and in half of the remaining households one person advocated the idea but both people discussed it. This process is the same in both samples. Only one of the couples in the study said that they disagreed over the decision to have a Home Energy Analysis. Among programme participants, the two decisions to have a Home Energy Analysis and to take part in Buy Back were made simultaneously in half the households. Four-fifths of those simultaneous decisions were made by the partners together. The other half of the participating households decided to take part in Buy Back after having had a Home Energy Analysis. Almost nine-tenths of those subsequent decisions to weatherize the house were made jointly by both partners. Again, only one of the couples said that they disagreed sharply over the decision to take part in Buy Back. Regardless of when the decision to participate in the Buy Back Programme was made, however, about half of the couples obtained information from sources outside the household before reaching their decision. The most common sources of such information were newspaper and magazine articles, literature distributed by EWEB, and personal friends.

To obtain an overall picture of the process through which couples reach decisions about saving energy - regardless of whether or not they had participated in the Buy Back Programme - they were asked to think about all the household conservation actions they had taken during the past two years and to indicate who generally made those decisions. By far the most common pattern is joint decision making by both partners, which occurred in two-thirds of the households. There is a noticeable difference between the two samples in this decision making, however. Joint decision making occurred in three quarters of the participating households, but in slightly less than three fifths of the non-participating households. Within both samples, joint decision making about energy conservation is much more frequent among households in the middle income bracket of $20,000 to $29,999 per year than in households with either lower or higher annual incomes. Joint decision making is also most common among people under age 40, and least common among people aged 40-49.

*Factors influencing conservation decisions:* A fourth fundamental aspect of household dynamics affecting conservation programme participation is the set of factors that influence decisions about weatherization actions. These findings include both two-adult and one-adult households.

All respondents were first asked about the main reasons that led to their decision to request a Home Energy Analysis. By far the most important factor was (1) a desire to same money by reducing their electric bills, which was mentioned by over three-fifths of the households. Two other important factors that were each mentioned by one third of the households were (2) a desire to have more comfortable and/or healthy home, and (3) a responsibility to help alleviate the national energy problem and/or conserve scarce natural resources. Next in importance was (4) finding out if the household could qualify for the Buy Back Programme, which was mentioned by nearly one quarter of them. The two factors of (5) obtaining technical information about how to reduce household energy consumption, and (6) maintaining the quality and resale value of the house, were each expressed by one-sixth of the respondents. Non-participating households were somewhat more likely to say that immediately reducing their electric bills was a reason for requesting a Home Energy Analysis, while all the other factors were mentioned more frequently by programme participants - especially saving energy and/or resources and obtaining technical information about weatherization.

Participating households were then asked about the factors that had influenced their decision to take part in the Buy Back Programme. Over four fifths of them said that the financial assistance available rough the programme was a major factor in their decision to participate. The second most common factor mentioned was a desire to keep their future electric bills as low as possible, which was expressed by over one third of the households. Nearly one fifth of them mentioned other features of the Buy Back Programme, such as the energy management planning assistance and the post-action inspections provided by EWEB, and the comprehensive nature of the Buy Back Programme. In addition, a personal belief in the importance of energy conservation was cited by one tenth of the respondents, while another one tenth wanted to preserve the resale value of their house. Beyond these specific factors, more than one quarter of the people said they believed energy conservation was so important that they would have weatherized their house even if the Buy Back Programme had not been available.

Table 7.2
Factors influencing the decision to weatherize

Average Importance Score[*]

| Factors | All Respondents | Non-participants | Participants |
|---|---|---|---|
| Keep energy bills lower in the long run | 2.4 | 2.2 | 2.5 |
| Immediately lower energy bills | 2.4 | 2.6 | 2.3 |
| Improve personal comfort of home | 2.4 | 2.4 | 2.4 |
| Protect resale value of the house | 1.2 | 1.2 | 1.2 |
| Reduce environmental pollution | 1.2 | 1.4 | 1.1 |
| Avoid constructing more power plants | 1.3 | 0.9 | 1.4 |
| Help solve the energy problem | 1.1 | 1.1 | 1.1 |
| Make the house more healthy | 1.1 | 1.4 | 0.9 |
| Preserve oil and gas deposits | 1.0 | 1.0 | 1.0 |
| Be a good community member | 0.7 | 0.6 | 0.7 |

[*] Most important=4,
Very important=3,
Important=2,
Somewhat important=1,
Not important=0

All respondents were next given a list of ten potential benefits of household weatherization, as shown in Table 7.2, and were asked to indicate how important each of those factors had been in their decisions to take whatever weatherization actions they had done, either with or without the Buy Back Programme. The first column in Table 7.2 gives mean scores for all households on a scale ranging from 4 = most important factor to 0 = not an important factor. The second column gives mean scores for non-participants and the third column gives scores for programme participants.

Overall, reducing household energy costs immediately and in the long run are clearly the most important factors in most people's decision to weatherize their house. Other personal concerns - home comfort, resale value of the house, and health - are also quite important considerations for a large proportion of the respondents in this study. Somewhat surprising, however, is the considerable importance given to public concerns and problems such as avoiding constructing more power plants, reducing environmental pollution, solving the energy problem, and preserving oil and natural gas deposits. Buy Back participants have somewhat higher scores than non-participants on keeping energy bills lower in the long run and avoiding constructing more power plants. In contrast, non-participating households score higher than participants on immediately lowering energy bills, reducing environmental pollution, and making the house more healthy.

In addition to the goal of lowering one's household electric bills, several other financial considerations may also be important in deciding whether or not to take weatherization actions. Four of these considerations are the total cost of the actions, regardless of who pays for them; the actual cost of the actions to the household; whether the household has enough cash in hand to pay its portion of the costs, or has to borrow those funds; and the cost effectiveness of the actions, in terms of how long it will take to repay their cost through lower electric bills. All four of these financial considerations are considerably more critical for non-participating households than for programme participants. Especially noteworthy is the finding that having enough cash in hand to pay for these actions is quite important to non-participating households, whereas programme participants are much more willing to borrow the funds for their portion of the costs under the Buy Back Programme (and a number of them said that they had indeed borrowed the money). Also striking is the fact that the cost effectiveness of weatherization actions is by far the least important consideration among all the respondents - but especially for Buy Back participants. Many participants said that conserving energy is so important that they were completely unconcerned abut the lengths of the payback periods for the actions they had taken.

Because of the nature of the samples in this study and the request of the sponsoring agency that the analysis be interpretive rather than statistical in nature, the findings were examined in a qualitative manner. This analysis sought basic themes that would help to explain why some households have participated in the Eugene Residential Weatherization programme and others have not. Seven basic themes emerged from this analysis. They do not express absolute or drastic differences between programme participants and non-participants, but they do provide several insights into the contextual and dynamic influences that likely influence the decision to weatherize one's home.

The *first theme* which characterizes Buy Back participants more than non-participants is that their current living conditions probably impose fewer routine homemaking demands on them. On the average, they have as much total income as non-participants and their monthly housing costs are no higher. Consequently, because of their smaller household size they have somewhat more income per person ($8900 compared to $8300 for non-participants), and presumably more resources for household expenses. They also have fewer children living at home and in many cases they consist of a single adult. They are older, on the average, and a considerable number of them are retired. In addition, their houses are somewhat smaller and older and hence may not require as much time and effort for tasks such as furnishing, decorating and gardening.

The *second theme* observed among programme participants is a strong personal commitment to conservation as a vital goal. These people are more likely to have an ideological commitment to conserving energy, to favour governmental action to deal with ecological problems, to be personally concerned about helping to alleviate the national energy problem, and to support mandatory conservation programmes. They also want to conserve energy regardless of the cost involved or the cost-effectiveness of those actions. In addition, a number of them said that conservation was so important to them that they would have taken weatherization actions on their own even if the Buy Back Programme had not been available.

The *third theme* is holding a long-term rather than an immediate perspective on the benefits of energy conservation. Programme participants are more concerned about keeping electric costs lower in the long run and less concerned about immediately lowering their bills. They are not very concerned about the immediate direct costs of weatherization actions are are willing to accept a longer payback period for those actions. A desire to protect scarce natural resources for future generations is also important to them.

The *fourth theme* is joint sharing of household tasks and energy decision making. Participating couples tend to share home maintenance and upkeep tasks, they jointly initiate ideas for improving the house, and they tend to make joint decisions about major expenditures. These couples are also more often equally interested in and knowledgeable about ways of saving energy, and they jointly make decisions about most weatherization actions. One finding that does not at first appear to support this theme is their relative infrequency of discussing energy issues and problems in the home. A possible interpretation of that finding is that when couples are in full agreement about the importance of weatherization they feel no need to frequently discuss the matter in order to reach a joint decision. This interpretation is supported by the observation made by all of the interviewers that the couples who had participated in the programme rarely disagreed in any way about the importance of taking conservation actions or the wisdom of their decision to weatherize.

The *fifth theme* that emerged from this analysis is the importance of indirect or impersonal influences from others to take conservation actions. Buy Back participants are more likely to believe that their friends and neighbours approve of conservation actions, to belong to community organizations that have taken steps to promote energy conservation actions, and to be concerned about complying with the city's Residential Weatherization Ordinance. Personal discussions about energy conservation with friends, relatives, and neighbours, meanwhile, are less common among participants than non-participants.

The *sixth theme* is that most households are taking weatherization actions in an intentional effort to reduce their energy consumption and to lower their electric bills, especially in the long run. In other words, they are directly addressing the problem of how to use less energy in the home. They are not merely taking conservation actions as a consequence of some other decision such as remodelling the house, as argued by Wilk and Wilhite (1983). Moreover, most Buy Back participants explicitly stated that their primary reasons for taking part in the programme were to obtain the financial assistance it offered for weatherization and to lower their electric bills in anticipation of rising electricity rates in the future. Nevertheless, since many programme participants are not greatly concerned about the immediate costs of weatherization, their decision to take part in the programme does not

222

appear to rest on direct cost-benefit calculations.

The *seventh theme* is that Buy Back participants appear to be more financially secure than non-participants. Participants are less likely to say that their financial condition has deteriorated rather than improved during the past five years, and they are less likely to have reduced their expenditures for all kinds of goods and services during that time. Participants are also less likely than non-participants to report having financial difficulties at the present time. They are more likely to say that they could presently afford to spend up to $750 for weatherization actions, and hence are less concerned about the direct costs of weatherization. In addition, many non-participants stated explicitly that the main reasons they had not taken advantage of the Buy Back Programme was that they did not have the cash available to pay their portion of the costs, and they could not consider borrowing those funds. Although the study did not investigate factors underlying the greater financial security of programme participants, one likely explanations that these people are better managers of their household finances. That is, they may be more skilful at making a household budget, keeping their expenses within that budget, and having some cash reserves on hand for unusual expenses such as weatherization improvements.

**Programme impacts**

We turn now to the question of how participation in the Eugene Household Weatherization Programme has affected these households. Three kinds of impacts are examined here: weatherization actions taken, daily living patterns, and electricity savings.

*Weatherization actions*

What types of weatherization actions have both participants and non-participants have taken in their homes? Table 7.3 includes only actions taken during 1982 and 1983 while the Buy Back Programme was in effect, but the following section includes actions taken prior to that period.

## Table 7.3
### Percentages of participants and non-participants taking various conservation actions during 1982-83

|  | P | NP |
|---|---|---|
| Caulking and weatherstripping: | 98 | 31 |
| Wrapping water pipes and/or hot air ducts: | 91 | 7 |
| Adding attic insulation: | 88 | 7 |
| Installing floor insulation: | 88 | 7 |
| Installing storm windows: | 32 | 10 |
| Wrapping the water heater: | 72 | 52 |
| Installing wall insulation: | 32 | 3 |
| Installing a clock thermostat: | 11 | 0 |
| Installing a solar water heater: | 5 | 0 |

The only actions taken by any sizable proportion of non-participating households have been caulking and weatherstripping (which is very inexpensive) and wrapping the water heater (which is done by EWEB as part of the Home Energy Analysis). Among participating households, large proportions have taken all the common weatherization actions except installing storm doors and wall insulation. Few of those households, however, have taken the less common actions of installing a clock thermostat or a solar water heater.

*Number of actions taken*

How many weatherization actions have been taken by various kinds of households in both samples? These tabulations are limited to the same ten weatherization improvements discussed above, but are not restricted to recent actions. Table 7.4 reports four different mean figures for each sample: the number of actions taken prior to 1982; the number of actions recommended in the Home Energy Analysis; the percent of those recommended actions that have been taken; and the number of all actions taken during 1982-83. In addition to total figures for each sample, the table also gives breakdowns by three household characteristics: the number of adults in the household; the age of the respondents; and annual household income.

## Table 7.4

Household weatherization actions among buy back non-participants and participants by selected household characteristics

### Mean Weatherization Actions Per Household

| Household Characteristics | Non-Participants | | | | | Participants | | | | |
|---|---|---|---|---|---|---|---|---|---|---|
| | Prior to 1982 | Recommended by Analysis | % of Recommended Actions Taken | Total Actions Taken in 1982-83 | N | Prior to 1982 | Recommended by Analysis | % of Recommended Actions taken | Total Actions Taken in 1982-83 | N |
| Total Sample | 1.7 | 5.4 | 14% | 1.3 | 29 | 0.9 | 6.0 | 85% | 6.1 | 57 |
| Number of Adults | | | | | | | | | | |
| Two | 1.9 | 5.4 | 13% | 1.2 | 21 | 1.0 | 5.9 | 87% | 6.2 | 37 |
| One | 1.4 | 5.5 | 14% | 1.6 | 8 | 0.7 | 6.1 | 82% | 5.8 | 20 |
| Age of Respondents | | | | | | | | | | |
| 20-39 | 2.0 | 5.2 | 16% | 1.2 | 17 | 1.1 | 6.2 | 88% | 5.9 | 19 |
| 40-59 | 1.1 | 6.4 | 14% | 1.8 | 9 | 0.4 | 6.3 | 90% | 6.7 | 21 |
| 60 or older | ---* | ---* | ---* | ---* | 3 | 1.3 | 5.9 | 88% | 5.8 | 16 |
| Household Income | | | | | | | | | | |
| Less than $20,000 | 1.5 | 5.3 | 13% | 1.4 | 11 | 1.0 | 5.9 | 87% | 6.0 | 20 |
| $20,000-$29,999 | 1.9 | 4.3 | 0% | 0.6 | 9 | 0.7 | 6.2 | 93% | 6.7 | 23 |
| $30,000 or more | 1.7 | 8.0 | 33% | 2.4 | 7 | 0.7 | 6.3 | 78% | 5.5 | 11 |

*Too few cases to compute meaningful statistics.

The first line in the table unequivocally indicates that programme participants have taken many more weatherization actions than non-participants. On the average, non-participants took somewhat more actions prior to 1982 (1.7) than did participants (0.9). Consequently, the number of actions recommended by the Home Energy Analysis was slightly greater for participants (6.0) than for non-participants (5.4). During 1982-83, however, non-participants took only 14 percent of the actions recommended by their Home Energy Analysis, whereas participants took 85 percent of those recommended actions. In other words, non-participants took a total of only 1.3 actions on the average, while participants took 6.1 actions on the average.

Among non-participants in the programme, two-adult households took somewhat more actions than one-adult households prior to 1982. However, the number of actions recommended by the Home Energy Analysis was about the same for both types of households, as was the proportion of recommended actions taken. Nevertheless, one-adult households took slightly more total actions than did two-adult households during 1982-83. Among Buy Back participants, two-adult households also took somewhat more actions prior to 1982, but the number of recommended actions was about the same for both types of households. In addition, two-adult households took a slightly higher proportion of recommended actions and a greater number of total actions during 1982-83 than did one-adult households. This finding suggests that the Buy Back Programme is marginally more effective among two-adult households than among one-adult households.

Among non-participants, people under 40 took more actions prior to 1982 than did middle-aged people, and consequently had fewer recommended actions. The rate of completing those actions is about the same for both age categories. During 1982-83, younger people took fewer actions than middle-aged people. Among Buy Back participants, people over age 60 took the greatest number of actions prior to 1982, and middle-aged people took far fewer actions. Older people had slightly fewer actions recommended in their Home Energy Analysis because of those prior actions. Age is not related to the proportion of recommended actions taken by participating households. However, middle-aged people took a greater total number of actions during 1982-83 than did either younger or older people. Overall, therefore, age does not appear to be a useful predictor to taking conservation actions.

Among non-participants, households in the middle income category of $20,000-29,999 per year took slightly more actions prior to 1982 than did other people, and consequently had fewer recommended actions in their Home Energy Analysis. Households with incomes above $30,000 had a surprisingly large number of recommended actions, and they subsequently undertook a fair number of them. In contrast, middle income households took none of their recommended actions. Overall, therefore, high income households took the most number of actions during 1982-83 and middle income households took the fewest total number of actions. Among Buy Back participants, households with incomes under $20,000 took slightly more actions prior to 1982 than did those at other income levels. Consequently, they had slightly fewer recommended actions in their Home Energy Analysis. Income level has very different effects on the rate of taking recommended actions among participants than among non-participants, however. High income participating households took far fewer recommended actions and fewer total actions during 1982-1983 than did middle or low income households. Middle income households completed the greatest proportion of recommended actions and took the largest total number of actions during this period. Theses findings indicate that the Buy Back Programme is most effective among households with incomes between $20,000 and $29,999, and least effective among households with incomes greater than $30,000 per year.

*Daily living patterns*

Most of the households identified at least one or two effects of the conservation actions they had taken on their daily lives and routines. The majority of those effects are viewed by them as beneficial. For example, about one-fifth of the households said that conservation had become a total way of life for them, involving such activities as recycling various items; closing off and not heating unused rooms; maintaining and keeping an old car rather than buying a new one; carpooling, riding a bicycle, or walking to work and other activities; or moving to a smaller house. This kind of energy conserving lifestyle is twice as common among programme participants as non-participants. Another beneficial effect of weatherization is having the house warmer and more comfortable, which was also mentioned much more frequently by participants.

Several other effects of conservation on these people's daily lives were viewed in a relatively neutral light. The most frequently mentioned of these neutral effects were hanging laundry outside rather than using the dryer, which is done by almost one quarter of the households; wearing more sweaters and other warm clothing, which is done by about one-fifth of the respondents; using the dishwasher less, which was mentioned by about one-twentieth of the respondents; and taking showers rather than baths, which was also mentioned by about one-twentieth of the people. Only a few of the households indicated that they had experienced any undesirable effects from their conservation actions. Three people said that they were tired of nagging or being nagged about saving energy; two people complained that their house was now too cold; one person said it was too air-tight; and one person didn't like having to clean the additional storm windows.

*Electricity savings*

The electricity consumption of households that had participated in the Buy Back Programme were divided into two periods: a 'pre-action Period A' consisting of the 12 months preceding the completion of their weatherization actions; and a 'post-action Period B' consisting of all months following those actions up to the time of the study in August 1983. (The post-action period varied between 8 and 12 months, depending on when the actions were taken. Ideally, it should have been a full 12 months for all households, but because the programme was so new some of the households were not able to participate in it until late 1982 or early 1983. However, the method of computation described below compensated for the varying lengths of the post-action period). The consumption data of non-participating households were arbitrarily divided into 'Period A' from July 1981 through June 1982, and 'Period B' from July 1982 through June 1983.

With all households, total electricity consumption during each of the two time periods was divided by the total number of 'heating degree days' during that period to ascertain the amount of electricity used per degree day. (A heating degree day is a day in which the mean temperature is less than 65 F, multiplied by the number of degrees of mean temperature below that base temperature. Hence a day in which the mean temperature is 50 F is counted as 15 heating degree days, and three days with that mean temperature constitute 45 heating degree days.) With this procedure, it is possible to hold constant variations in outside temperature over a period of time and to measure the amount of electricity consumed by a household for each heating degree day regardless of the weather. This procedure also has the benefits of enabling us to express energy savings as a percentage increase in the energy efficiency of the house, and compensating for the varying lengths of the post-action period with Sample II.

How much electricity has been saved as a result of weatherization actions taken by households that participated in the Buy Back Programme? Expressed differently, to what extent have those actions improved the energy efficiency of these people's houses? Non-participating households in Sample I are used only as comparison cases in this analysis, to hold constant electricity savings resulting from weatherization actions taken outside the Buy Back Programme for reasons other than the financial benefits of the programme. Those reasons might include changing perceptions of the energy problem, rising electricity rates, and other conservation programmes such as or state and regional energy information programme. Sample I provides an excellent comparison group for this purpose, since all of those people are concerned about conserving energy and are aware of what actions are needed to improve the energy efficiency of their house as a result of their Home Energy Analysis.

*Overall findings*

The results of the analysis are reported in Table 7.5. Buy Back participants used an average of 4.32 kilowatt hours of electricity per degree day (KWH/DD) during Period A prior to taking weatherization actions through the programme. This figure varies considerably among households, however, from under 2 KWH/DD to over 8 KWH/DD. During Period B, after taking weatherization actions through the programme, their use decreased to an average of only 3.91 KWH/DD. This is a mean reduction of -0.41 KWH/DD between the two time periods. That amount of electricity savings represents an average increase of 9 percent in the energy efficiency of their houses.

We must also, however, take account of the energy savings realized by the non-participating households. Their use averaged 4.15 KWH/DD during Period A, or slightly less than participating households. This difference is not surprising, since the Home Energy Analyses found that houses of non-participants were initially a little more energy efficient than houses of participants. What is surprising is the finding that although non-participating households typically took only one weatherization action, they nevertheless reduced their electricity consumption during Period B to an average of 3.89 KWH/DD, which is only slightly less than the reduction by programme participants. The mean energy savings of non-participating households was therefore -0.26 KWH/DD, which represents an average increase of 6 percent in the energy efficiency of their houses. In other words, despite the fact that Buy Back participants took an average of six weatherization actions through the programme, their electricity savings were only marginally greater than the savings achieved by non-participants. These findings are obviously not encouraging for advocates of household weatherization programmes.

Table 7.5
Electricity savings by buy back participants
& non-participants

| Consumption Measures | P | NP |
|---|---|---|
| Period A: mean KWH per degree day[*] | 4.15 | 4.32 |
| Period B: mean KWH per degree day[**] | 3.89 | 3.91 |
| Mean reduction: KWH per degree day | -0.26 | -0.41 |
| Percent (%) increased energy efficiency | 6 | 9 |

[*] For Sample II, the 12 months prior to completing their weatherization actions. For Sample I, from July 1981 through June 1982.

[**] For Sample II, the 8-12 months after EWEB's inspection of their weatherization actions, depending on when that occurred. For Sample I, from July 1982 through June 1983.

The mean reduction in electricity consumption of -0.41 KWH/DD that occurred among participating households can be translated into average annual electricity and monetary savings for those households. Assuming 5000 heating degree days per year (which is approximately the Eugene norm), this improved energy efficiency should reduce their annual electricity consumption by approximately 2050 KWH per household. At the current EWEB rate of 2.6 cents/KWH, their annual household electric bills should be reduced by about $53 on the average. At that rate, the payback period for the approximate average total cost of $1750 per house for weatherization will be about 34 years, not considering interest or inflation. If the household pays $400 of those costs under the Buy Back Programme, its payback period will be about 7.5 years.

*Increased consumption households*

The mean electricity savings of -0.41 KWH/DD by programme participants masks considerable variation among households in reduced electricity consumption. The highest reduction observed among those households was -3.19 KWH/DD, while two households showed no change between the two time periods. More critically, 10 households increased their electricity use after weatherizing. In five of them, the increased consumption was less than 0.50 KWH/DD. But in the other five cases the increase was considerable, with the largest being 3.81 KWH/DD.

If those ten cases of increased electricity consumption are removed from Sample II, the average energy savings of the remaining cases increases considerably. The mean reduction in electricity consumption between the two time periods for those remaining cases is -0.77 KWH/DD, which represents an average increase of 18 percent in energy efficiency. Those households should have average annual electricity savings of approximately 3850 KWH per household, or monetary savings of about $100 per household. Such savings will result in an average payback period of about 18 years for the total cost of weatherizing a typical house, and a payback period of about 4.0 years for the typical household's share of those costs. In short, those few households that have increased their electricity consumption since participating in the Buy Back Programme make it appear that the programme is much less effective than it could be.

Why did those 10 households increase their electricity consumption after weatherizing? They had taken an average of about six weatherization actions, which is approximately the same as all other participating households. Moreover, they do not differ from the other households in the nature of their house, their socio-demographic characteristics, their household dynamics, or their financial conditions. Instead, their increased electricity consumption appears to have been an outcome of more-or-less intentional modifications they had made in their daily living patterns. Several of these respondents said that having the house warm enough was of great importance to them, and now that it was weatherized they felt they could afford to turn up the heat. That attitude was expressed by such statements as: 'We both like to be warm - its very, very important to us,' and 'I've been ill for some time, and need the house warmer than I used to.' In addition, two of these households explained that after having the house weatherized they used their wood stove much less than before. Although these ten households may not have intended to increase their electricity consumption, they had made deliberate changes in their living patterns that resulted in greater energy use.

## Discussion and conclusions

From a theoretical perspective, this study deals with the process of intentional social change. As outlined in the model that guided this multinational study, intentional social change can occur in either of two ways: (1) a 'top-down' process, in which a broad public policy is adopted and then specific programmes are designed and implemented to realize that policy; and (2) a 'bottom-up' process, in which groups of citizens and private organizations mobilize themselves to achieve a desired change. The Eugene Household Weatherization Programme is a top-down approach to promoting energy conservation, since its authorizing policy was set by the Eugene City Council and the programme is designed and directed by the Eugene Water and Electric Board. The public has had relatively little input into this process, although public opinion in Eugene strongly supports the EWEB programme.

### Programme design

Since this study was limited to one community, it is not possible to compare the design of the Eugene Residential Weatherization Programme with other programmes or to test the adequacy of its design empirically. We can, however, make several relevant observations about the nature of the Eugene programme.

*First*, this research had demonstrated that it is possible to conduct a relatively effective household energy conservation programme at the community level, as has also been done in Seattle (Olsen and Cluett 1982) and a number of other communities. These successful community programmes stand in sharp contrast to the marked inability of the US Department of Energy to carry out effective national-level energy conservation programmes. Two important strengths of these community programmes are the extent to which local residents identify with and support such programmes as desirable, and the greater potential of community programmes for flexibility and diversity to meet local conditions. At the same time, however, community programmes are subject to conflict among local interest groups and political leaders. Such conflict is more evident in relatively heterogeneous communities such as Seattle and much less evident in rather homogeneous communities such as Eugene, where support for the conservation programme is widespread throughout the population.

*Second*, credibility of the sponsoring agency is vital for programme effectiveness. The very high credibility of EWEB among Eugene residents is clearly a major contributor to the success of its programme. In contrast, because the Oregon Department of Energy, the Bonneville Power Administration, and the US Department of Energy all have much less credibility with Eugene residents, it seems unlikely that those agencies could have conducted a comparable programme in that community. The fact that EWEB is a municipal rather than a private utility is undoubtedly important in this respect, since EWEB is seen as serving the needs of the community, not making profits for its owners.

*Third*, a consumer energy conservation programme that utilises a wide variety of instruments will undoubtedly be ore effective than one that relies on only one or two instruments. The Eugene programme - which includes information dissemination, home energy audits, weatherization grants, and mandatory energy efficiency standards for all residences - illustrates this kind of comprehensive approach to promoting energy conservation.

*Fourth*, financial incentives can be highly effective in encouraging people to weatherize their house. Most of the participants in the Buy Back Programme were responding directly and intentionally to the financial benefits provided. Moreover, considerable previous research has rather conclusively demonstrated that information programmes, by themselves, are not very effective in promoting energy conservation (Olsen and Joerges 1983), and must be supplemented with additional instruments such as financial incentives. When offered in the form on no-interest weatherization loans, however, such incentives do not appear to be highly effective, primarily because many people do not want to go further into debt and have a lien placed on their house (Rosa and Olsen 1983). That finding argues strongly for the desirability of grant programmes like EWEB's. Therefore, why do utilities not simply pay the full cost of weatherizing houses? The rationale for partial-payment grant programmes (except for low income households) is social in nature, not economic. Utility managers commonly assume that if people are given complete weatherizations grants, many of them will either be suspicious of a 'give-away' programme and reject it for fear that it contains some kind of hidden trap; or make an unearned profit on the weatherization improvements when they sell the house. This research has demonstrated, however, that being able to spend approximately $400 for one's share of the weatherization costs is financially impossible for many households with modest incomes that are considerably above the poverty level.

*Fifth,* given the latter finding, it appears that utilities should consider providing full payment weatherization grants to all households regardless of their income. Such a programme would still be highly cost-effective for utilities, since the complete cost of fully weatherizing a house can produce energy savings at less than half the current cost of building new electric generating plants. In addition, such a programme would be fully compatible with the present thinking of energy planning bodies such as the Northwest Power Planning Council, which are now treating conservation as a cost-effective source of energy rather than simply as a means of reducing energy demands. As a result of this perspective, conservation efforts are presently being incorporated into the supply rather than demand side of energy demand-supply equations.

*Sixth,* the kinds of conservation actions addressed by a programme is crucial for its effectiveness in saving energy. Most early programmes simply gave consumers a long list of suggested energy-saving actions, with the implication that all of them were equally conserving of energy. A typical result was that many households did only a few simple things - such as turning off unused lights or closing curtains at night - that produce minimal energy savings, and then took no further weatherization actions (Olsen and Cluett 1982). In contrast, the EWEB programme pertains to only a few specified weatherization improvements that conserve the greatest amounts of energy, such as installing more insulation. These improvements can be moderately expensive, but once they are done they are permanent and do not depend on the residents continually remembering to take some action such as turning down the thermostat at night. By focusing on major weatherization improvements to houses, the EWEB programme is able to achieve the greatest possible energy savings with the least disruption of household living patterns.

*Seventh,* despite the relative effectiveness of the Eugene programme, it still contains several serious limitations. It is restricted to electrically heated houses and thus omits about half the homes in the community. The programme is designed primarily for owner-occupied dwellings and (with the exception of energy audits) includes no provisions for rental apartments or houses. To induce landlords to weatherize their rental properties, special financial and/or legal incentives must be specifically targeted at that population. Nor does the EWEB programme identify any other target populations and offer special provisions for them. Such populations included the elderly, single-parent families, single adults, and ethnic minorities. All of these groups contain disproportionate numbers of renters and low- and modest-income households, and they also have many other special characteristics and conservation needs.

*Invalid assumptions*

Designers and implementors of household energy conservation programmes frequently make a number of assumptions about various factors that may influence programme participation. This study has demonstrated that several of those assumptions are invalid in regard to programmes such as Eugene's.

*First*, many previous studies have found that socioeconomic status is important in determining rates of participation in conservation programmes (Olsen and Joerges 1983), but virtually all of that research dealt only with information programmes. Since the participants and non-participants in the EWEB programme have similar average educational and income statuses, these characteristics do not appear relevant for explaining participation in weatherization grant programmes.

*Second*, it is often assumed that older people are more resistant to taking household conservation actions. This study found no support for that assumption, provided that those people have an income adequate to afford weatherization improvements.

*Third*, it is sometimes assumed that because weatherization actions fall within the traditional male domain of home maintenance, men are more interested in this topic than women and conservation programmes should be aimed primarily at them. This research discovered that when traditional gender roles are enacted in energy management decision making, households are less likely to participate in weatherization programmes. Instead, when traditional gender roles are set aside and conservation decisions are made in an egalitarian manner, programme participation tends to increase.

*Fourth*, the common assumption that interpersonal communication promotes participation in conservation programmes is not supported by this study. On the contrary, participation in the Eugene

235

programme is influenced by the belief that one's friends and neighbours approve of taking conservation actions, while non-participants are more likely to discuss this topic with their friends and neighbours. In other words, reference group norms are of greater importance than interhousehold communications. Furthermore, frequent discussions about energy problems between households may inhibit taking conservation actions.

*Fifth*, the results of the Eugene study suggest that informal opinion leaders may not play a critical role in promoting programme participation. However, support of these programmes by formal community leaders seems to be extremely important. In Eugene, the City Council, City Manager, and the EWEB Director are all publicly committed to energy conservation, as are the leaders of most of the neighbourhood associations, many interest organizations, and numerous business leaders. This discovery is congruent with recent community leadership studies that emphasize the role of multiple overlapping formal leadership influences in the adoption of innovations. This conclusion is also supported by the finding that people who are actively involved in local community organizations are more likely to participate in the Eugene Household Weatherization Programme.

*Sixth*, many energy professionals are quite concerned about the length of the payback period for various weatherization improvements, and assume that consumers share that concern. This study found that people do approach the EWEB programme with an explicit concern for reducing their energy bills, especially in the long run as these costs are expected to continue rising. However, most people do not calculate the cost effectiveness of weatherization actions in terms of their payback periods when deciding whether or not to participate in a conservation programme. Instead, they accept the recommendations of professionals that specified weatherization actions will save energy, and base their participation decision primarily on whether or not they can presently afford to take advantage of the programme.

*Participation influences*

This study of the Eugene Residential Weatherization Programme indicates a variety of critical factors that appear to influence households to participate in what is obviously a financially beneficial programme. Those influences are summarized in terms of seven major themes that distinguish programme participants from non-

236

participants. In general, households that have thus far taken advantage of the Buy Back Programme can be characterized in the following ways:

* Their current living conditions likely impose fewer routine homemaking demands of them.

* They express a strong personal commitment to energy conservation as an important activity regardless of its cost.

* They take a long term view of the potential benefits of conserving energy, both for themselves and for society as a whole.

* They have established a pattern of joint discussion and decision making about household improvements and conservation actions.

* They take account of energy conservation information obtained from impersonal and formal sources, as well as prevailing neighbourhood norms.

* They intentionally seek ways of reducing their household energy consumption and lowering electric bills, especially in the long run.

* Their household financial condition is relatively secure and they have the funds available to participate in the programme, which may be a result of more effective household financial management practices.

*Programme consequences*

Participation in the Eugene Programme results in households making numerous weatherization improvements in their houses. A typical participating household takes six weatherization actions, including caulking and weatherstripping around doors and windows, adding more attic insulation, installing insulation in the walls and floors, wrapping the water heater and water pipes and/or hot air ducts, and installing storm windows and doors. In contrast, a typical non-participating household takes only one weatherization action, usually wrapping the water heater (which is done for them free at the time of the Home Energy Analysis). or caulking and weatherstripping.

In addition, most households that have participated in this programme report that it has had desirable effects on their lives, in addition to lowering their electric bills. In general, these people have become more concerned about saving energy, and conservation has become a way of life for many of them.

The ultimate goal of all energy conservation programmes is to reduce energy consumption. Thus far, however, most calculations of potential energy savings from weatherization improvements have been taken not from actual meter readings, but rather from engineering calculations of expected consumption reductions. These estimates usually predict rather large potential energy savings, often as great as 30 to 40 percent. When actual energy consumption data are examined, however - as in the Eugene study and an earlier study in Seattle, Washington (Olsen and Cluett 1982) - the energy savings attained by participating households are much less than predicted. Despite the many weatherization improvements made by the Eugene households, the average energy efficiency of their houses have risen by only nine percent, compared to six percent among non-participants.

These are at least three possible explanations for this situation. The weatherization improvements that are actually being made may not meet the technical standards assumed in the engineering calculations. There may be negative interaction effects among weatherization actions, so that when several improvements are made simultaneously their combined energy savings are considerably less that the sum of their separate potential savings. Some households do not reduce their energy consumption after taking conservation actions, and may even increase their total energy consumption. The latter explanation - which is clearly relevant in Eugene - requires much more study. Why do people weatherize their house and then increase their energy consumption? Are they aware of what they are doing? How can this be prevented? This problem clearly demonstrates that energy conservation is never simply a mechanical process of stopping air leaks in houses. This process of reducing energy consumption always involves a dynamic relationship between buildings and the people who live in them.

In addition to eliminating heat losses, successful energy conservation programmes must also educate consumers concerning efficient and wise use of energy in their homes. One way of accomplishing this would be to provide all households that participate in a weatherization programme with an annual record of their total electricity consumption for the past year, as well as the year preceding their weatherization actions. These consumption reports should be standardized for heating degree days during each time period, and should be clearly presented and easy to understand. Households could then keep track of how much electricity they were saving each year. Moreover, if a household increased or failed to decrease its electricity consumption after taking weatherization actions, that fact should be explicitly pointed out to the residents.

In addition, many households - but especially those that increase their energy consumption after weatherizing - might welcome and benefit from assistance in managing their energy use in a more effective manner. Such assistance might be provided by a professional Household Energy Management Consultant, who would meet personally with the household members to review their living patterns, show them how those activities were affecting their energy consumption, and suggest modifications in their living patterns that would use less energy. It would be highly cost effective for utilities to provide this service at no charge, since it could considerably increase the energy saved through conservation programmes.

*Final conclusion*

From a broader perspective, this research indicates that various household dynamics are a crucial intervening link between community conservation programmes and making weatherization improvements in one's house. A utility or other community agency cannot simply establish a conservation programme and assume that households will eagerly participate in it, even though the programme may provide highly lucrative benefits. To ensure that these programmes achieve their goals, programme managers must give serious attention to household dynamics such as established role expectations, interpersonal communications, decision-making patterns, personal values and ideological commitments, time-perspectives, interactions with others, and past and present financial conditions and problems. In short, a crucial consideration in designing energy conservation programmes is how well households function as social units and as financial and energy management systems.

**References**

Anderson, C. D. and McDougall, G.H.G. 1980. *Consumer Energy Research: An Annotated Bibliography*. Faculty of Administrative Studies, University of Manitoba, Winnipeg, Canada.

Bonneville Power Administration. 1981. *Pacific Northwest Electric Power Planning and Conservation Act: A Summary.* Portland, Oregon.

Hirst, E. et al. 1983. *Evaluation of the BPA Residential Weatherization Pilot Program.* Oak Ridge National Laboratory, Oak Ridge, Tenn.

Olsen, M. E. 1978. Public Acceptance of Energy Conservation. In Warkov, ed., *Energy Policy in the United States: Social and Behavioral Dimensions.* Praeger, New York.

Olsen, M. E. 1983a. Public Acceptance of Consumer Energy Conservation Strategies. *Journal of Economic Psychology*, 4:183-196.

Olsen, M. E. 1983b. *Phase I report for the United States and the Pacific Northwest Region* to the Multinational Study of Consumer Energy Conservation Policies. Social Research Center, Washington State University, Pullman Wash.

Olsen, M. E. and Cluett, C. 1982. Voluntary Energy Conservation Trough Neighborhood Programs: Design and Evaluation. *Energy Systems and Policy*, Vol. 6, pp. 161-192.

Olsen, M. E. and Joerges, B. 1983. Consumer Energy Conservation Programs. In Edward Seidman, ed., *Handbook of Social Intervention.* Sage Publications, Beverly Hill, CA.

Pease, S. R. 1982. *An Appraisal of Evaluations of Utility-Sponsored Programs for Residential Energy Conservation.* Rand Corp., Santa Monica, Calif.

Rosa, E. A. and Olsen, M.E.. 1983. *Washington Water Power Company Home Weatherization Study.* Social Research Center, Washington State University, Pullman, Wash.

Synergic Resources Corporation. 1982. Pacific Northwest Conservation Assessment, Ch. 3. Part II of Independent Review of WPPSS 4 and 5, Study Module 1B, *Supply Alternatives and Costs.* Pullman, Wash., Washington Energy Research Center, Washington State University.

US Department of Energy. 1981 and 1983. *The National Energy Policy Plan.* US Government Printing Office, Washington D.C..

Wilk, R. R. and Wilhite, H.L. 1983. *Household Energy Decision Making in Santa Cruz County, California.* Berkeley, Calif., University Wide Energy Research Group, University of California, Berkeley, CA.

# PART III
# THE INTERNATIONAL
# EXPERIENCE

# 8 Policy analysis: the 'top-down' approach

ERIC MONNIER and HARALD MUELLER

## Introduction

In this chapter we investigate the ways in which programme characteristics shape programme impacts. This we have called the 'top-
down' approach which refers to the analysis of programme formulation and implementation and the relations of these features to overall
programme outcomes. Before doing so a few general remarks about
programme evaluation will be made. Although assessment of the actual outcomes of a programme is a prerequisite of any evaluation, it
is not on its own sufficient. The ultimate aim of an evaluation should
be the identification of the causal factors determining the success or
failure of a programme. Some researchers have made a useful distinction between evaluations that are limited to the results, or
'outcome evaluation' and those which set out to understand the
process by which the results were obtained, or 'process evaluation'
(Freeman 1977; Soderstrom et al. 1981).

While many process evaluations try to identify the characteristics of
participating and non-participating households, few go beyond this
to analyse the outcomes in the light of the actual characteristics of
the programme itself. A study by the Mellon Institute of Research
(1983) shows the importance of such an approach. An evaluation of a
pilot project to promote energy efficiency in dwellings suggested
that the project had failed: energy savings were only one half of the

projected figure. However a detailed analysis of the causes of this failure pointed to poor programme organization and to lack of competence of the personnel employed. At the same time they found that consumer acceptance of the programme was higher than expected.

In a meta-evaluation of more than 200 reports of evaluations in California, White et al. (1984) note that the vast majority fail to give even the basic description of the programme. Thus, the case studies in this multinational project which give a 'top-down' analysis, stand out from the normal run of studies and may contribute both to the understanding of the process of energy conservation and to evaluation methods generally. The diversity of programmes studied and the detailed analyses of the process of programme realization described in the case studies allows us to draw at least tentative conclusions about the relations between programme characteristics and outcomes.

**Two comparative perspectives**

In order to gain a greater understanding of the role of programme characteristics we will analyse the case studies using two related perspectives. In the first of these, four stages in the process of programme realization are reviewed. Without assuming a strict temporal order, these cover the stages of

* selecting objectives: the nature of the goals (both explicit and implicit) of the programme, that is energy conservation actions, other policy goals, and target groups;

* designing the strategy: the strategy adopted, the communicative, financial, regulatory or technical instruments and channels used;

* mobilizing resources: the type of organizational structure set up, the role of the agencies participating in the programme;

* implementation: finally, the process of implementation of the programme, the way in which planned operations were carried out and difficulties were resolved.

Following this, and by way of a detailed conclusion we address the seven structural issues set out in the first chapter. These are the extent to which the effectiveness of a programme varies with:

* its comprehensiveness

* the degree of matching programme services to the requirements of specific target groups

* the degree of commitment of programme staff, with regard to energy conservation issues and the needs of specific target groups

* the credibility of the programme agencies

* the number of linkages which the programme agency establishes with other actors

* the availability of conflict management techniques and mechanisms

### Selecting programme objectives

Energy conservation is a broad and general goal which must be specified and detailed before actions can be taken; it also has to be put into the overall goal system of the agency involved. It is for this reason that, under the umbrella goal of energy conservation, the fine-tuning of programme objectives was rather diverse across the programmes studied.

*The policy goals of local programmes: combination and superimposition*

It will be noted that in general the local programmes studied aimed at several policy goals simultaneously. Sometimes the variety of the agencies taking part in the programme necessitates this combination of goals. The initiators of a programme were often forced into this situation in order to be able to take advantage of available sources of funding from different public bodies. Because many 'access points' emerged with the development of welfare state functions, it has been possible to enlarge the small resources dedicated specifically to energy conservation programmes. This, however, means that sponsoring institutions' goals must be taken into account in the design and implementation of the programme: such as creating employment

(Veynes and La Rochelle in France, municipal programmes in Sweden, Zutphen in Netherlands and the NEA in Britain), helping the poor (in Britain), improving the community image (Conflans in France), protecting the environment or consumers (Eugene in the USA, or in Tuebingen in FRG).

However, increasing funds by such means may involve a trade-off in terms of goal comprehensiveness. Multiple goals need not be detrimental to energy conservation objectives: they can even increase public participation because they reflect the variety of needs of the people themselves. Compartmentalization is in itself a weakness of administrative systems, a point which will be discussed later in the conclusions. To integrate different policy goals is, in this sense, a challenge, and this feature of the local programmes must be kept in mind in evaluating their energy conservation effects.

For example, the US and British cases show that energy savings fell short of expectations, because clients took advantage of the programme benefits in the form of enhanced comfort; but these programmes can still be judged successful with reference to consumer policy goals. This indeed was the main objective of the British programmes. There is the danger, however, that energy conservation may loose priority altogether in a multiple goal system. This danger is by no means trivial given the ebb and flow of public policy issues in public attention. We are now in a period of an energy policy ebb, and, the existence of multiple goals may well swallow the last remnants of attention of energy issues at the local level.

In conclusion, however, it seems a particular attribute of local programmes that they cannot avoid having a multiplicity of goals which does not necessarily facilitate the implementation of the programme as it is shown in the following sections.

*Target groups: spatial and socio-economic criteria*

In contrast to this accumulation of goals, it emerged that the local programmes are targeted far more strictly than most national programmes (see the conclusions of Joerges and Mueller 1984). This attribute of local programme is probably due to the fact that the more restricted the target is, the easier multiple policy goals can be fulfilled. It is moreover, less costly to design instruments adapted to a target group if it is homogeneous, that is if the targeted households have numerous common characteristics.

The targets of the local programmes evaluated in the studies, were always defined on some criteria of location; and only a few are targeted on socio-economic criteria.

The Swedish programmes have been loosely targeted: the loans and grants were substantial and made available to whoever was interested. The same was true in the Conflans/France programme which involved 54 percent of households in a specific area and induced energy conservation actions in 37 percent of participating households (at this time only 17 percent of the households at the national level were taking conservations actions). The programme in Eugene/USA, apart from offering special conditions to lower income clients, did not develop a specific approach to channel the programme to this group.

Our case studies document again the well known fact that lower income consumer groups concentrated in the rented sector and other marginal groups like the elderly, with their specific problems in communication and in dealing with technical changes, will be missed if not targeted consciously. The British projects are the most specifically (and exclusively) targeted on difficult groups and made notable achievements. The programme in Zutphen/NL which chose two limited areas, was restricted to tenant-houses. Its achievement of insulating 40 percent of eligible dwellings in the target area is remarkable. While endowed with relatively scarce financial resources, it succeeded in achieving high participation rates and significant growth in energy conservation.

These two programmes succeeded because they concentrated their limited resources. They by-passed the problem of developing fine-tuned strategies for very different client groups, because their prospective clients shared relatively uniform attributes. In addition, the limited area made the dissemination of information through the neighbourhood and through the housing association almost cost free. Nevertheless, the British and the Dutch cases show that targeting specific disadvantaged groups requires careful measures to overcome communication barriers - channelling information through local voluntary organizations and the social networks of clients - and, just as important, removing cost barriers by providing services cost-free or at very low cost instead of the usual tax and loans schemes.

The bottom-up analysis (see Chapter 9) underlines these conclusions. Furthermore, in some cases this analysis revealed rifts in the public based on political or cultural criteria. In the French and German cases, groups are identified whose political and cultural ideology leads them to reject 'official' programmes, either from a general 'anti-state' stance or in the context of 'green' opposition on hard/high technology energy policies. This phenomenon, which leads to the exclusion of part of the potential clientele by generalized official approaches, could be attenuated using appropriate targeting: programmes clearly tailoring their services to such specific orientations are apt to reach groups otherwise indifferent or even hostile to official conservation programmes. It should be noted, however, that the generously funded utility programmes in Eugene/USA, Tuebingen/FRG, and in Sweden which did not practice sophisticated targeting, still achieved good participation and adoption rates among the general public.

It can be concluded that while generous funding allows particularly attractive services to be offered and communication actions to be multiplied of a programme have only limited funds at their disposal.

## Designing programme strategy

The cases studied show considerable variation in this respect. In Veynes/France, the strategy was rather limited: persuasion (through exhibits) to use solar devices was the only instrument employed; in Eugene/USA, in Conflans/France or the utility programme Tuebingen/FRG, the strategies were sophisticated, combining instruments such as audits, advice, technical arrangements, financial incentives, and a certain degree of regulatory coercion.

*Energy conservation services: varying degree of comprehensiveness*

The most determining difference between the programmes, lies in the fact that some programmes only offer advice on the different conservation measures, for instance in Tuebingen/FRG or in France. Others carry out, on behalf of the householders, the relevant improvements for energy conservation, for instance in Eugene/USA, in Britain and in Zutphen/NL. In the latter cases, the instruments of the programme cover the whole process of energy conservation actions, and the impact of these programmes in terms of home improvements is thus greater.

Concerning the comprehensiveness of the technical services offered to consumers, the main issue raised by the studies is whether it is more cost-effective for the programme to carry out the home improvements for free or to devote the funds to convincing households to take conservation actions on their own. This point will be discussed at the end of the section. Besides that, the efficiency of services is related to their fit with the needs of the target groups: in the Swedish programme, an advisory service was taken more frequently by the younger home-owners; in the British schemes, a limited number of measures performed at low or no cost for a rather circumscribed target group of mainly old-age pensioners; in the German ecologists' programme, a service particularly geared to the expectations of ecologically aware, notably low income student households.

It is remarkable that the majority of programmes focused exclusively on house improvements and did not include advice on behavioural changes in favour of energy conservation. One can speculate whether such a combination would have further improved programme efficiency.

*Communication instruments: information and community mobilization*

Virtually all programmes studied employ more than one way to get the message of energy conservation across. Media, exhibitions, letters, phone calls, home visits, demonstration houses, social networks – all are used. While a clear ranking of 'degree of channel comprehensiveness' is not possible, evidence suggests that programme success is indeed related to it, provided channels are orchestrated and information is handled in the framework of a single programme. As the Tuebingen/FRG case shows, problems of information overload arise if conflicting and contradictory information is given by rival programmes.

A comparison between similar programmes carried out in France at La Rochelle and at Conflans shows, moreover, that the cost of the information campaign used increases less rapidly than the rate of participation in the population exposed to the programme: the information campaign in La Rochelle cost 300,000 FFr and resulted in the participation of 5 percent of the exposed population at the regional level, whereas in Conflans it cost 1,000,000 FFr and led to the participation of 54 percent of the exposed population at the local level. This is a striking illustration of the snowball effect made possible by the local level of organization of the programme: the programme can really mobilize the community to participate.

It must be emphasized, however, that in terms of the energy conservation actions taken, the La Rochelle programme comes off best in a comparison of the cost benefit ratio of the two programmes. The ratio - total cost of the home energy improvements for energy saving carried out by households divided by the total cost of the programme for the organizers - is more favourable in La Rochelle than in Conflans. In La Rochelle, the participants were fewer, but were more motivated and hence the cheap audit offered was sufficient to convince them to take energy conservation actions. In Conflans, the snowball effect mentioned above was probably an ongoing process at the time the evaluation was carried out and thus had additional effects afterwards.

It seems that there is an optimum cost which unfortunately can be defined only for a given type of programme (that is to say in relation to the goals and the local context) and based on evaluations of several identical programmes. As such it is difficult to establish in advance. Furthermore, numerous studies have show that, where sensitization to energy savings is concerned, proselytizing is one of the most effective methods. Friends or neighbours often set an example and help a great deal in spreading information. As a result, a two-track strategy is desirable. Broad, unspecific offers are likely to be taken up by more attentive people, as indicated by the fact that pre-programme awareness is generally higher for participants than for non-participants. Concentrating on the 'easy cases' in order to create 'snowball effects' through communication by existing participants to potential participants may be a reasonable strategy if the funds available are meagre. A better strategy would be to design a general programme for the 'easy cases' or 'converts' (seen next chapter), and a targeted programme for the problem cases. Regrettably, such complementary relationships between programmes are difficult to establish as evidenced particularly by the German case.

*Financial instruments: clients' needs and 'free-riders'*

Financial instruments are often used to stimulate programme adoption by consumers. Several instruments can be combined: direct financial help such as buy-back arrangements in Eugene/USA favourable credits in Conflans/France, or indirect financial help through free technical services or even through beneficial electricity tariffs in Tuebingen/FRG, or arrangements for tenants in Zutphen/NL. (Here they had to pay a small increment to the rent instead of a heavy investment for conservation measures). Such financial instruments are able to overcome clients' reluctance to risk personal sacrifices. Cost considerations are reported by all studies to be a very important factor in decision-making for the majority of consumers, and particularly the less well-to-do, or those pessimistic about their future financial conditions, who may hesitate to commit cash to conservation actions, or to borrow money.

However, whether it serves this purpose depends on the quality of targeting in relation to financial instruments chosen; in the German case, for instance, the free services offered by the utility programme did not fare better than the more frugal consumer and ecologists' programmes, the main reason being lack of targeting. The same problem is raised by the Swedish study which stresses that a considerable portion of 'loan users' would have improved their home even without state subsidies. This 'free-rider' effect is corroborated by the fact that consumers utilising the loans and grants are slightly better educated, have more income available and that they don't really change their conservation investments.

In Eugene/USA on the other hand, the abundance of funds at the local level helped the Eugene Water and Electricity Board to circumvent constraints due to strict targeting rules of the main funding programme sponsor (Bonneville Power Administration). Still, potential clients were missed because the board's special scheme for low income customers - a full buy-back programme, was tied to a strict statistical measure (125 percent of US poverty level): the poverty level was arbitrarily set, and among consumers constraints due to lack of cash exist well beyond that limit.

As a conclusion to this section about strategy, we will discuss the efficiency of the combined instruments. It might be thought that the more exhaustive the instruments employed, the better the chances of the programme achieving its goals. The truth is, unfortunately, not so simple due to the so called 'rebound effect' : that is consumers take advantage of the home improvements carried out at low cost to raise their level of comfort (Hirst and Berry 1983; Condelli et al. 1984). In the case of Eugene/USA for example, the extensive instruments used did indeed make it possible to achieve a high rate of participation (home improvements), but the results in terms of energy conserved remained well below the initial objectives. The same phenomenon was noted in the British programmes for the elderly, though in this case the raising of the internal temperature can be considered not as a 'perverse' effect but as one of the objectives of the programmes, given the fact that the health of the old age pensioners was affected by their poor thermal comfort.

Conclusions differ concerning this rebound effect amongst the various national studies: the American study recommends that the organizers of the programme should increase the extent of financial support for the home improvements for energy conservation, whereas the French and Swedish cases concluded the opposite, that the financial involvement of the consumer in the process should be increased, to avoid the 'free-rider effect'. Obviously, such conclusions must be assessed in their respective national context: American and French or Swedish households are reacting in very different ways.

## Mobilizing resources

In analysing the local programmes it is necessary to draw a distinction between the different types of actors, according to the role they play within the organizational structure. First of all there is the actor, called the leading implementing agency of a programme. In most cases this is a local organization of a political nature or an association, though it can also be the local branch of a national organization, as in Sweden or Conflans/France. The leading implementing agency needs to gain the support of more powerful agencies having political, financial or administrative power (called 'legitimizing agencies'). These legitimizing agencies are mainly on the national or regional level and the linkages are therefore 'vertical' in nature. The leading implementing agency should also maintain 'horizontal linkages' with other organizations established at the local level which may be able to help in the implementation of the programme. These different aspects of the organizational structure in turn, implementing agencies legitimizing agencies and horizontal linkages, are discussed below.

### Implementing agencies: commitment and personality factors

In most of the studies, a conclusion is drawn that the commitment of the leading agency or of the key persons within the programme has been a crucial factor.

For projects in Britain and Zutphen/NL project commitment can be assumed to exist because there are non-profit making associations. In La Rochelle and Conflans/France, the key person whose commitment counted was not part of the programme agency, but rather in an upward-linkage organization: the city council in La Rochelle, and AFME in the case of Conflans. If strong linkages are maintained

252

during the whole implementation process, such a situation appears not to impede the success of the programme. Commitment of programme staff also can blend into a general community commitment, as in the case of Eugene/USA. Here, a kind of 'conservation culture' seems to have evolved, that is, the leading figures not only of the programme agency and the city council, but also of supporting groups all hold strong convictions about energy conservation as a public policy goal. The study stresses the importance of this pattern for the scope and the take-up of the Eugene effort.

The municipal programmes in Sweden have been more or less successful depending on the type of involvement of the municipalities. The essential factor was the local techno-economic context. If a municipal district heating scheme exists, the energy conservation goal can ruin its economy, this is the case of Gothenburg. There may be exceptions, as in Uppsala, where the context is similar to Oregon: the municipal energy utility company wants to improve energy efficiency in order to avoid investing in a new supply system.

Obviously, the commitment discussed above concerns energy conservation as the primary goal. In some cases, however, energy conservation as such was a means to an end for a programme's commitment to other objectives. If the agency staff is aware of such instrumental relationships or if the logical connection is self-evident, as in the case of environmental goals, commitment to energy conservation is implicit. If, however, the focal commitment is to social policy goals not strongly tied to energy issues, like improving living standards of the poor or providing jobs, such commitment may divert a programme away from conservation objectives, as the British case indicates. It seems safe to conclude that the 'personality factor' plays an important role, both in getting local programmes off the ground and in keeping their momentum over time.

*Legitimizing agencies : determining vertical linkages*

Almost all local programmes have linkages to regional or central governments, which help with the necessary legitimization. Cases in point are the role of AFME (Agence Francaise pour la Maitrise de l'Energie) for the role of AgV (National Consumer Union) for the Consumer Union's advice programme in Tuebingen/FRG, and both the Department of Energy and the NEA (Neighbourhood Energy Action) in the case of local projects in Britain. From these 'upward linkages' emerges guidance, that is, a framework and direction within which programme agencies can develop more detailed, or, if necessary, supplementary patterns for solving unexpected obstacles. Upward linkages can also integrate a variety of funding sources into the programme as in the British schemes, where the official legitimizing agency (the Energy Efficiency Office) is not the major funding body.

When programmes are novel and organized by newly established implementing agencies, a credibility gap may arise, as shown for Veynes/France. In such cases, the gap can be bridged by 'borrowing' credibility and reputation from the principal supporting agencies. The French case strongly stresses the necessity of getting the support of an agency at the national level which is perceived by a majority of citizens as capable and serious. Although France, with its highly centralized political system, may appear an untypical case, similar effects were observed in other countries. The Swedish case ascribes the success of local schemes largely to the competence and credibility of the established Regional Housing Board through which the Central Housing Board initiated municipal programmes (in Sweden, the public seems to have more faith in the central government than in other countries: USA, FRG). The British local projects heavily depend on the ability of NEA to deliver information, advice, and brokerage services. In Zutphen/NL, a network of highly respected and well established organizations (such as Zutphen Council, Zutphen Housing Association, the Provincial Gas Board...) lent strength to the programme.

Upward linkages may, under certain circumstances, delegitimize rather than enhance legitimacy. If programme agencies and goals are ascribed to certain political parties or personalities, the programme becomes an object of politics. The Socialist Party's endorsement of the Veynes solar programme undermined local credibility among conservative citizens; the association with the statist AFME alienated anti-interventionist citizens in La Rochelle and Conflans/France.

The ecologists' programme in Tuebingen/FRG, on the other hand, loosely connected only with the national association of environmental groups, functioned quite well considering its limited sources and exhibited the highest degree of consumer satisfaction with its services among the four German cases. The reason may be that for consumers with 'green' preferences, the high value afforded to decentralized local self-reliance obviates the need for high-level legitimization.

254

*Horizontal linkages: integration of local resources*

Horizontal linkages refer to linkages within the community, for example connections to local government offices, or local associations and organizations, including local groups such as neighbourhood associations, pensioners clubs and the like. Linkages to local authorities are vital if information needed for conducting a programme is only available at that source, as in the case of the gas utility in Zutphen/NL. They are also important if funds on which local programmes must draw are channelled from central governments through local authorities as in the British case; there insulation grants are administered through local offices. Such linkages are important, moreover, to deal with conflicts. The poor performance of the municipal advisory service in Tuebingen/FRG may be due in good part to the fact that it was set up as a rival, rather than a supplement to existing programmes, particularly that of the local utility. Linkages to local non-governmental groups serve different purposes. First, they can add to a programme's credibility if such groups are not suspected of having political interest. Public support by respected organizations, for example local unions, the Chamber of Commerce and banks, lends seriousness to programmes and can prevent possibly damaging opposition. This 'additional legitimization' is quite evident in the careful build-up of local support networks in La Rochelle and Conflans/France, and it was essential for the initiative of a local group of unemployed in Zutphen/NL.

Horizontal linkages can also help in programme implementation. Their support can consist of financial incentives not available from the programme as such. The French cases underline this: two programmes drew local banks into the supporting linkage network, to provide clients with favourable credit terms.

Another kind of direct support is mobilizing the technical competence of traders and craftsmen. Data from Tuebingen/FRG show that - with no strong horizontal linkages developed by the four local programmes - local installation companies accounted for more conservation advice, and had a higher 'adoption rate' even among socially disadvantaged groups, than all but the utility's energy conservation programme. It makes good sense therefore, to work with those local companies, as was done in La Rochelle/France. Clients can be referred to the appropriate companies for major work and be saved the time and cost of getting the relevant information themselves. It is the same for the British projects which appear to be more efficient if they have more operational linkages at the local level for promoting the services of the project. However it seems to be a characteristic of local utility programmes that they can do without horizontal linkages. Eugene/USA, Tuebingen/FRG, and municipal programmes in Sweden are examples. In at least three of these cases, the lack of linkages did not impede their functioning. There are exceptions in Gothenburg/Sweden, it seems that the failure to link-up the utility company with the municipal energy adviser's office, because of conflictual interests, impeded the programme. Since utilities possess many assets - financial sources, technical expertise, customer relationships - they can create their own functional equivalents of linkages. The variety of intra-organizational capabilities and the strictly hierarchical integration of programmes within the utilities' company structure entails a degree of organizational effectiveness not easily emulated by other programme agencies.

### Implementing programmes

Many unforeseen difficulties can arise in the process of the implementation of a programme. An important issue in a programme success is though to lie in its flexibility, its capacity to resolve the difficulties encountered such as: inappropriateness of the strategy designed, conflicts between social actors or negative reactions in the target groups.

*Actor games: different interests and conflict management*

Each actor has specific interests on which his existence in an organization is based (cf. Britan 1981). A programme structure is set up in the course of a social process which brings into play power conflicts within the framework of formal and informal relations (Pettigrew 1973). The local dimension of these programmes tends to exacerbate, in the circumstances, politico-ideological micro-conflicts. In the case of Veynes/France, a conflictual dynamic developed to the point where the programme broke off, even though the implementation had been successful. For this reason, the French study recommended the necessity of having methods of conflict management within the programme structure.

Some programmes anticipating conflicts between supporting organizations integrated them into the structure of the programme. The British programmes, Zutphen/NL, La Rochelle and Conflans/France have taken this strategy. It remains open whether this strategy does not result simply in transforming inter-organizational conflict into conflict within programme agencies. Therefore, a governing body comprising relevant actors is sometimes established, as in the case of the Funding Bodies Liaison Group of NEA in Britain, and may be a good way to reach early compromises without jeopardizing the programme itself. Compromise may well mean paying a price, the constraints upon conservation measures permitted in the Zutphen/NL programme in order to prevent 'unfair competition' were the price for the Chamber of Commerce's support of the programme.

A steering body including all important supporting organizations comes close to a kind of conflict management: mediation. Mediation depends on the position of one of the supporting organizations, or the programme agency itself, or the main legitimizing body. If there is one organization trusted and accepted by the others, it can mediate between contending parties and foster compromise. The French programmes in La Rochelle and Conflans, for example, had especially complex linkage systems which required a good deal of conflict management. In Conflans, setting up a local outlet of AFME provided for this mediating function.

*Community interactions: feedback processes*

As was emphasized in the former section, a programme is an interactive process with the social context in which it takes place. As such it can give rise to new social phenomena. Political and cultural rifts which turn groups of consumers against a programme because they simply do not like its thrust and main justification have been mentioned above. The development of 'value fronts' such as materialistic versus postmaterialistic, is a well-known phenomenon in highly industrialized countries. As the case of Tuebingen/FRG shows, it is not easy to address both groups through one single programme. However, this can be done if the programme is large and comprehensive enough to embrace several 'value fronts'; in Eugene/USA household economizing was a dominant motive for most participants (94 percent ), but environmentalist orientations were also endorsed by a majority (60 percent ) of programme users. The programme had attractive features for both orientations. Energy conservation was presented as a contribution to a healthy environment, a credible proposition given the pro-conservationist community culture of Eugene. On the other hand, the financial incentives of the buy-back arrangement made sense to the more traditionally-minded consumers too.

Sometimes consumers' distrust is strongly directed against an implementing agency itself. Anti-statism in La Rochelle and Conflans/France, misgivings about party politics in Veynes/France, and lack of trustworthiness of the utility among environmentalists in Tuebingen/FRG precluded simple interactive response. In the latter case an alternative programme was set up by ecologists, explicitly competing with the utility programme. This may be interpreted as a form of interactive process which translates an ineffective political stalemate into creative activity; while it does not solve the conflict, it is still a sensible response to it. The high participation rate of the ecologists' programme among students and young academics - the leading 'adversary' group to the utility programme - underlines the usefulness of this strategy in an antagonistic constellation. It goes without saying that it is virtually impossible to initiate such a two track strategy from above.

*Organizational difficulties: structural and instrumental flexibility*

If a programme runs into difficulties it must be able to adjust its strategy and instruments. The British Study concludes that one of the most important characteristics of the successful projects is their financial flexibility for employment of specialist staff and provision of extra help to clients. A permanent feedback process between programme implementation and programme effects, as in Eugene/USA, is sensible only for a highly flexible programme. The lack of flexibility on the other hand, impedes Swedish local housing boards from inquiry into the reasons for non-use of approved home insulation credits; because almost 20 percent of approved applications are never called upon, programme success is unnecessarily reduced.

Household situations and context vary widely. This implies that a given instrument, appropriate in one situation, may entirely miss the requirements of households in different circumstances. Only if programme agencies are at liberty to match their instruments to varying household conditions will the programme goals can be achieved. Cases in point are Eugene/USA and Tuebingen/FRG. The Eugene utility is able not only to give advice on the whole range of heating and hot water use, it is also permitted to conduct on-site demonstrations and to offer financial support (and, although this seems to be of less importance, to use the future ordinance requirements as an incentive). In contrast, the Tuebingen/FRG programmes are almost entirely confined to advisory services. Not surprisingly, the Eugene programme had a much higher success rate.

The Conflans/France programme tried in particular to adapt its communication actions to the usual events of the local community (the annual cultural festival, local sports events...). But, and this is the most important point, the organizers of the programmes managed to vary the instruments, mounting demonstrations and exhibitions of materials whenever the demand was felt from the customers. They also knew when to stop all activities when there was a risk of rejection by the public because they had reached saturation point. This risk was perceptible when information from the programme came into competition with the election campaign.

On the basis of a trial project the Zutphen/NL programme achieved a degree of flexibility by offering a second programme package involving a series of lower cost actions. Moreover, when the estimations of expenses and savings appeared to be too optimistic, the implementing agency reached an agreement with the gas supplier to secure a deduction on the bill based on the savings estimated.

This conclusion, the need for flexibility, must be qualified. If rules for fund distribution and targeting are loose, local offices may redirect money from energy conservation to other preferred purposes, or they may favour special target groups for political reasons. The ingenious misuse of federal funds assigned to specific objectives by local administrations is a well-known subject, particularly in the USA. A second consideration concerns the requirements placed on programme staff: flexibility works only with highly qualified sincere and committed implementors. The adaptation of instruments to a rather complex situation without guidance by clear rules requires a high degree of organizational competence in order not to result in arbitrariness and disorganization.

## Conclusions

After the preceding comparative view of processes in formulating and implementing programmes, it is possible to assess the main hypotheses concerning the seven structural programme attributes formulated at the outset.

## Comprehensiveness

The comprehensiveness of programme goals, instruments and channels has proved conducive to programme efficiency for the following reasons:

* it provides the basis for flexibility
* it enhances the general legitimacy and acceptability;
* it helps local actors to economize scarce resources by working towards multiple goals simultaneously;
* it reduces the consumers' time to supplement the programme by own efforts, and, thereby, leads to better adoption rates.

There is a risk of information overload in the case of comprehensive programme. It has also to be recognized, that comprehensiveness usually means higher programme costs. Comprehensiveness is generally less important than tailoring a specific combination of instruments to specific contexts and special target groups.

## Targeting

Targeting has been the most important attribute of successful programmes drawing on small resources. Targeting specific groups:

* saves the costs involved in addressing a very diverse, diffuse public:
* utilises highly effective small-scale communication networks;
* helps to reach groups which are hardly accessible to generally-communicated programmes;
* avoids the risk of subsidizing 'free riders'.

Targeting is less of an absolute necessity, the more financial resources are available.

## Commitment

While commitment may be not a necessary condition for programme efficiency in the case of highly skilled, well-organized and abundantly funded programme agencies, in other cases the engagement of key staff for programme objectives has been a highly effective substitute for the lack of other resources. The utility of commitment lies in:

* its ability to get a programme started against the resistance of bureaucratic inertia;
* to keep a programme going its initial impact declines and when the programme is threatened by being overwhelmed by bureaucratic routine;
* to overcome unexpected difficulties in the course of programme implementation.

*Credibility*

Credibility of the programme agency is an attribute which is crucial:

* to persuade consumers to take the risks involved in energy conservation
* to get through to disadvantaged consumers inclined to distrust government

If the credibility of the programme agency is insufficient, linkages to more credible institutions can help to overcome this handicap.

*Linkages*

Linkages of several types have proved to be essential to programme success, because they serve:

* to provide legitimacy to the programme
* to mobilize financial resources and technical skills
* to prevent and mediate conflicts
* to accumulate and connect communication channels useful to disseminate programme information.

In a few cases it must be recognized that upwards linkages run the risk of delegitimizing the programme in the eyes of specific (anti-interventionist or pro-decentralization) target populations.

*Flexibility*

The findings suggest that programme effectiveness grows with programme flexibility. Such flexibility serves:

* to achieve a high quality of targeting if the population addressed is diverse
* to meet unexpected situations
* to improve the quality of the programme in a kind of learning process

Flexibility can limit programme effectiveness if it is granted to actors with multiple goals without sufficient supervision.

*Conflict management*

Conflict management is essential to achieve programme success particularly for more comprehensive, multi-linkage programmes, because:

* it preserves a consensus on goals and priorities
* keeps support of a variety of organizations
* prevents time-consuming bureaucratic infighting
* mitigates the effects of cultural cleavages.

Conflict management is evidently less essential in small programmes conducted by a few people united by a very strong commitment. It has to be recognized that conflict management is not cost-free; nor are all conflicts manageable.

Our results indicate that the differential success of energy conservation programmes must be explained with reference to a political and an organizational dimension. In the political arena, as Barrett and Hill (1984) describe, implementing public policy programmes is a continuing process of negotiation, bargaining and compromise between actors seeking to change both the actions of their clientele and of other interested groups. At the organizational level programmes are a particular kind of system whose success is based on flexible modes of operation, the commitment of staff, fostering public credibility and being able to strategically match services to client's needs.

Neither official institutions nor grass roots initiatives have proved sufficient to these political and organizational challenges. It seems

262

that programmes have been successful only where imaginative combinations of the formal (established bureaucracies) and informal (voluntary groups, citizens action) have been achieved.

## References

Barrett, S., and Hill, M. 1984. Policy, bargaining and structure in implementation theory. *Policy and Politics*, 12, 3, 219-240.

Britan, G.M. 1981. *Bureaucracy and Innovation: An Ethnography of Policy Change*. Sage Publications: London

Condelli, L., and Archer,D.A., Aronson, E., Curbow, B. McCleod, B.. Pettigrew, T., White, L. and Yates, S. 1984. Improving utility conservation programs: outcomes, interventions and evaluations. *Energy*, 9, 6, 6, 485-494.

Freeman, H.E. 1977. The present status of evaluation research. *Evaluation Studies Review Annual*, 2, 17-51.

Hirst, E., and Berry, L. 1983. Evaluating utility conservation programs. *Evaluating and Program Planning*, 103-113.

Joerges, B., and Mueller, M. 1984. Energy conservation programs for consumers: a comparative analysis of policy conflicts and program response in eight western countries. In P., Ester, G., Gaskell, B., Joerges, C., Midden, W.F., van Raaij, T., De Vries, *Consumer behavior and energy policy*. North Holland, Amsterdam.

Mellon Institute of Research 1983. Project evaluation, residential energy efficiency program, pilot demonstration in Lakewood, New Jersey. DOE, Washington D.C.

Pettigrew, A.M. 1973. *The politics of organizational decision making*. Tavistock:London

Soderstrom, J., Berry, L. and Hirst, E. 1981. The use of meta-evaluation to plan evaluations of conservation programs. *Evaluation Program Planning*, 4, 113-127.

White, L.T., Archer, D., Aronson, E., Condelli, L., Curbow, B., McLeod, B., Pettigrew, T. and Yates, S. 1984. Energy conservation research at California's utilities - a meta-evaluation. *Evaluation Review*, 8, 167-186.

# 9 Consumer contexts and programme impacts: the 'bottom-up' approach

PETER ESTER and CEES MIDDEN

## Introduction

In this chapter we analyse the way in which consumer and community characteristics have influenced programme awareness, programme participation and the conservation behaviours of target groups. As has been outlined in the introductory chapter this analysis is conceptualized as 'the bottom up' approach in which programme impacts are seen as mediated, that is constrained or facilitated, by a set of contextual factors which shape consumers' responses.

The relationship between programme take-up and personal, household, and community characteristics will be analysed in three sections. The first section looks at programme impacts as related to consumers' dispositions and attitudes; the second section analyses the relation between programme impacts and household and socio-economic characteristics for example micro-economic position, and social interaction; in the third section, a number of community characteristics including the homogeneity of the community, spatial mobility, interhousehold communication, support by local opinion and community leaders, the role of community organizations and community identity are related to programme impacts. The final section will summarize the main findings from the case studies.

## The personal context

Understanding the role of the personal context, including the influence of attitudes and values, past experience of energy conservation and expectations of programme use is important in the analysis of consumers' responses to existing energy conservation programmes, in identifying possible target groups for new initiatives and in the design of programmes themselves. It is well-established in consumer and diffusion research (Rogers 1983) that consumers cannot be conceived as a homogeneous group with similar attitudes, beliefs, values and needs. It is therefore of relevance to both social-scientific theory and practice to trace those consumer characteristics which either facilitate or impede the adoption of opportunities offered by local conservation programmes.

This section will contrast findings from the six case studies in order to determine whether social segmentation occurs with respect to consumers' awareness of, participation in, and take-up of the local programmes. An adopter/non-adopter or client/non-client comparison regarding a number of personal characteristics will be the main analytic approach. As the various local programmes studied were already operating, the researchers could not make use of sophisticated before and after experimental designs. Therefore, most studies are at best ex post facto experiments or perhaps more accurately comparative group studies using an adopter/non-adopter comparison. As a result of this our analysis of consumers' attitudes and beliefs is based on measures taken after the programmes had been implemented. Since the very act of participating or not-participating may change people's attitudes we can only draw tentative conclusions about the role of such personal characteristics before the programmes were implemented.

### Attitudes and values

As noted it is misleading to conceive of consumers as a more or less homogeneous group sharing similar attitudes, beliefs, norms, personal and social values. Gaskell and Pike (1983) showed that people differ with respect to energy literacy and that such differences are related to energy conservation behaviours in the home. At issue here is whether adopters and non-adopters of local conservation programmes differ in terms of energy conservation attitudes and behaviours, personal commitment to conservation, personal and social values directly or indirectly related to energy conservation and knowledge of residential energy use.

265

Moreover, it might be expected that adopters and non-adopters would have different beliefs about the advantages and disadvantages of programme participation, about the credibility and perceived expertise of programme agencies, as well as about the programme itself. Of immediate relevance in this context is the question whether adopters and non-adopters differ in their energy conservation attitudes and related social values. In most of the studies the findings show that general energy related attitudes do not differentiate between adopters and non-adopters, a result which is in line with observations from many other behavioural energy studies (Ester 1985; Olsen 1981). However, in Conflans/France there is a clear attitudinal difference between those who accepted the audit and those who refused it. The former group were more likely to believe that energy saving is an important matter and to be more knowledgeable about energy use in the home. Thus while positive attitudes do not lead automatically to adoption, negative attitudes may be related to the rejection of new energy saving measures.

There is also evidence that adopters are more personally committed to energy conservation than non-adopters. According to the US case they feel more personally responsible for helping to alleviate energy problems, favour governmental action to deal with environmental problems, such as limiting economic and population growth and wish to avoid the need for constructing new electric generating plants. The German study showed that adopters of ecologists' services have a stronger attitude toward conservation than adopters of services by other, more formal organizations. In France too, the adopters were more concerned about energy saving in their town.

*Past experience of energy conservation*

The next issue is whether adopters and non-adopters differ with respect to energy saving actions in their household before programme participation. There is evidence for such differences.

On the one hand in Eugene/US case it was observed that, on average, non-participants had taken slightly more conservation actions prior to the programme than had participants, but that as a result of the programme the participants subsequently took six times as many actions as the non-participants. The Zutphen/NL study found no differences between adopters and non-adopters in pre-programme conservation behaviours.

However, in the French and three of the German cases it was

found that consumers who participated in the programme had implemented significantly more conservation measures prior to the programme than non-participants. Thus there may be a self-selection effect in the sense that conservation programmes seem to attract consumers who are already involved in conservation behaviour. This effect may be related to the earlier finding that adopters are more personally committed to energy conservation than non-adopters.

A possible explanation for the US case is that all the people in the study had had a home energy audit, thus the participant/non-participant distinction came from involvement in the Buy-Back programme. It is likely that those who did not participate found that the audit more or less confirmed what they already knew or had acted upon. Although their homes were still relatively poorly insulated they may have considered that they had done enough already.

Almost by definition, programme use follows familiarity or knowledge of the programme and favourable initial attitudes towards it. Most studies indicate that adopters had more positive attitudes toward it, as compared to non-adopters. However, knowledge and positive attitudes may be a necessary but not a sufficient condition for programme take-up. In Zutphen/NL, for example, it was found that the majority of adopters of the insulation programme held favourable attitudes toward the programme, but favourable attitudes were also more common than unfavourable ones among the non-adopters. As will be discussed below other factors influenced the non-adopters decision.

*Expectations about programme participation*

Thus far we have found that adopters tend to hold more positive attitudes about energy saving, to be more committed to conservation and to have been more involved in energy saving actions prior to programme participation. We now look to see whether adopters and non-adopters differ in their expectations about the likely costs and benefits of programme participation.

All studies provide strong evidence that such differences occur. Moreover, it appears that these differences are quite consistent across the programmes. The two most important considerations to participate in a conservation programme appear to be:

* the expectation of savings on the energy bill
* the expectation of increased comfort or better housing quality

In comparing the decision making criteria of adopters and non-adopters it is clear that these groups of consumers differ in their estimates of the costs and benefits of programme participation. Adopters expect more positive outcomes of programme adoption, whereas non-adopters expect more negative outcomes, and vice versa. Thus, adopters believe that improved comfort, savings on the energy bill, and fewer draughts are likely consequences of accepting the services offered by the conservation programme, whereas non-adopters are less convinced and feel that negative impacts -especially financial costs - are quite likely.

As far as collective advantages are concerned, for example reduction of environmental pollution, saving energy for future generations and job creation the findings are less consistent. The Zutphen/NL case found no evidence that considerations of collective advantages differentiated between adopters and non-adopters. However in the German case all the user groups rated the environmental benefits of energy conservation highly and in Eugene/US it was found that public concerns were important in deciding to participate in the programme. Eugene in Oregon has a history of environmentalism as has Tuebingen and thus the inconsistent findings between the German and American cases on the one hand and the Dutch case on the other, may reflect more general differences in public sentiments about energy conservation and environmental protection.

**The household context**

In this section three aspects of the household context will be addressed in relationship to programme participation and programme impacts:

* the micro-economic position of households: the relationship between programme adoption and household income, perception of future budget position, budget management, payback estimates.

* socio-demographic characteristics: the relationship between programme adoption and education, socio-economic status, marital status and life cycle position.

* social interaction in households: the relationship between programme adoption and assignment of household roles, decision making regarding adoption and non-adoption, joint or individual decisions and intra-household communication.

Before turning to the findings some general remarks are in order. As observed many times price is one of the most important reasons for consumers to conserve energy. A number of earlier behavioural energy studies reported positive relationships between income and conservation efforts (Bultena 1976; Milstein 1976). Some studies, on the other hand, found a nonlinear relationship between income and conservation with middle-income consumers demonstrating greatest conservation efforts (Kilkeary 1975; Morrison, Keith and Zuiches 1979).

One explanation for the existence of such a nonlinear relationship has been offered by Cunningham and Lopreato (1977). According to their explanation high income consumers use more energy and can better afford to keep doing so at higher energy costs. At the same time they can decrease their energy consumption without major life style implications. Low income consumers, however, cannot do so since their energy consumption is already minimal and further cutbacks would create serious lifestyle threats. Middle income consumers are therefore believed to be the most active income segment with respect to taking conservation actions, as they are sensitive to price increases and are able to decrease their consumption of energy without major lifestyle alterations.

The case studies do not suggest a straightforward relationship between household income and programme adoption. In the French, German and Swedish studies higher income consumers were found to be more likely to participate in the conservation programme(s) compared to lower income consumers, whereas the British study - though having a more homogeneous sample in the sense of income distribution - observed that clients had somewhat lower incomes 'than non-clients. In turn, the US and Dutch cases found no relationship between household income and programme adoption.

The interpretations of these findings changes somewhat, however, if one relates the outcomes to the nature of the programmes. If programmes include low-cost/no-cost conservation measures (as in the Dutch and British programmes) or other significant economic incentives (as in the US programme), there are not substantial differences in programme adoption between different income segments. However, loans and preferential interest rates (as in Sweden and France) are not sufficient to overcome the financial constraints faced by low income households.

Thus, it cannot be concluded that the mere implementation of a local element in conservation programmes is a sufficient condition for reaching low income consumers. Other factors, including low-cost conservation measures appear to be necessary.

Within this context of the micro-economic position of households it is also important to note that, apart from a more or less objective variable like income, consumers' subjective perception of their economic situation may effect their decision taking. Some interesting evidence for the importance of such perceptions is offered by both the US and Dutch cases. Although these studies did not find any effects related to income, it was observed that adopters are less likely than non-adopters to report a deterioration of their financial situation in the last three to five years.

Furthermore, adopters were more optimistic about their incomes in the immediate future. The US case found that an important reason not to participate in the programme was cash problems. With people in the same income bracket it was suggested that adopters may be better managers of their household finances, that is, they may be more skilful at making a household budget, keeping their expenses within that budget, and having some cash reserves on hand for unusual expenses such as weatherization improvements.

Finally, expecting fast paybacks from household investments is an important barrier for participation in conservation activities, since such investments may only produce relatively long-term financial advantages to the household. This assumption is substantiated by the US study which observed that non-adopters were more likely than adopters to expect a very short payback period (three years or less), while adopters were willing to wait at least five years or longer for conservation investments to pay for themselves.

*Socio-demographic characteristics*

Evaluation studies of national energy conservation information campaigns have observed quite consistently that such campaigns often fail in reaching lower educated and older consumers. This appears to be especially the case with campaigns which rely heavily on transferring written conservation information for example conservation leaflets and advertisements. It is well-known from communications theory that consumers with lower educational levels can be less easily reached with written information. It is often observed that these groups experience difficulties in interpreting, for instance, numerical

270

information, which is usually an elementary part of such campaigns (cf. Ester 1985). Therefore, it is interesting to analyse whether local conservation programmes involving personal contact, informal local channels and social networks are better able to overcome these problems and to reach these consumer groups. Also from a more general policy point of view it is important to relate programme adoption (or non-adoption) to specific demographic characteristics. Thus this section will look at a number of demographic variables, including education, socioeconomic status, age, marital status and life cycle as possible mediators of programme awareness, participation and conservations behaviours.

As with micro-economic characteristics of adopters and non-adopters, findings with respect to differences in education and socioeconomic status are varied but the overall conclusion points in the same direction. The Dutch and US cases found no relationship between programme adoption and education and socioeconomic status, whereas the French and German cases - and to some extent also the Swedish case - observed an over-representation of those from the higher education and socioeconomic groups among adopters. The finding that both the Dutch and US programmes were equally able to reach varied educational and socioeconomic consumer segments is, again, related to the favourable economic incentives offered by these programmes.

Not all studies report about differences in adoption in relationship to age, marital status and life cycle of the target population. In the British case, for instance, such differentiation is absent given a fairly homogeneous target sample of old age pensioners. The most elaborate analysis of these variables is offered by the French study and to a lesser degree by the German study. In France it was observed that gender differences are important: men living alone were very active in programme participation, whereas women living alone were quite passive. The most favourable life cycle position for programme adoption is generally 35-49 years which can be characterized as a stable and prosperous period in their life cycle. The German case also provides evidence for the importance of life cycle. It appears that marriage and the presence of children are major determinants of a higher-than-average programme participation (number of conservation measures taken). Retired persons show the opposite pattern: they are underrepresented among those using the advisory services offered by the programme and took fewer conservation actions. Moreover, in this case there is strong evidence that higher income and older households turn to a different type of programme, in this case that of the utility, while younger and lower income households tend to prefer the ecologists' service.

According to the Eugene/US case adopters are more likely than non-adopters to be one-adult or two-persons households and to have fewer children. By considering the economic demands in the different age categories, it is suggested that programme adoption is lowest in the middle years of life when such demands are typically greatest.

On the whole these findings point to the conclusion that it is during stable and prosperous periods of the life cycle that the greatest energy conservation efforts are made. In different countries the actual age profile of this period varies due probably to economic demands of house purchase, the schooling of children etc.

*Social interaction in households*

Although numerous survey studies have been conducted since 1973 on consumers' attitudes toward energy conservation (Ester 1985; Olsen 1981), very few studies have investigated household decision making processes with respect to conservation actions (Perlman and Warren 1977). A recent study by Gaskell and Bates (1986) shows that males and females attach different levels of importance to attributes of energy conservation decisions; males giving greater importance to energy savings while females are more concerned about improvements in comfort levels. It seems reasonable to assume that decisions are taken within the family, after consultation and discussion rather than by one individual alone. At present the bulk of research has focused solely upon individuals but little is known about household dynamics. For example how salient is energy conservation the household agenda? How do households function as energy management systems? How do they decide about adoption or non-adoption of conservation programmes? Are these decision taken jointly or not? In what way is the distribution of household roles related to decision making characteristics?

By interviewing different members of the same family in Eugene/US the study addresses these questions in relationship to local conservation programmes as does the Dutch study albeit to a lesser degree. One of the most interesting findings from the US case is that joint decision making and responsibility sharing between adults is more common among households which adopted the conservation programme as compared to households which did not adopt the programme. These joint decisions and shared responsibilities include household maintenance and upkeep tasks, initiating new ideas for improving the house, major household expenditures, and taking conservation actions.

Thus, it appears that traditional role distribution and decision making vis-a-vis household tasks is more characteristic of non-adopting households. Also, it was found that couples participating in the local programme are more equally interested in and knowledgeable about energy conservation, as well as more strongly committed to conservation goals than non-participating couples.

The Dutch study on the Zutphen conservation programme also provides evidence for the importance of joint decision making between adult members of a household with respect to programme adoption. It was observed that in the adopters group both adult members had positive attitudes toward the programme, whereas 80 percent of the home companions of the interviewed non-adopters had negative attitudes toward the retrofit programme. It appears, therefore, that take-up of conservation programmes in the typical household is more likely when decisions are made jointly and when both adults are persuaded of the benefits of energy conservation. Given the findings of Gaskell and Bates (1986) it would seem necessary to design strategies focused at both male and female interests.

Discussions within the household about participation in conservation programmes are clearly an important process affecting decision making about programme adoption. However, frequency and intensity of programme discussion are not necessarily related to programme participation. The US study, for example, found that although adopters more than non-adopters believe that their friends and neighbours approve of taking weatherization actions, they are somewhat less likely than non-adopters to discuss such topics with their family members, friends, and neighbours. The explanation is probably that when households are in full agreement about the importance of weatherization or taking other conservation actions they feel no need to discuss the matter in order to reach consensus.

**The community context**

In this section some characteristics of the local communities that have affected the initiation, organization and effectiveness of the conservation programmes in the six studies will be analysed.

Community characteristics may have a more active or passive role. In local programmes it is possible to make deliberate and active use of the small-scale social structures by taking account of specific community characteristics in the design stage. Thus for example a heterogeneous community requires a communication plan which differentiates between the different target groups; a system with high mobility must take account of the special cost-benefit structure of conservation instruments for residents who expect to move soon. The organization of a programme should take account of political sensitivities to avoid getting involved in local conflicts. Perhaps more typical is the passive role. Community characteristics are not acknowledged in programme design but act either to promote or inhibit programme effectiveness.

Thus we hypothesize that the awareness of and participation in a programme and the behaviour change it promotes will be strongly influenced by the structure of the community's social networks and the communication which takes place through such networks. Two basic elements of the communication processes can be identified:

* the diffusion effect: the spread of awareness about a programme
* the social influence effect: social pressures on attitudes and behaviours relevant to programme participation.

With respect to the process of diffusion our analysis builds on the theory of social networks (Rogers and Kincaid 1983; Knoke and Kuglinsky 1982).

In a social system people may have weak or strong connections. The interaction channels between the individuals form an entity of direct and indirect social ties which is called a 'communication network'. The nature of a system can be social (a cultural association) or spatial (a neighbourhood). Larger networks can be dense at particular points and more loose at others. Small homogeneous groups with a dense network of strong ties are called cliques. Within cliques communication will diffuse quickly. Between cliques, however, diffusion will be slower and dependent on the few persons who connect the cliques. Often within cliques often a central person can be identified who has many connections, high social status and often many external contacts. Opinion leaders can play an important role in making a social system aware of a programme and convincing people of its usefulness, but also the opposite direction by stimulating rejection of the programme (Rogers 1983; Leonard-Barton 1981).

Openness to the outside and the number of outside connections are another important aspect of a social system (Warren and Warren 1980). An open system has more and easier entrances than a closed system. A conservation programme should take this into consideration, especially during the early stages of implementation.

As already mentioned the diffusion of information is not the only goal of a conservation programme. More important is that people change their attitudes, participate in the programme and take conservation actions. To reach these goals the social network plays a crucial role, but to use it optimally the analysis needs to go beyond the diffusion of information and to include social influence processes. In social psychology, social influence processes have been studied from different perspectives: from learning theory (modelling), from communication theory (persuasion) and from conformity theory (social norms). It is not possible to discuss all these theories at length in this chapter (Bandura 1962; Winett et al. 1982 for modelling; Janis and Hovland 1959; McGuire 1969 and Ester 1985 for persuasion; Fishbein and Ajzen 1973, and Midden and Ritsema 1983 for normative approaches). There are however, some interesting applications of these theoretical approaches.

An application of modelling can be found in the use of demonstration houses where people can see how neighbours in comparable situations adapt their house to make it more energy efficient (Olsen and Cluett 1979). Another example is the introduction of a practical workshop in which people learn to apply conservation techniques. An example of persuasion is the use of opinion leaders in the Dutch village Gasselte where high status inhabitants convinced others to participate in the local conservation programme (De Boer et al. 1982). An example of conformity is the diffusion of solar technology. The possession of this technology by neighbours proved to be the best predictor of adoption in a US study (Leonard-Barton 1981). Finally, normative processes can be used by publishing testimonials in local media.

For all social influence processes the effectiveness will be greatest if the system has a high level of interaction and if people are homogeneous and comparable to each other. Furthermore, the stability of the system is important: in a system with high spatial mobility it will be difficult to develop the network channels which are necessary for information diffusion and social influence processes.

Based on these more theoretical considerations the following indicators are used for the analysis of community effects on local conservation programmes:

* level of homogeneity
* spatial mobility
* interhousehold communication
* normative support by opinion leaders
* normative support by community leaders and community organizations
* the compatibility between community identity (as a set of common norms and values) and the conservation programme

First, we will discuss how each of these community characteristics are taken into account in the design and implementation of conservation programmes. Secondly, ways in which these characteristics influenced programme impacts will be determined. As far as possible from the available data we will consider the following programme impacts:

* programme awareness: which community characteristics contribute to awareness of the conservation programme and to what extent?

* programme participation: which community characteristics contribute to household participation and to what extent?

* conservation actions: which community characteristics contribute to households taking conservation actions and to what extent?

*Homogeneity*

This characteristic refers to the relative heterogeneity or homogeneity of the populations which have been selected as target groups for the local programmes. This may be the community, a specific social category (renters, pensioners) or a geographic category (a neighbourhood), or a combination of both. Target groups, of course, may differ with respect to social, household, technical or economic characteristics. In general it can be assumed that the more homogeneous the target group the more effective conservation programmes can be tailored to the needs and characteristics of the target group.

The British programmes were tailored to a very homogeneous target group. Nevertheless the authors conclude that one informational strategy was not sufficient to reach all eligible clients and particularly the more socially isolated. Apparently, more careful targeting is necessary for this category of consumers. The US study found that a homogeneous population supported the goals of the programme. This finding is in contrast to, for example, the Seattle City Light programme (Olsen and Cluett 1979) where several policy options led to political opposition, rooted in the heterogeneity of Seattle's population. Thus, programme organization and development may also benefit form a homogeneous population which can result in a more supportive legitimating body.

The same phenomenon appeared in Conflans/France. Here some political position arose among the conservative higher class inhabitants who opposed the energy conservation programme because it was perceived as an initiative of the socialist mayor. In addition the heterogeneity of the target population inhibited sufficient participation throughout the population, particularly among disadvantaged consumers. In Tuebingen/FRG however, the three major programmes covered all shades of the ideological opinion. Each programme attracted a specific group, the ecologists' programme attracted more ecological interested citizens than the utility programme.

In sum, the findings suggest that it is easier to promote programme awareness and participation in a homogeneous target group. Since communities will tend to be relative heterogeneous pluralistic approaches as seen in Tuebingen/FRG are likely to be more successful.

*Spatial mobility*

The second community factor is spatial mobility. The guiding hypothesis is that the higher the level of mobility in the target group, the fewer residents will be interested in energy conservation actions, particularly in programmes that require investments in energy savings. People who expect to move within some years will not be eager to invest in longer term investments. In Conflans/France a mobility effect was visible with respect the the adoption of an energy audit. The group which expected to move within some years took less audits. The US case concluded that residents who lived longer in the neighbourhood showed more interest in conservation actions. In the Dutch study the residents living in 'maisonettes' had a higher mobility rate. This was also the group with the highest percentage of people who 'never heard about the scheme'. This finding should be interpreted with some care, as the residents of maisonettes differed from the other inhabitants in more than mobility rates, for example they also had fewer social contacts. In Sweden it appeared that the number of years that residents already lived in their homes was not related to the number of conservation actions taken. No differences were found between active and non-active households in terms of the number of years they already lived in their homes. It appeared that the future perspective was more dominant: active residents felt more certain to stay in their present dwellings for at least another five years.

It can be concluded that in cases of a high mobility population a programme should take this into consideration. An example is provided by the Dutch case where no relation existed between adoption and spatial mobility. The special programme feature was that the financial commitments were not connected to the renter as a person but to the house: the rents were increased somewhat as a consequence of the home improvements but this increase was compensated by a reduction in the energy bill. As soon as the tenant wanted to move, he was freed of the investment consequences which were automatically transferred to the next renter.

*Interhousehold communication*

This variable is probably one of the most central factors with respect to the impact of the community context. As was noted in the introduction to this section, the level and pattern of interaction and communication are vital factors for the diffusion of information and the acceptance of the programmes. In the British study 40 percent of the target group said they had become aware of the local insulation project through informal contacts within their social networks. In addition 47 percent of the adopters had recommended the programme to other residents. The study concludes that in the most successful scheme, the social network was used most intensely. The researchers note that the effects of social network processes become more visible after a project had run for some time. In Germany, too, personal contacts were more important than impersonal information services. In the Swedish case, however, friends and neighbours were not a very important source of information. A partial explanation might be that here it concerns 'national' programmes which are relevant to individuals but not to a specific local social system. Hamler (as quoted in the Swedish study) demonstrated that in a more specifically local conservation programme tailored to residents of apartment flats, social interaction was very important.

In the Dutch case the importance of informal communication between residents is clearly confirmed. Adopters talked more often about the programme and had also heard more positive reactions from other residents than non-adopters. This result should be interpreted with care. It does not necessarily mean that social contacts cause adoption. It does show that social support is related to adoption. Social support can intervene between attitude and behaviour but can also promote adoptive behaviour independent of existing attitudes. The findings indicate that residents talk more often about the programme after adoption. Non-adopters who had never heard of the programme had less social contacts than adopters, which indicates that social contacts improve programme awareness.

In the US study a contradictory result was found: non-participants in the programme were more likely to talk about it with their friends and neighbours than were participants. A possible explanation of this finding is that participants were convinced of the desirability of the programme and hence felt little need to discuss it with others, while those who were sceptical about the programme did discuss it with others in an effort to corroborate their viewpoint. The German study observed that communication about the programme correlated positively with energy conservation actions taken and also with the search for additional information about conservation. In Conflans/France the non-adopters of the audits were often isolated people who had only a few contacts in the community. Programme participation correlated strongly with the degree of social involvement as measured by membership rates of local clubs, organizations and political parties. This study found a snowball effect in the diffusion of programme adoption while in other areas the opposite effect occurred: a growing opposition toward the programme. Thus, spatial and social factors influenced both the nature of the diffusion process of programme adoption and non-adoption.

In summary it can be concluded that interhousehold communication plays a crucial role in most programmes investigated. The main functions are represented in Figure 9.1

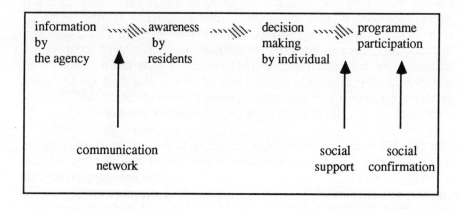

Figure 9.1 Functions of interhousehold communication in the adoption process.

The first function of interhousehold communication is increasing programme awareness in the community. The social network is an important channel for calling people's attention. The second function is mediating social support which stimulates residents to participate in the programme and take action. The third function is social confirmation. Residents communicate about their actions and exchange experiences to ensure the wisdom of their actions and to reduce possible behavioural dissonance.

*Opinion leaders and community leaders*

A distinction can be made between opinion and community leaders. Opinion leaders operate more on a smaller-scale level which can be a neighbourhood or a local social organization. Opinion leaders have primarily informal influence. Community leaders exert influence through their formal position on local initiatives like a conservation programme. Of course both roles can be integrated in one person, but not necessarily so.

In the case studies the distinction is not easy to pursue because opinion leaders on the neighbourhood level are not identified in most studies. However, community leaders played an important role in many programmes and in a number of cases also acted as opinion leaders. In Conflans/France, for instance, the Union of Traders and Craftsmen supported the programme and this proved to be crucial. The town hall on the contrary was reluctant to participate anticipating negative public opinion.

Closely related to the community leaders is the support by community organizations. In Conflans, again, it was found that the members of community organizations like the labour union, political parties and cultural organizations took more actions. Integration in the local community leads to higher programme awareness, to a more positive identification with programme goals and to more participation.

In the British study membership of local organizations was part of the constructed index of social integration which discriminated between adopters and non-adopters. The evaluation of the Eugene/US programme showed the importance of support by business leaders and leaders of neighbourhood associations. It also showed that the co-operation of the city manager, the EWEB director and business representatives was a vital condition for programme success. In the Netherlands and Sweden the community programmes are not considered as politically 'hot' issues. So, although it was important that community organizations were involved in the organization of the project (see also the Chapter 8) the support of these organizations in a psychological sense does not seem crucial in the various programmes.

*Community identity*

The identity people attribute to their community can play an important role in both a positive and negative sense. Its relevance depends on the possible relationship between the dominant identity, and the content and scale of the programme. As an example of the first point one might imagine a situation in which energy conservation is in contradiction to present norms and values in a community. In Veynes/France for example, the dominant feeling was that Veynes was a 'railway town' with many residents working as railway employees. The conversion to an image of 'solar city' was not compatible with the existing dominant identity.

Similar phenomena could be expected in relation to the type of conservation action. Some actions are considered fashionable and others are not. In many high income areas solar technologies are very popular, while other less visible actions are less so. Compatibility with existing values and behavioural patterns is an important factor in adoption processes (Darley and Beniger 1981). On the community level this implies that if a programme is in conflict with dominant values and commitments which are reflected in the community identity, this can be an inhibiting factor.

The identity of an energy conserving community can also be a very desirable one. It might create jobs but may also function as a barrier to outside constraints. A clear example of the last point is the Dutch village, Gasselte, which runs an impressive conservation programme as an answer to attempts by the national government to select Gasselte as a storage place for radioactive waste from nuclear power stations.

Community identity is of less relevance in cases in which the programme focuses on only part of the community like a specific neighbourhood or social category. This explains why in the Netherlands and Britain the community identity did not seem to be an important factor, while in France ('Veynes, solar city', 'the Conflans Challenge') and also in Eugene/US the community identity played a role. In Sweden this aspect was not very relevant mainly because the programmes are organized on a national level and cannot be attributed to local initiatives.

**Conclusions and policy recommendation**

In this comparative analysis investigating the ways in which the contexts of consumption mediate programme impacts we have looked at the various aspects of the personal, household and community contexts separately. The arguments in this chapter are 'ceteris paribus' that is relationships are interpreted and instanced one by one. In reality, of course for each household there is a very complex interaction between these different contexts.

This is perhaps best illustrated in the study of reactions to the programme in Conflans/France. Here four types of consumers were identified, each type being characterized by a variety of personal, household and community attributes. Amongst the non-participants two types were observed, the not-interested and the opponents. The not-interested group were unfamiliar with the national energy con-

282

servation campaigns, had done little to save energy in the past and were not concerned about energy saving. They were of low socio-economic status and lived in either terraced or rented homes. Thus for a variety of reasons they felt that the programme was irrelevant. On the other hand the opponents reaction was motivated by political ideology, coming from the conservative upper middle classes they objected to an initiative by the socialist mayor. Although they were familiar with the national programmes and had well insulated homes they perhaps could afford to feel that energy saving is not important. Of the participants two types were observed, the consenters and converts. The consenters had positive attitudes to energy saving, were economical in their habits and were satisfied with the programme. These middle class people lived in areas of the town in which there was a snowball effect amongst the community. However with declining standards of living they preferred to rely on behavioural actions rather than more costly home improvements. The converts are the typical well-educated middle class early adopters. They have positive attitudes to energy saving, are familiar with existing programmes and are well integrated in the community. They had already carried out many home improvements and took advantage of the new services on offer.

Thus we see the interplay of a number of different contextual factors which together are related to people's reactions to a particular energy conservation programme. We can only speculate about the most influential of these in determining the reactions of the different groups. Setting aside the converts whose enthusiastic participation would be welcomed by any programme implementor it is possible that the major constraint to participation for the not-interested was tenure, for the opponents, political beliefs and for the consenters, economic considerations.

This example shows the complex relationships between programmes, consumers' actions and their context. Attitudes towards programmes and past energy conservation actions influence programme acceptance, programme content is likely to influence attitudes toward the programme and attitudes toward new conservation actions. The programme encourages conservation actions, actors seek confirmation of their actions in the programme itself. Because of these complex cyclic processes it not possible to directly derive conclusions from our data about causal relationships. Where causal relationships are suggested these must be considered as more or less plausible interpretations.

Highlighting the findings concerning the personal, household and community contexts, a number of points emerge which must be taken into account in the formulation and implementation of programmes. First with respect to the differences between typical adopters and non-adopters we find that adopters are more likely to:

* believe savings to be more likely
* expect improved comfort and better housing quality
* have more favourable cost-benefit estimates
* make joint decisions about energy conservation
* feel economically more secure
* accept longer payback periods

This points at the centrality of economic decision making in energy conservation. Whatever other goals are pursued be they ecological or social policy oriented the importance of this aspect will be neglected at great cost.

In turn the micro-economic position of target groups may lead to constraints to programme participation. In this respect the Dutch programme offers an interesting answer to payback barriers, especially when the target group is characterized by low incomes and high mobility. Here the tenants did not pay for the insulation measures as the rent increase of those measures balanced their energy savings. More experimentation with this kind of solution to investment barriers is therefore recommended for the rental sector.

The subtle interactions between community characteristics and the functioning of local programmes do not lead to clear cut conclusions. It is safe to say, however, that the more similar the socio demographic characteristics of a target group, the easier it will be to reach them and encourage participation. Correspondingly, the higher the political homogeneity of the legitimating body, the better the programme can be anchored and supported in the community.

It is important to note that the existing community identity can interfere with conservation programmes because of value or commitment incompatibility. In such cases community identity will function as a cultural local barrier to programme acceptance.

In spite of existing possibilities very little account is taken of specific community aspects in the programmes studied. In particular differences in homogeneity and problems resulting from by high mobility have been ignored. Little or no use is made, in a conscious way, of informal and formal social networks, nor is the nature of the social networks used as a selection criterion for an adequate communication strategy.

Finally we should like to address the issue of possible interactions between personal and community context factors. It would be erroneous to conclude that a homogeneous and cohesive target group will automatically lead to programme success. Highly important is the precise tuning of a programme to existing attitudes, beliefs, knowledge and financial barriers within the target group. At this point a relation exists with community characteristics. For instance, in a cohesive social network negative attitudes toward the programme can develop into normatively supported resistance. On the other hand positive dispositions can also be reinforced in a cohesive target group. The effect of a strong social system can therefore go in two directions: stimulating positive dispositions and diffusing information efficiently; or enhancing effective resistance, confirming misjudgements and increasing the risk of programme failure.

Summing up, we find that take up of energy conservation services is influenced by the configuration of contextual factors operating at three levels: the personal dispositions of individuals, the socio-economic position of households and the wider community structures. To this extent it must be accepted that no one programme will fit the diversity of all possible configurations. Realistically there will be always difficult cases defined on all of the three levels and inevitably programme users are the easy cases. It must be kept in mind too that in selecting communities for study we have an inbuilt bias towards interesting and even 'privileged' examples. Even in these settings successes were largely found amongst the economically more advantaged groups. Irrespective of socio-economic position it is these consumers with both commitment and past experience of energy conservation that tend to be the typical user. Thus while we have evidence that local programmes attenuate the social selectivity effects of public policies for energy conservation, without much more effort and funds invested the frontiers will not be pushed back very far.

**References**

Bandura, A. 1962, Social learning through imitation. In M.R. Jones (ed.) *Nebraska symposium on motivation*, Lincoln University Press.

De Boer, J., Ester, P., Mindell, C., and Schopman, M. 1982, *Consumer energy conservation programs in the Netherlands*. Paper presented at the International Conference on Consumer Behavior and Energy Policy, Noordwijkerhout.

Bultena, G. 1976, *Public response to the energy crisis: A study of citizen's attitudes and adaptive behaviors*. Unpublished manuscript, Iowa State University, Department of Sociology and Anthropology, Sociology Report 130, Ames, Iowa.

Cunningham, W.H. and Lopreato, S.C. 1977, *Energy use and conservation incentives: A study of the Southwestern United States*. Praeger:New York.

Darley, J.M. and Beniger, J.R. 1981, Diffusion of energy conserving innovations. *Journal of Social Issues*, 33, 2, 150-171.

Ester, P. 1985, *Consumer behavior and energy conservation; A policy oriented experimental field study on the effectiveness of behavioral intervention promoting residential energy conservation*. Dordrecht: Martinus Nijhoff.

Fishbein, M. and Ajzen, I. 1973, Attitudinal and normative variables as predictors of specific behavior. *Journal of Personality and Social Psychology*, 27, 41-57.

Gaskell, G. and Bates, J.J. 1986, *Energy saving investments: consumers decision making strategies*. In E. Monnier, G. Gaskell, P. Ester, B. Joerges, B. LaPillonne, C. Midden and L. Puiseux (eds.) *Consumer Behaviour and Energy Policy*. Praeger: New York

Gaskell, G. and Pike, R. 1983, Residential energy use: an investigation of consumers and conservation strategies. *Journal of Consumer Policy*, 6, 285-302.

Hemrica, H. Inkomen en gasverbruik van gezinshuishoudingen. *Gas*, 1981, 101, 67-74.

Janis, I., and Hovland, C.I. 1959, *Personality and persuasibility*. New Haven, Yale University Press.

Kilkeary, K. 1975, *The energy crisis and decision-making in the family*. National Technical Information Service, PB-238-783.

Knoke, D. and Kuglinsky, H. 1982, *Network analysis*. London: Sage.

Leonard-Barton, D. 1981, Diffusion of energy conservation and technologies. In J.D. Claxton, D.C. Anderson, J.R.B. Ritchie, and G.H.G. McDougall, (eds.) *Consumers and Energy Conservation*. New York: Praeger.

McGuire, W.J. 1969, The nature of attitudes and attitude change. In G. Lindzey and E. Aronson (eds.) *The Handbook of Social Psychology*, 2nd edition, 3, Reading, Mass: Addison-Wesley.

Midden, C.J.H. and Ritsema, B.S.M. 1983, The meaning of normative processes for energy conservation. *Journal of Economic Psychology*, 4, 37-55.

Milstein, J.S. 1976, *Attitudes, knowledge and behavior of American consumers regarding energy conservation with some implications for governmental action*. Paper presented at the National Meeting of the Association for Consumer Research.

Morrison, B.M., Keith, J. and Zuiches, J.G. 1979, Impacts on household energy consumption: An empirical study of Michigan families. In C. Unseld, D. Morrison, D. Sills and C.P. Wolf (eds.) *Socio-Political effects of energy use and policy*. National Academy of Sciences, Washington D.C.

Olsen, M.E. 1981, Consumers' attitudes toward energy conservation. *Journal of Social Issues*, 37, 108-131.

Olsen, M.E. and Cluett, C. 1979, *Evaluation of the Seattle City Light Neighborhood conservation program*. Battelle Human Affairs Research Centers, Seattle.

Perlman, R. and Warren, R. 1977, *Families in the energy crisis: Impacts and implications for theory and policy*. Ballinger, Cambridge M.A.

Rogers, E. 1983, *Diffusion of innovations*. Free Press: New York.

Roger, E. and Kincaid, D.L. 1981, *Communication networks: toward a new paradigm for research*. Free Press: New York.

Warren, D.I. and Warren R.B. 1980, *The neighborhood organizer's handbook*. University of Notre Dame: London.

Winett, R.A., Hatcher, J.E., Fort, T.R., Leckliter, I.N., Love, S.Q., Riley, A.W., and Fishback, J.F. 1982. The effects of videotape modelling and daily feedback on residential electricity conservation, home temperature and humidity, perceived comfort and clothing worn: Winter and summer. *Journal of Applied Behavior Analysis*, 15, 381-402.

# PART IV
# CONCLUSIONS AND IMPLICATIONS

# 10 A social scientific and policy perspective on energy conservation and research

GEORGE GASKELL and BERNWARD JOERGES

## Introduction

In this chapter we review the implications of this research for policy and social science. With respect to policy we discuss the strengths and weaknesses of local programmes: make specific recommendations about programme formulation, implementation and evaluation, the three key stages in conducting energy conservation programmes: and finally, make suggestions for national and supranational bodies about ways in which they might contribute both to the development of local energy conservation schemes and multinational research. In the context of social science we discuss the problems and vexations inherent in applied multidisciplinary research and set out some modest proposals for future research. Finally we note some general issues about the nature of social change and identify various issues for further research.

## The strengths and weaknesses of local conservation programmes

In 'Energy Use: The Human Dimension', Stern and Aronson (1984) from the US National Research Council, while noting the remarkable growth of local energy action in the United States, some 2,000 examples in a decade, comment that there has been a striking inattention to this important phenomenon by evaluation researchers.

Reviewing the limited literature they felt unable to draw any firm conclusions about the prospects and achievements of local energy action yet they argue that local energy action merits careful research since it may be one of the most exciting policy strategies for the future. The present research can be seen as at least a partial answer to their question regarding the potential of local energy action to contribute to the solution for national problems.

When viewed as a whole the case studies confirm the value of local programmes as a policy initiative in two particular arenas. Firstly as an implementing structure for central policy, secondly in the development of alternative community level instruments for energy conservation policy.

Both of these opportunities are predicated on the existence of strong upward linkages between local actors and central authorities and agencies, for only in exceptional circumstances local programmes are viable without these.

The advantages local programmes offer are as follows, although it must be recognized that all these are seldom realized in any one programme.

* targeting different consumer groups by the tailoring of services to their needs;

* adjusting flexibility and capitalizing upon the particular circumstances of the community;

* mobilizing the various community resources to achieve programme goals;

* providing for feedback from participants to the programme agency for the purposes of programme development and change.

* serving the needs of less advantaged consumers.

The last of these opportunities is perhaps unique to local programmes allowing them to achieve not only energy policy but also social welfare goals. However, some qualifications are necessary. Reaching less advantaged clients is not an automatic product of localization. Without special provisions tenants, low income families and the elderly will fall through the net of local schemes just as they often do in the case of central programmes.

Our studies show that a strategy of localization of policies and programmes has emerged as one promising institutional response to energy conservation, and by implication to environmental conservation. Still, on the basis of our evidence the institutional battle can hardly be considered won. Local programmes are not only novel and, with the exception of Sweden and the United States, distinctly experimental; they are in themselves precarious undertakings as long as they are not linked to municipal policies and local authorities. Furthermore, the contribution of either the national or local energy utilities is related to their longer term success. How these requirements can be achieved on a broad scale is unresolved, both from the perspective of programme development and with regard to policy research.

In Europe, on the whole, municipal administration and local authorities are in a difficult position. In one respect they are 'organizations in decline', losing or shedding control, on the other hand they meet with a mounting number of 'social crises' and citizens' expectations to tackle these crises. Possible institutional responses in such situations are a major issue for future research (Czarniawska and Hedberg 1985).

## Recommendations for the design of local programmes

There are three ways to derive policy-related conclusions from our material. One is to present it to policy-makers, programme-designers and practitioners, and to develop policy requirements interactively. This would be ideal, but is hardly possible in an international, or supranational, setting. A second approach is to work from the specific recommendations spelled out in the case-studies, and to extract from them, as it were, elements common to all countries. A third and somewhat different approach is to draw on the comparative analyses of findings presented above.

In the following section the latter two approaches are combined in addressing what we consider to be the three main stages of conducting energy conservation programmes: programme formulation, programme implementation, and programme evaluation.

*Programme formulation*

Generally we are led to the conclusion that no one type of local programme studied can be considered as an exemplar for implementation across the wide range of local conditions and consumer requirements represented in our cases. Confronted with a choice either to organize comprehensive community-wide schemes or to allow for a variety of schemes catering to particular social groups and tapping particular local resources, the second strategy seems to be more promising, provided a modicum of co-ordination is involved and a mechanism for arbitration in case of conflict can be instituted. The following recommendations refer to more specific aspects of programme formulation.

*Combining energy conservation and other goals:* While programmes will typically have multiple goals, a distinction must be made between those initiated within official energy policy regimes and those initiated under other policy regimes, such as environmental protection, social welfare, and employment creation. The issue of combining goals presents itself differently for these two cases.

Where non-energy goals form an integral part of programme structure, particularly in combining energy services with more comprehensive social services for low income groups, retaining a longer term focus on energy conservation may prove difficult and will require strong upward linkage with and the support of some national energy conservation agency. Conversely, where non-energy goals are included, but subsidiary in status, programmes require conscious policy decisions and formal links with agencies representing these subsidiary interests and requisite resources to maintain a broad policy orientation. The fact that programmes are organized at the local level is in no way sufficient to achieve the degree of simultaneity in goal orientation which central programmes fail to achieve and which is a prerequisite for mobilizing local resources, reaching disadvantaged consumer groups, and for minimizing external costs.

A particular risk that single purpose conservation programmes face comes from the cyclical nature of both public attention to energy issues and the absolute and relative prices of fuels. Assuming that energy conservation actions have, within the time horizon of most private households and particularly less advantaged groups, a rather long lead time, and assuming that the present complacency in view of lower oil prices will sooner or later give way to a new 'crisis', energy conservation policies and programmes need to be stabilized by embedding them as a matter of routine in wider policies and programmes. An obvious candidate in this respect remains environmental policy. At an early age of introducing energy conservation policies it was quite obvious that 'the best environmental policy was energy conservation policy', and it must be considered a failure of energy conservation programmes not to have translated this maxim into local practice. Today, when environmental issues are becoming more prominent on political agendas, the reverse can be said from the point of view of energy conservation policy, that is, 'the best energy conservation policy is environmental policy'. Translating this maxim into local schemes which originate under the auspices of environmental policy will give continuity to a line of public policy which has hardly begun to evolve as an established and stable feature of local policy making.

*Choice of implementing agencies:* The most effective implementing agencies will be those which are part of the ongoing life of the community, or, at minimum, situated within its geographical location. Such agencies can either conduct an informal social diagnosis, or have expert knowledge of the political tensions, important networks and opinion leaders, all of which may have a direct bearing on the success of a programme. Without support from key political actors in the community, the help of other opinion leaders and the use of existing community networks, a programme will struggle to establish credibility. However, community based programmes benefit from a central advisory and support agency to provide guidelines for implementation and other consultancy services which are common to any such operation. Without a central advisory body there is a danger that every new community programme 're-invents the wheel', passing through the problematical development stages which others have successfully overcome.

Beyond these considerations, the issue of shifting experimental programmes typically originating in the voluntary/assisted sector to a more permanent base will often arise once these programmes are extended in scope either geographically and/or with respect to the serves they offer. This will often be a risky operation, because their vitality and particular approach might not be easily transported to more bureaucratic/official settings. On the other hand it may be the only way to put them on a permanent basis and to ensure a measure of adaptability to a changing policy environment. This aspect should therefore be taken into consideration at quite early stages of programme formulation and choice of implementing and co-operating agencies.

*Target group specification:* While a programme may be based on an overall strategic approach, sub-strategies within the programme must be tailored to the needs of particular target groups. For example, if the target group is owner-occupiers, known to be pro-energy con-servation, then a mass media-based information campaign will be sufficient for awareness and participation. However, if the target audience of a programmes also includes tenants, disadvantaged con-sumers, or those who in the past have had little involvement in energy conservation, then there is a need for additional and much more specific communication instruments directed at them.

It should be underlined again here, that the decision to decentralize conservation policies, and even the adoption of an explicit policy to address 'difficult' consumer groups, in no way guarantees in itself that these groups are actually reached. In many cases, it will be dif-ficult to enlist the active participation of specific consumer groups through programmes that cater mainly to the requirements of what we have called the 'converts', or are perceived to do so.

*Selection of programme instruments:* This issue hinges on the nature of the target groups. Advice bureaus and home audits will be suffi-cient for higher income groups. However while home energy audits are valuable in showing clients what to do, they do not inform people how to do it, and what to do next. A home audit is not an end in itself, but should be seen as part of an ongoing programme which includes demonstration homes, additional information on recom-mended building firms or about home improvements and a follow up visit to advise on problems arising from the audit. Such information services will not be effective for lower income groups without the additional provision of financial support subsidies and/or practical services such as the installation of energy saving equipment. Since most communities include those in difficult economic circumstances, the case for selective intervention either in the form of grants or free services is unquestioned.

Selective intervention has a number of benefits. It is more cost-effective than undifferentiated schemes because it excludes the well-to-do free riders; it is socially more equitable, and finally the very existence of selective subsidies may encourage others outside the eligible group to take action.

Here again a dynamic aspect enters. Programme instruments adequate and sufficient at an early stage of a programme's develop-ment may become inadequate and insufficient at a later stage, with characteristic shifts in policy orientation, organizational build-up and early targets having been achieved. Successful programmes in particular will experience a need to adjust their instruments to post-investment requirements of clients and to technically more sophisticated measures once basic conservation services have been adopted on a broader scale.

*Programme implementation*

Our studies suggest two overriding factors operating in programme implementation: the extent to which programmes manage to establish linkages, join forces, and mediate conflicts with other agencies and groups, and the extent to which programmes are seen as credible and competent by their potential clienteles. While the art of linkaging and creating confidence can hardly be prescribed by way of formulating abstract recommendations, a few features making for effective implementation clearly emerge.

*Channelling information:* The most practical way to 'get across' a programme is to establish channels of communication with and through important social, business and political groups and relevant agencies within the community. Such communication links, formal and informal, are essential for building community support and thus promoting consumer confidence, for opening up established channels to reach and maintain contact with prospective clients, and for keeping in touch with reactions to a programme. A successful programme will, in other words, seek to orchestrate its promotion through available high credibility channels and existing social support systems, using focal points to target particular groups.

*Delivering programme services:* Information about a programme must be distinguished from the specific information services pertaining to alternative conservation actions and other non-informational services programmes might offer. In order to fully exploit the potential of local programmes, care must be taken to develop the full set of services required by a given clientele. As a rule, information and advisory services must be complemented with actual remedial and installation services, financial services and follow-up services; in similar vein predominantly remedial and retrofitting services must be complemented with advisory services.

With respect to the issue of who should bear the costs of conservation measures, we are not able to draw firm conclusions. While it seems clear that special subsidies, incentives or pay-back provisions for low income/tenant households should be provided as a matter of course, they do not guarantee programme take-up by such groups; on the other hand, a strategy of 'free services for everyone', includ-

297

ing installation costs, may be a plausible alternative to investment in energy generating capacity, notwithstanding free-rider effects.

*Timing and imaging:* Local programmes have a particular advantage in being able to time their launch to build upon with other important events and developments in a community. Local fairs, markets, anniversaries etc., in which community identity and aspirations are expressed and reinforced, have proved to be excellent opportunities for programme implementors to capitalize upon. Indeed, if a programme itself manages to become an element of community identity - 'The Conflans Challenge', - then support, acceptance and participation, possibly imitation by other communities will be enhanced.

Established programmes will experience a need to evolve their services in two directions. They will progressively have to address more 'difficult' groups, turning from what we have called 'converts' to 'indifferent' or even 'opposed' segments of their target populations; and they will have to respond to a growing demand for more than basic investment services, such as offering follow-up and quality control, energy-use advice as opposed to conservation-decision advice, and providing conservation feedback to clients. These two issues may apply generally to the 'next generation' of conservation programmes, because a large proportion of potential client households will have taken basic conservation measures before coming into contact with a specific programme.

*Key persons and staffing:* All of these points concerning the art of implementing local programmes call for special qualities in the persons running them. The management of the peculiar type of organizations such programmes represent is a demanding task, almost entrepreneurial in one respect, highly committed to public interests in another. Diplomacy in dealing with community, political and business leaders, skills in the recruitment, training and motivation of staff, innovative approaches to social marketing and promotional activities, a way of relating to consumers, and broad technical/engineering competences are typically combined in cases of successful local programme development. While such factors are not easily turned into policy recommendations, they underline the requirement for local programmes to retain the degree of flexibility and restraint with respect to bureaucratic apparatus essential for bringing these elements to bear. They also suggest that 'hiring-out' the implementation of programme services to primarily commercially interested, if technically competent, staff is not a promising course of action.

298

*Programme evaluation*

None of the programmes featured in the case studies had built-in evaluation procedures. Yet programmes of this kind are highly complex types of organizations and by their very nature must be dynamic, responsive to the concerns of their clients, and sensitive to feedback from the community. Without a systematic understanding of the nature of programme impacts programme organizers can hardly determine if the targeting is effective or make rational decisions about adjustments in goals and implementing strategies.

It is unrealistic to burden local programmes with the task of elaborate evaluation procedures, but clearly some institutional mechanisms must be found to give them the necessary day-by-day feedback and more systematic management information services. How this can be achieved is an unresolved issue but it is one which should be taken up with practitioners in successful local programmes.

## Policy implications for national and supranational bodies

*A catalyst for multinational comparative research*

This multinational study was made possible only by the grants awarded by the Commission of the European Communities (CEC). They served to stimulate interest in the project outside the contractors, Germany and Britain, to help secure national funds of considerable magnitude for the different studies by giving the overall project official support and legitimation, and to co-ordinate the intellectual efforts of the participants in the design, execution, analysis and interpretation of the findings.

In this way the CEC acted as a catalyst for the research, for without this support the project would not have reached a successful launch let alone conclusion. We believe that the CEC and other supranational bodies could play a continuing role in this context, providing seed corn and other funding for co-ordinated multinational research enterprises. In such a role, they could make an important contribution to the direction of future European research on consumer, energy and environmental issues.

*As supporters of social demonstration projects*

While demonstration projects of a technical nature attract substantial funds, the wider implementation and diffusion of technology is largely neglected. We envisage a role for the CEC in supporting 'social demonstration projects'. Proposed projects which involve either novel instruments or new approaches to promoting energy conservation at the community level would qualify for such funds. Evaluation would need to be a formal element of the overall scheme. Such a scheme for social demonstration projects would encourage the design of innovative proposals which as such have difficulty raising financial support but when legitimized by the CEC would be more able to tap national sources.

*In setting up international information exchange on community programmes*

Our study selected a small number of community programmes from a growing movement. In different countries schemes are being set up with a variety of interesting programme objectives, instruments and implementation strategies. Yet programme initiators often know little about other developments in their own country and beyond. Thus new schemes often start by solving problems which others have successfully tackled. A valuable role for the CEC would be to help establish an information exchange on community programmes which would collect and disseminate information about local programmes in different countries. Such an operation would need to go beyond simple statistics but concern itself with details of schemes - target groups, instruments etc. - so that the information is of relevance and utility to those developing initiatives.

**A strategy for applied social research**

The formulation of our research strategy combining the 'top-down' and 'bottom-up' perspectives for the evaluation of energy conservation programmes was a reaction to what we and others perceived as weaknesses in much current evaluation research.

Traditionally research in this field has adopted the approach of the consumer survey to determine how successful a particular intervention or programme was in terms of achieving its stated goals. However, the answer to this question, while useful for short-term cost-benefit considerations, is relatively useless to the development of the programme itself, or to other groups working in similar areas. Without an appreciation of why a programme worked or did not work the understanding of the process of social intervention is not furthered. To answer this more complex question calls for the fusion of the traditional policy analytic and evaluation research perspectives in a systematic appraisal of relationships between organizational context, design, implementation and impacts of a programme. Such a comprehensive approach to the evaluation of energy conservation programmes has been advocated elsewhere (Monnier et al 1986). More generally Cronbach (1980) calls for a complete reformation and transformation of both the institutional arrangements and practices of programme evaluation. The metaphor of reformation is pursued by introducing 95 guiding theses for programme evaluation and reading between the lines of these a trenchant critique of current evaluation research is apparent. Rather than describe the failings of the past or indeed on the basis of one study to prescribe a detailed model of programme evaluation for general application, we would like to draw upon our experiences and comment on some aspects of the nature of applied social research with particular reference to the conflicting demands of social theory and policy application.

## The nature of applied research

Although the term applied social research is generally understood to cover the endeavours of social scientists to contribute to the understanding and ameliorating of social issues it is a somewhat overinclusive term for analytic purposes. Under the umbrella of applied social research are a variety of distinct research foci and styles which carry with them different implications for the nature of applied research and its links, both to social scientific theory and to social policy.

In Figure 10.1 a basic model of applied research is depicted. This defines two dimensions, research style and research focus which can be used to characterize a particular piece of research. Research focus differentiates between research which is primarily theory or problem driven. The extremes of this continuum are, on the one hand, the specification, elaboration or application of theoretical concepts in relation to social issues and, on the other, the formulation of specific answers or solutions to a social issue, in a sense social engineering or design. The former is a longer term enterprise seeking to influence the public debate. The latter is short term and directed toward solutions.

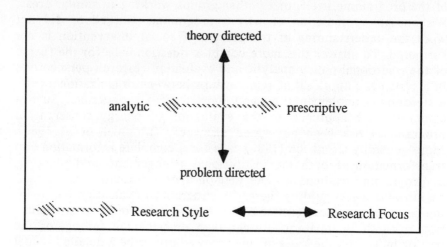

Figure 10.1 A model of applied social research

Research style captures another orientation within the research enterprise running from the analytic or explanatory perspective to the prescriptive or value explicit approach. It is not proposed that this continuum of research style is a simple value free/value laden distinction since it is assumed that values enter into all scientific endeavours. Rather it sees applied research as more or less inspired by certain conceptions as to how society should be organized. Those adopting the analytic style tend to take the present state of affairs as starting point for research and accept a consensual view of both problems and social goals. In this somewhat liberal-democratic approach scientists are the servants of society. Their role is to give an 'objective' analysis of social phenomena, a description of 'what is', and through this to contribute to the evolution of more informed social change. The roles of scientist and policy maker are strictly distinct. Social science informs but is not part of the policy making process.

In contrast the prescriptive style is more political. To the extent that as social science it seeks to exert direct influence on policy, science and social policy become interrelated since researchers take an explicit position regarding either the nature of man or an image of society. They ask not merely 'what is possible' but in addition 'what ought to be'. Within this prescriptive style are a number of traditions. For example, there are those promoting the utilitarian underpinnings of self interested classical economics - the pursuit of the rational society based on the principle of economic man: others can be described as the radicals or utopians who may question the value and legitimacy of existing policy goals and assume the role of advocates of alternative end-states. While differing in their specification of the millennium these traditions are linked in using social science as a proactive influence in the process of social change.

At first sight this model suggests a four fold typology of applied research but in reality this would be too insensitive. The tradition of empirical research having aspirations both to theory and application and perhaps the most well developed area in the field of applied social research lies, in terms of the focus continuum, between the poles of theory and problem directed research. Since the present discussion concerns certain conflicts inherent in the pursuit of theory and application the working typology is extended to include three research foci namely: theory, empirical analysis and design, while the two styles of research, analytic and prescriptive are maintained. The resulting six types of applied social research are depicted in Figure 10.2.

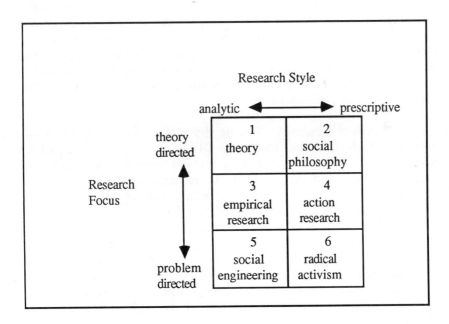

Figure 10.2 Six types of applied social research

Let us briefly elaborate on these six types of research with some examples:

*Type 1 Theory:* Here the concern is for the conceptual nature of the phenomenon in question and the development of logically interconnected relationships between specified variables. The objective is the specification of theories of the middle range defined by Merton (1961) as 'intermediate to the minor working hypotheses involved in abundance during the day-by-day routines of research, and the all-inclusive speculations comprising a master conceptual scheme'. As examples consider the work of Rogers (1983) on the processes of social change and the diffusion of innovations and the theoretical models of the energy economy reviewed by Stern and Aronson (1984). The study of energy conservation can fall into this category as it is an example of a number of theoretically similar processes that operate in different areas of policy concerns or everyday life.

*Type 2 Social Philosophy:* Here the process of theorizing embraces an ethical dimension. As in the analytic tradition assumptions about some aspect of man or society are part of the theoretical perspective. However, here these assumptions are more akin to stipulations or normative prescriptions and take on the status of desired end states. Of course there are social philosophers whose writings shore-up the present order but the more visible are typically involved in shaping alternative visions of the future creating the counter-myths for the post-industrial society. The analysis by Sachs (1984) of energy intensive life styles and of Illich (1974) on equity and energy fit into this category of social philosophy.

*Type 3 Empirical Research:* This is the main focus of applied research in psychology and sociology. Here, using current scientific knowledge and methods researchers investigate problems within the current paradigm and the work of the research community fits into Kuhn's characterization of 'normal science'. The role of the scientist is that of an indirect contributor to the empirical/rational strategy of social progress, in which it is assumed that policy makers and the public are rational and will act accordingly on the basis of the available evidence. The objective of research is the pursuit of superior factual knowledge but without consideration or responsibility for its use. Much research on residential energy use fits into this category (Ester et al. 1984; Monnier et al. 1986). It is applicable rather than directly applied research.

*Type 4 Action Research:* In action research the emphasis is on improving some aspect of the human condition through intervention strategies designed and implemented by the researcher. The researcher acts as a social catalyst using research based change strategies to maximize desired and minimize undesired goals. By investigating the process of change an attempt is made to pinpoint the critical variables influencing the result. Action research was introduced by Kurt Lewin (see Marrow 1969) and today its proponents are found in the area of organizational development. The researcher becomes a collaborator with the target of change. In analysing the opportunities for and institutional constraints to new schemes for collective action in energy production and energy savings, Monse (1986) moves close to this type of research.

*Type 5 Social Engineering:* This is the instrumental orientation of the social technologist. Here, the research objective is the specification of procedures which would achieve some relatively small scale means-ends relationship. There a few good accounts of research in this area because social engineers are doers rather than writers. The particular problem is 'out there' in the minds of policy makers and the researcher acts in the role of an expert. What would be the elements of an effective campaign to raise public awareness? How could people be persuaded to insulate their lofts? These are the types of issues for which policy makers and their clients expect solutions and get them from researchers. This is the application of research rather than applied research per se.

*Type 6 Radical Activism:* The radical activist tradition combining the prescriptive style and problem oriented focus is best exemplified by the field of conflict intervention. Laue (1981) defined conflict intervention as 'the process by which an outside or third party enters into a conflict in order to influence its outcome in a direction he or she defines as desirable...all interveners are advocates - for a specific party, a particular outcome, or a preferred process...' The boundaries between the intellectual pursuit of ideas and political activism become blurred. Whether this, in a pure form, can be considered social science is a debatable point but it is not at issue here since as will be argued strands of radical activism may appear in other more 'legitimate' social science pursuits.

This typology presents a static picture on to which the dynamics of the research process can be described by combinations of the different types. To put it another way applied research often has multiple objectives with some more important than others in different

305

phases of the research. Thus for example someone working on energy conservation in the residential sector might focus at different times on the impact of a particular programme (type 3), theories of social change (type 1) the specification of strategies to achieve a consensually agreed goal (type 5). The empirical research on consumption feedback determining its potential to influence energy use fits into type 4, and specifying the processes involved in consumption feedback using theories of skills learning (type 1).

Some having analysed fuel expenditure among low income groups from the perspective of rational economic models (type 2) were led to the conclusion that the exercise is pointless and have moved toward types 4 and 6 to advocate new policies to remove structural constraints against disadvantaged consumers.

In our study a variety of dynamics of research can be observed. Some started with strong philosophical concerns of either an environmentalist or consumerist nature, others were more attuned to theory. What emerged was a movement from type 2 to type 1 as the conceptual framework was formulated involving an integration of aspects of policy analysis, sociology and social psychology. The social philosophies were neutralized due to the research group's different views and priorities arising out of academic interests and funding. The empirical research conducted falls into type 3. The evaluations of the local programmes using both quantitative and qualitative methods were analytical rather than prescriptive in style. Finally, the conclusions move in different directions. Some concern the process of intentional social change (type 1), others fall in type 5 - specific recommendations regarding the design of local programmes; yet at the same time elements of the radicalism of type 6 are apparent in, for example, social policy issues in the realm of disadvantaged consumers.

Partially, at least, the positions which people assumed were a function of their institutional affiliations and outlooks. Those coming from academic backgrounds worked primarily in types 1 and 2, from governmental and other official research bodies in types 3 and 5 and from non-governmental consumer or environmental associations in types 4 and 6. These differences in research perspective may lead to characteristic tensions and cross-pressures in co-operative research.

*The Pressures on applied research*

It is generally accepted that the joint pursuit of theory and practical application is not a straightforward undertaking, however it is seen as the ideal strategy for the applied research. 'There is nothing so practical as a good theory' a phrase coined by Kurt Lewin is often quoted as the rallying cry for social scientists who have moved outside the strictly academic traditions towards the real world of social problems. Given time, so the conventional wisdom implies, good theory and relevant application will emerge and essentially there is no conflict between theory and application. In contrast what will be argued here is that there are simultaneous pressures on empirical researchers to move towards the theory and problem solving foci and that these pressures are very much at odds.

Applied research integrating theory and design might appear attractive as a regulatory ideal but it is far from certain that it can be achieved in practice.

Pressures towards theory are linked to the overall objectives of science as perceived by researchers. Extending the corpus of scientific knowledge through the development of theory is generally held to be the rationale of science, and those who contribute most are accorded highest prestige. Furthermore since the social sciences are rather strictly compartmentalized in universities there is also pressure for disciplinary purity - for working in and/or developing the existing, but often narrowly focused, paradigms specifying consensually defined issues, concepts, terminology and methods. These disciplinary pressures are mediated by the researchers peer groups, indirectly through the current literature and directly through career structures, the peer group review system for research and the editorial preferences of journals.

In the contexts of design and relevance the pressures are exerted by funding agencies who call for 'relevant research' and policy makers who expect social scientists to provide concrete solutions to problems that confront them. In addition social scientists themselves often feel that a logical outcome of their research is the specification of ways and means of achieving certain ends. Having invested considerable time and effort in the study of an issue, and become an 'expert' it is tempting to take the opportunity of going beyond the 'data' to formulate policy. Depending on the research style this may take the form of 'what could be done' (type 5) or 'what should be done' (type 6).

More complex still, to the extent that researchers get involved in 'relevant' research and policy is the inescapable dilemma as to whom they serve. 'Whose relevance' involves a new set of pressures, sometimes of a irreconcilable nature. These involve conflicts between meeting the expectations of politicians, decision makers and practitioners versus those of clients and particularly marginal clients. In some circumstances it is a matter of far reaching consequences whether the researcher is working for the political system in which power resides or for those to whose benefit a programme is carried out.

These pressures pull researchers into very different worlds. Moving towards theory entails unidisciplinary approaches, theoretical abstraction and the language of conceptualization. In contrast design calls for multidisciplinary strategies and a pragmatic and concrete approach couched in the languages of politics and common sense.

Much applied research operates within the rational-economic framework on the assumption that there is a reasonable convergence between public issues and private concerns. However if our thesis is valid applied research must be seen to sit uneasily between three related but different worlds, those of science, of politics and policies, and of everyday life.

*Some modest proposals*

If applied social science is to meet its objectives of both theory and application it must relate to these different worlds. Approaches like our 'top down' and 'bottom up' perspectives are an attempt to achieve this. In the 'top down' perspective the issues are described in the terms of the politician. The objective is to identify how those elements of programme design and implementation that are accessible to control can be most appropriately constructed to reach particular goals. The outcome is a set of recommendations, couched in the language of policy, enlightened by taking note of the recipients of the policies. In this 'top down' approach we see the relatively well articulated links between science and policy. Science and applied science particularly is becoming a more public enterprise and as politics becomes increasingly data dependent a commonality of interests has developed.

In the 'bottom up' approach the concerns of citizens as consumers are addressed. We analyse consumers' capabilities to deal with their concerns and the variety of obstacles that may explain differential

308

responses to public policies. This approach encourages both science and policy to adopt a more differentiated approach to the world of everyday life, to recognize the notion of standard survey respondents and model citizens as a crude and often misleading characterization. By integrating the two approaches we attempt to inform the policy process and represent at least some of the concerns of the common man.

If this description of the vexations of applied research is valid what can be done about it? Let us make clear that we believe that theory is the sine qua non of social science and that the social sciences have much to contribute to concerns of everyday life, and that solutions which bridge the gap between science, policy and the concerns of ordinary people are desirable. In the following paragraphs we concentrate on what the social science community might contribute to this bridge building.

First, there is a need for a broader, almost multilingual training of researchers. Specialism in research skills must be matched by a social awareness and appreciation of the policy process. The academic dealing with esoteric matters in arcane language will share little common ground with those whose role it is to organize public policy or with common people. Social scientists must be able to articulate their ideas in a style accessible to others, hoping for the reverse processes is quite unreasonable.

Secondly, how might research efforts be organized? It is very seldom that social problems of the type that become the focus of applied research present themselves in neat packages amenable to an exhaustive analysis by one of the current social scientific disciplines and to this extent many of the issues that confront policy makers are multidisciplinary. As a result of this, interdisciplinary approaches are often the recommended strategy . Yet interdisciplinary research is almost never achieved in practice, in part because the theoretical synthesis across disciplines and the requisite methodological tools for this type of research are not yet well developed. In analysing energy conservation programmes, for example, we have found that sociological, policy analytic and social psychological theories are all relevant. However, since there are no broad explanatory perspectives embodying these approaches, proposing unified theories about such a complex social system is either pretentious or trivializing.

In the light of this, we believe that there is a case for a greater emphasis in applied research on the formulation of conceptual frameworks as a prelude to theorizing. In such frameworks an attempt is made to identify the key elements and possible functional links between them so that the issue is simplified into a manageable heuristic representation. The framework presented in chapter 1 is an example of this. Its purpose is not to specify causal relationships between the elements but rather to describe and formalize what may be important in analysing the process of energy conservation. The value of such frameworks is to be found in both the research and policy contexts and in building bridges between them.

In research it is a guide to research strategy and to the types of explanation that may be relevant to different aspects of the phenomenon in question. In terms of policy it provides practitioners with a clear and concise description of the elements that should be considered in policy formation, implementation and evaluation, and the links between them. As a way of structuring a problem it is an aid to communication, on the one hand between researchers from different disciplines and on the other between researchers and practitioners. Although the world of science is united by certain abstract principles and general guidelines at the level of analysing particular issues, there are considerable divides between those anchored in the different disciplines. Thus, for example, what an economist takes for granted in modelling patterns of consumption is sometimes the key issue from the perspective of the behavioural researcher and the reverse is equally true. The task of developing a conceptual framework can provide a structure and focus for an emerging consensus as to the central issues, terminology and appropriate procedures. The same type of benefits are found in bringing together the perspectives of researchers and practitioners. It was certainly our experience that the conceptual framework outlined in chapter 1 facilitated discussions between us and those actively involved in programme design and implementation.

**Final conclusion**

In this research we have investigated one area in which public policies impinge in private concerns. Our particular focus was that of energy conservation, but, in passing, we see our project as having lessons for a number of issues and social problems which for their resolution require social change. Although at a technical level the problem of energy conservation is solved it is apparent that in most countries more than a decade of a mix of traditional policies and programmes has yielded only moderate results. Even with 'average' households there is still on a long way to go but for the more 'difficult' groups the task has hardly started. The tensions and con-tradictions between the public and private spheres have been reduced but if progress is to be continued further efforts to under-stand how to create a better 'fit' between those two spheres are required.

We have found that local programmes are a promising policy mechanism which for a variety of reasons may be more effective than the typical centrally administered and implemented campaign. Furthermore, with special provisions local programmes can achieve notable and dramatic results among disadvantaged consumers. This opportunity we see as arising from their proximity to their target audience, a proximity which allows them to bridge the gap between the public and private spheres. In our study the public and private are encapsulated in the 'top down' and 'bottom up' perspectives.

These two approaches are pragmatic devices to simplify the inter-pretation and evaluation of the complex policy and social system of an energy conservation programme. What is more, these perspectives correspond to the viewpoints of policy makers, on the one hand, and on the other, the programme users. To this extent, the 'top down' analysis is typically of primary interest to the policy maker and programme designer but it is just as important for them to under-stand the perspective of the client. While programme design may be given much consideration and is often thought to be decisive, from the user's point of view this is not the reality. Our studies demonstrate that programme effectiveness is a result of the constant interplay between programme design and the personal and social con-text of the users. Since the personal and social context are the paramount reality for consumers, the 'givens' in which a programme must operate, the conclusion is that a programme must accommodate to the existing situation. An otherwise well-designed and rational scheme will fail if this is not appreciated.

Finally, in modelling the overall social process of energy conserva-tion we have been forced to confront a number of unresolved issues on which further research might focus.

* for consumer research: to concentrate on the poorly understood issues of complex goods and services which require for their ac-quisition and use a high degree of co-operation by consumers;

* for research on the informal economy, of which energy use

forms an important part: to look, not only for factors facilitating and indeed pushing technical change in the home, but for its broader social and ecological impacts; to identify promising new forms of 'co-production' of social services between public and private enterprises and informal, self-organized groups;

* for policy research: to focus on the issues of linking community energy conservation programmes with other municipal programmes, particularly energy supply planning, land-use planning, housing policy, and policies for new industrial developments; to explore further the question of 'simultaneous policies', that is, analyse the links and conflicts between policies affecting energy end-use in view of enhancing conservation and preventing the production of external environmental and social effects necessitating costly remedial policies.

We hope that our proposals for applied social research may be of value to those investigating these issues. All the topics call for multidisciplinary approaches and can be conceptualized in terms of 'top down' and 'bottom up' perspectives. To this extent the formulation of conceptual frameworks maybe of value in bridging various gaps between researchers, policy makers and everyday life.

## References

Cronbach, L.J., 1980. *Toward reform of program evaluation: Aims, methods and institutional arrangements.* Jossey-Bass: San Francisco.

Czarniawska, B. and Hedberg, B. 1985, Control cycle responses to decline. *Scandinavian Journal of Management*, 19-39.

Ester, P. Gaskell, G., Joerges, B., Midden, C., Van Raaij, W.F. and DeVries, T. (eds) *Consumer Behaviour and Energy Policy.* North Holland: Amsterdam.

Illich, I. 1974. *Energy and equity.* Harper and Row: New York.

Laue, J.H. 1981. Conflict intervention. In M.E. Olsen and M. Micklin. *Handbook of Applied Sociology* 4, 67-90. Praeger: New York.

Marrow, A.J. 1969. *The practical theorist: the life and work of Kurt Lewin.* Basic Books: New York.

Merton, R.K., 1961. *Social theory and social structure.* Free Press: Glencoe, Ill.

Monnier, E., Gaskell, G., Ester, P., Joerges, B., LaPillonne, B., Midden, C. and Puiseux, L. 1986, *Consumer Behaviour and Energy Policy: an International Perspective.* Praeger: New York.

Monnier, E., Vallet, B. and Bordenave, C. 1986, Evaluation methods for energy conservation in the residential sector. In E. Monnier, G. Gaskell, P. Ester, B. Joerges, B. LaPillonne, C. Midden, and L. Puiseux, *Consumer Behaviour and Energy Policy: An International Perspective.* Praeger, New York.

Monse, K. 1986. Institutional barriers to new forms of collective action aimed at saving energy. In E. Monnier, G. Gaskell, P. Ester, B. Joerges, B. LaPillonne, C. Midden, and L. Puiseux, *Consumer Behaviour and Energy Policy: An International Perspective.* Praeger, New York.

Rogers, E. 1983. *Diffusion of Innovations.* 3rd Edition, Praeger: New York.

Sachs, W. 1984. Are energy intensive life images fading? The cultural meaning of the automobile in transition. In P. Ester, G. Gaskell, B. Joerges, C. Midden, W.F. Van Raaij and T. DeVries (eds) *Consumer Behavior and Energy Policy.* North Holland: Amsterdam.

Stern, P.C. and Aronson, E. 1984. *Energy use: The human dimension.* W.H. Freeman: New York.